D1238736

The
EMPEROR ROMANUS LECAPENUS AND HIS REIGN

The
EMPEROR ROMANUS LECAPENUS
AND HIS REIGN

A Study of Tenth-Century Byzantium

BY

STEVEN RUNCIMAN

CAMBRIDGE

AT THE UNIVERSITY PRESS

1963

PUBLISHED BY
THE SYNDICS OF THE CAMBRIDGE UNIVERSITY PRESS

Bentley House, 200 Euston Road, London, N.W. 1
American Branch: 32 East 57th Street, New York 22, N.Y.
West African Office: P.O. Box 33, Ibadan, Nigeria

First printed 1929
Reprinted 1963

First printed in Great Britain at the University Press, Cambridge
Reprinted by offset-litho by Bradford & Dickens Ltd, London. W.C. 2

CONTENTS

MAP

THE
EMPEROR ROMANUS LECAPENUS
AND HIS REIGN

PROLOGUE

Sources for a History of the Emperor Romanus Lecapenus

T HE original sources for a history of the Emperor Romanus Lecapenus and his reign divide themselves naturally into four categories, according to language: (i) the Greek and Slavonic, the latter being either translated or almost wholly derived from the former, (ii) the Latin, (iii) the Armenian and Caucasian, and (iv) the Arabic.

(i) The Greek and Slavonic sources are infinitely the most important; indeed the Greek chroniclers must be the fundamental authorities of any period in Byzantine history. Chronographically the reign of Romanus I has a curious importance, as it was then that there lived his friend the mysterious Logothete, whose chronicle was the basis of all the other chroniclers dealing with that age. Before embarking on a discussion of them it is well to remember Krumbacher's often-quoted remark: "In Byzantium such works were never regarded as finished monuments of literary importance, but as practical handbooks which every possessor and copyist excerpted, supplemented and revised just as he pleased".[1] Consequently there was always a network of synoptic chronicles, whose relative value it is very difficult to gauge. The Logothete, whom I have mentioned above, was almost certainly called Symeon and was perhaps Symeon Metaphrastes, the hagiographer. He wrote a history of the world from the creation to the year 948, the date of the death of Romanus; one of his main characteristics was a strong affection for that Emperor which outlasted his fall. This chronicle does not exist in its original form, but we have four copies which probably represent it with fair accuracy and which are almost

[1] Krumbacher, p. 362.

identical with each other. Of these perhaps the closest is the
Slavonic version recently published by Sreznevski; it is actually
headed by the name of Symeon Metaphrastes the Logothete, and
quite possibly this title is not a later interpolation but the whole
work (as far as 948—there is a continuation) is a literal translation. The Greek versions are those known by the names of
Georgius Monachus (or Hamartolus) Continuatus,[1] Leo Grammaticus (said to have been written in the year 1013) and Theodosius of Melitene.[2] The chronicle called in the Bonn series
Symeon Magister has no right to the name, and seems to be a
later and unimportant copy. The work of the Logothete was
clearly used again by the author of the last book of the *Continuation* of Theophanes (Book VI, dealing with the reigns from
Leo VI to Romanus II) who may have been Romanus I's secretary, Theodore Daphnopates. It was probably written under
Nicephorus Phocas, but it reproduces the same facts and the
same curious Lecapene sympathies. It is a rather fuller work
than the earlier chronicles, including a few unimportant facts
that must have been common knowledge at the time,[3] a few
more comments on its heroes,[4] and a few stylish interjections on
morality and fate. The main later chroniclers that deal with the
period are the early twelfth-century Cedrenus, who for this
period copies the (as yet unpublished) chronicle of Scylitzes—
who provides some new facts from unknown sources:[5] Zonaras
who wrote, rather uncritically but with sarcastic comments, an
epitome of previous chronicles; both he and Cedrenus are hostile
in tone to the Lecapeni and also to the Porphyrogennetus: and
finally Manasses, whose verse chronicle is also an epitome,

1 There are one or two slight divergencies between the Georgius Monachus
Continuatus of the Bonn series (edited by Combesis) and the text (Georgius
Hamartolus Continuatus) edited by Muralt.
2 The only divergencies during these years (912–948) occur over the date of
Symeon's interview with Romanus, about which no chronicle is convincing,
and over the identity of Euphrosyne Curcuas's intended bridegroom, whom
the Slavonic version calls the son of Constantine Porphyrogennetus and the
other three and Theophanes Continuatus the son of Constantine Lecapenus.
Here the Slavonic version must be right.
3 E.g. Agatha Lecapena's marriage to Romanus Argyrus.
4 Especially about John Curcuas and his brother Theophilus.
5 E.g. his information about Southern Italy during the reign of Romanus I.

though it seems to have been the best seller among the chronicles; it only deals briefly with the early tenth century.[1]

The Greek sources, apart from the chronicles, present no great difficulties. Most important are the works of the Emperors Leo the Wise and Constantine Porphyrogennetus, the *Novellae* and *Tactica* (a monumental work on warfare) of the former, and the *De Ceremoniis*, the *De Thematibus* and the *De Administrando Imperio* of the latter;[2] the *De Administrando*, indeed, is one of the most important books in the whole history of the early Middle Ages. We also possess some valuable correspondence, a few letters of Romanus himself and a vast series written by Nicholas Mysticus the Patriarch, of which those to Symeon the Bulgar and to the Pope are especially vital for the history of his times. There are also some important lives of the saints, particularly that of the rival Patriarch Euthymius, which, though fragmentary, is essential for the history of the reign of Leo VI and the early regency. The other Greek sources require no special comment, with the exception of the epical novel of Digenis Akritas, written one or two generations later, that gives a romantic but probably not inaccurate picture of life on the eastern frontier during these times.

The only important Slavonic source (apart from the translation of the Logothete) is the chronicle called wrongly by the name of Nestor.[3] It is derived partly from the Greek chroniclers and partly from Russian sources—e.g. the records of Kiev—now lost. There are also several Bulgarian translations of various Greek works, made during the tenth century and two short original works, Chrabr on the Slavonic Alphabet and John the Exarch's preface to the *Shestodniev*, which are invaluable for the picture that they give of Bulgarian civilization under Symeon.

1 Of the other chronicles that cover the period, the so-called Synopsis Sathas (and, I presume, the unpublished Theodore of Cyzicus, which is said to be closely related to it), Glycas and the unimportant verse work of Joel, treat the period too briefly to need notice.
2 Constantine's purely *historical* works do not concern us, with the exception of one or two stray passages in the *Vita Basilii* and the last pages of the least important, the *Image of Edessa*. The De Ceremoniis and the De Administrando both present some very important problems, but they have both been admirably treated by Bury and need no further comment here (see bibliography).
3 Leger's critical edition deals fully with its problems.

(ii) With one exception the Latin authors are unimportant, consisting of chroniclers dealing with the history of Italy, Illyricum and Hungary; their contributions to the central history of the Empire are rare. The one exception is Liudprand, Bishop of Cremona, who wrote two invaluable works, the *Antapodosis*, a history of his own times up to the year 950, and a report on his embassy to Constantinople a few years later. He twice visited Constantinople, and his father and stepfather had been ambassadors there before him; he thus had admirable opportunities for collecting firsthand information. He was, however, credulous and gossipy and rather prejudiced,[1] and saw love affairs wherever he looked; so, though he is the most entertaining as well as one of the most vital of the sources, he must be treated with a little circumspection.

(iii) The Armenian and Caucasian sources deal solely with Armenia and the Caucasus; but, as the Armenian question was always, and especially now, of supreme importance to Byzantium, a study of the Armenian authorities is essential. They are all careless, ingenuous and unfair, and have to be believed with caution. The most important is John the Catholicus, who wrote a history of his own times in which he was a principal actor; he is verbose and never gives any help about dates. Nevertheless he cannot be ignored, and it is usually easy to make due allowances for his patriotism and self-glorification.

(iv) The Arab authorities are absolutely essential for the history of the Asiatic and Italian frontiers and of the tribes of the Caucasus and the Steppes; Maçoudi in particular, gives a most useful account of the Arab world and the countries round about. As yearly chronicles they are of great value, though they are inclined to overlook any Christian triumphs in war (of the details of the truces they are more honest). The contemporaries Maçoudi and Eutychius of Alexandria also deal with the internal history of the Empire; but there, dependent as they were upon rumour and hearsay, they are quite unreliable.

These are the main original sources for the period. To discuss

---

1 The *Legatio*, for example, is far more anti-Greek than the *Antapodosis*—Liudprand had been well received by Constantine Porphyrogennetus, but badly by Nicephorus Phocas, and was angry.

their relative reliability in greater detail would occupy too many pages; much has been done by modern writers in discussions or in critical editions, to which I refer in the bibliography. For the rest the historian can only estimate according to his own experiences and instincts.

Modern works on the subject need little comment. Only two cover the period in any detail, Hirsch's *Konstantin VII* and Rambaud's stimulating though careless monograph on the same Emperor. Both, however, are more concerned with Constantine as an author than with the history of his or Romanus's reign. The older historians, Gibbon and Finlay, dismiss Romanus briefly and contemptuously, but latterly his importance is being realized (e.g. by Professor Oman and still more Mr Bussell). The *Cambridge Medieval History* passes the period in four pages (vol. IV, chap. III, pp. 59–63) that are unbelievably full of unwarrantable errors:[1] though when dealing with local aspects —the eastern frontier, Armenia and the Steppes (vol. IV, chaps. IV–VI) and Italy (vol. III, chap. VII) it is more creditable; nevertheless as a standard work it is sadly inadequate. I have spoken in my first chapter of the tendency of Byzantinists to write 'vertical' rather than 'horizontal' histories; but, though I regard the latter as being really more useful, many of the 'vertical' histories are of supreme value, notably Gay's study of Byzantine Italy, and Vasiliev's study of the Arab wars. Zlatarsky's history of Bulgaria and his articles on the Bulgaro-Byzantine diplomatic correspondence are of monumental help, though I do not always agree with his conclusions. There are also a number of excellent monographs dealing with various points and aspects. Particularly one must be grateful to the late Professor Bury for his monographs and his appendices to

---

1 Whenever Ashot may have come to Constantinople, it was certainly not in 923 (p. 62): the terrible winter was 928 not 933 (*ibid.*). The vacancy in the Patriarchate lasted fifteen months not eighteen, and ended in 931, though Theophylact was not ratified from Rome till 933 (p. 63). The Image of Edessa reached Constantinople in 944 not 942; Curcuas got it in exchange not for one but for two hundred prisoners (*ibid.*). Theodora was probably crowned in 920 not 921, and there is no reason to suppose that she did not die, as the chroniclers say that she did, in 922 (Feb.) and Sophia was crowned next month not in 923. It is difficult to see why M. Vogt should trouble to invent so much.

Gibbon, which are perhaps the most permanent modern contributions to Byzantine history.

Throughout my text I have endeavoured to support my statements with references to the original authorities. Where, however, the original authorities are obscure or contradictory, I have referred, where possible, to modern works which elucidate their meaning. I have also occasionally, where the original sources are diffuse and hard to obtain, referred to modern works which have collected and made a digest of them; in dealing with the Arab writers' information about the Caucasus and the Steppes I have given many references to d'Ohsson's *Les Peuples du Caucase*, a fairly modern work in the form of fiction, which is, however, a reliable compendium of the Arabic works on those districts during the tenth century. With regard to the Greek chronicles, where they are in harmony, I have made my references to Theophanus Continuatus, as being the fullest and most easily obtainable. I append a bibliography with a few comments, and a list of abbreviations used in the references in the footnotes.

In conclusion I wish to announce my debt to the personal help of the late Professor Bury, who started me on this road and guided my first steps, of Mr Norman Baynes, and of Professor Zlatarsky of Sofia. My thanks are also due to Miss R. F. Forbes, for helping me over my proofs.

I have deliberately omitted any account of the art of the period. The history of Byzantine art cannot be neatly divided up according to the Emperors' reigns. Actually Romanus I's reign occurred in the middle of a richly active artistic period; but it is almost always impossible to assign any definite artistic work to any definite decade, and any artistic discussion of these decades would lead to a discussion of the art of the whole Macedonian dynasty and would at once exceed the limits obligatory to such a book as this. Fortunately Byzantine art is attracting an increasing amount of attention and appreciation, and many competent books have recently been devoted to it. I have therefore restricted myself to mentioning a few of the most useful and relevant of these in my bibliography.

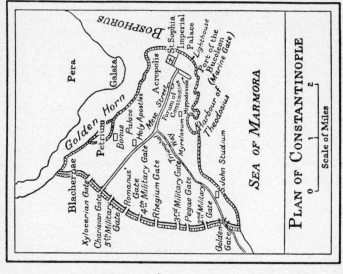

BOSPHORUS

Pera

Galata

Golden Horn

Blachernae

Xylocerian Gate

Charisian Gate

5th Military Gate

Romanus' Gate

4th Military Gate

Rhegium Gate

3rd Military Gate

Pegae Gate

2nd Military Gate

Golden Gate

Petrium Palace

Bonus

Holy Apostles

Mese Street

Acropolis

St. Sophia

Imperial Palace

Lighthouse

Port of the Bucoleon (Marine Gate)

Forum of Constantine

Hippodrome

Myrelaeum

Triumphal Way

Harbour of Theodosius

S. John Studium

SEA OF MARMORA

PLAN OF CONSTANTINOPLE

Scale of Miles

0   1   2

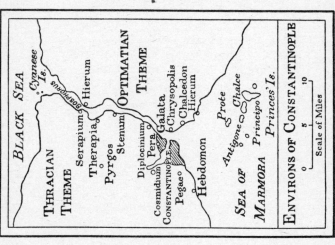

BLACK SEA

Cyanese Is.

THRACIAN THEME

Serapium

Hierum

Therapia

Pyrgos

Stenum

OPTIMATIAN THEME

Diplocinium

Pera

Galata

Chrysopolis

Chalcedon

Hierum

Cosmidium

CONSTANTINOPLE

Pegae

Hebdomon

Prote

Chalce

Antigone

Principo

Princes' Is.

SEA OF MARMORA

ENVIRONS OF CONSTANTINOPLE

Scale of Miles

0   5   10

CHAPTER I

Life in Byzantium at the Beginning of the Tenth Century

IN the battles between truth and prejudice, waged on the field of history books, it must be confessed that the latter usually wins. The armies of prejudice march under the banner of loyalty; loyalty to their country, to their religion, to the standards and traditions of their fathers—these are things that stir men to their hearts. Loyalties live deep down in them; and when they write their histories, prejudice, even against their intention, will not pass away, but stays to cloud and obscure the true mirror of facts.

At the hands of such prejudice many historical epochs have suffered, and most of all the epoch known as the Later Roman or Byzantine Empire. Ever since our rough crusading forefathers first saw Constantinople and met, to their contemptuous disgust, a society where everyone read and wrote, ate food with forks and preferred diplomacy to war, it has been fashionable to pass the Byzantines by with scorn and to use their name as synonymous with decadence. In the eighteenth century, refinement was no longer considered decadent; but decadence remained the Byzantine characteristic. Montesquieu and his more brilliant contemporary Gibbon, searched for new justification. Taking the superstition and bloodthirsty intrigues that were typical of all mediaeval Europe, and harnessing them to Byzantium, they gave new life to the synonym. Gibbon's dark shadow has long weighed on posterity; his sweeping epigrams and entertaining sneers frightened even gentle nineteenth-century phil-hellenes into the adoption of an air of disapproval. All the historians in chorus treated of a thousand years of empire as a short sinister unbroken decline.

Now, at last, thanks to the first appreciation of Byzantine art and the growth of sober scholarship, Byzantine history is finding its truer level. But it is still an interrupted story, with gaps breaking even the period of its highest grandeur; and it is in an attempt to fill one of these that this book is written.

In dealing with Byzantine history, one fact must be kept prominent—that the Byzantine State was probably the most centralized organization of such a size that the world has known. It is fashionable now to deplore the ways of the old historians, how they laid stress on the accessions and deaths of monarchs and told of all the personal dramas of the past. History is now become a staid impersonal science; and biography is a thing apart. Such a reaction is inevitable and healthy, but is not of unadulterated value; for history, after all, is only a mosaic of biographies, and some stones are large and affect the whole design. In Byzantium, where the whole government centred on the person of the Emperor, the Emperor's life and character were of paramount importance. Other elements played their part, providing the material on which he worked and the tools ready to his hand, but it was on him, his ability or his incompetence, his strength or his weakness, on which the Empire's fate depended. His reign therefore marked an epoch, and, in so far as any short period of history, can be treated as a unit. And such a treatment has a further advantage. In dealing with so short a period, the historian is compelled to take what might best be called the 'horizontal' view of history. In the case of Byzantium many histories have been written of particular aspects—histories that deal 'vertically' with, for example, the eastern frontier, or the Byzantines in Italy; but, to understand the methods and significance of Byzantium, it is essential to correlate every provincial incident with the contemporary story of the central government at Constantinople, and through the central government to the other provinces. The 'vertical' histories cannot take so wide a view, and thus half their value is gone. A far better insight into Byzantine history can be gained by taking the legitimate unit of an Emperor's reign, and by keeping continuous watch during these years over every province from Naples to the Caucasus, focussing the eyes centrally on Constantinople, and the Imperial Court.

The lesson has not yet been learnt; in the long procession of the rulers of Constantinople there are still many shadowy figures, and in consequence their reigns remain in shadow. Even in the tenth century, the century in which the Byzantine Empire attained its zenith, there ruled for twenty-five years an Emperor so mysterious that Gibbon could say of him that "in his licentious pleasures he forgot the safety both of the republic and of his family":[1] whom Finlay could call "a man of weak character, who was distinguished neither by his birth, his talents nor his services",[2] but whom a modern historian considers to have been "a sedulous and businesslike administrator...a capable master of those jealous and unruly services which the Empire employed and feared".[3] The Emperor Romanus Lecapenus cannot have combined all these qualities; but the history of his times will never be understood until the mystery is cleared.

Romanus Lecapenus was crowned Emperor in December, 919. But his reign, in common with the reign of every usurper, had its prologue too closely bound up with it to be ignored. To understand his rule, we must go back to the source of most of his difficulties, to the day in May, 912, when Leo VI's reign was ended, and the sickly child Constantine Porphyrogennetus was launched on his stormy minority. And, even then, before we begin the drama, we must paint in the back-cloth, bring up the accessories, and enumerate the rôles that are to be filled.

The Empire which Leo VI bequeathed to his successors, though shrunken greatly from the old Roman Empire whose name it yet bore, was still diverse and powerful; and for the last two centuries its area had not much changed. It was divided, in administration as well as by geography, into two main divisions, the Asiatic provinces and the European. Of these the Asiatic were the larger and considered the more important. It is impossible to give at any one date the exact position of the frontiers; we can only make a rough calculation. In Asia Minor, in 912, the line ran approximately from the mouth of the river

1 Gibbon, *Decline and Fall*, ed. Bury, v, p. 209.
2 Finlay, *History of Greece*, 11, p. 291.
3 F. W. Bussell, *Constitutional History of the Roman Empire*, 11, p. 208.

Tsorokh on the Black Sea, about a hundred miles east of Trebizond, to the Upper Euphrates near Kharpurt. It left the Euphrates north of Melitene and went parallel to the river some fifty miles to the west, excluding Marash, down to the Taurus range, along which it ran, past the Cilician Gates, and eventually turned down the river Lamus to the Mediterranean, a little to the east of the Cilician Seleucia. Seleucia itself was in Leo's time too isolated a possession to have been raised to the dignity of a theme; so probably the Saracens commanded one if not both of the passes over to Barata.[1] Under Basil I, a few years previously, Cyprus had been recovered from the Moslems, but only very ephemerally. Beyond the frontier, on the north-east, lay the various principalities of Armenia and the Caucasus, all officially counted as vassals of the Empire. But they were, most of them, equally willing to call themselves vassals of the Califate, and at the moment Moslem influence was in the ascendant.

In Europe, on the northern frontier, lay the immense bulk of Bulgaria, pressing down the imperial territory to a narrow strip, some fifty miles in width, along the coasts of the Aegean and Adriatic Seas. The frontier left the Black Sea at the south end of the Gulf of Burgas, the chief towns on which, Develtus and Anchialus, had for some time been recognized Bulgar possessions: though the peninsula port of Mesembria, further north, remained in imperial hands.[2] It passed close to the north of the imperial city of Adrianople, and ran along the Rhodope range to the environs of Thessalonica; Berrhoea, slightly to the northeast of Thessalonica appears in John Cameniates' time as a Byzantine town, but by the reign of Basil II was in Bulgar hands, ceded no doubt by the peace of 927.[3] Exactly where the frontier crossed the Greek watershed it is hard to say. Constantine VII's remarks about the themes leaves the impression that the Empire possessed very little of the hinterland of Greece, and certainly in the war of 912–927 districts as far south as

1 *D.T.* p. 36.

2 Develtus and Anchialus had been ceded to the Bulgars by Theodora (Theoph. Cont. p. 165). Mesembria in Basil I's reign was still Byzantine (*ibid.* p. 308) and clearly remained so throughout the Bulgar war (see below, pp. 85, 97).

3 Cameniates, *De Excidio*, p. 496. Cedrenus, II, p. 344.

Phocis suffered as frontier provinces.[1] On the Adriatic coast the mountains of Albania protected the narrow themes of Nicopolis and Dyrrhachium, to the north of which, by Lake Scutari, the Bulgarian frontier ended, to make way for the Serbo-Croatian. Henceforward, to the north, the imperial territories were scanty; the theme of Dalmatia consisted merely of seven Latin-speaking towns in a semi-hostile, Slav hinterland, and themselves paying more attention, and tribute, to the Slavs than to the Emperor—the ports of Ragusa (with Cattaro which was probably its vassal), Spalato, Trau, Zara, Arba, Veglia and Osero. The Serbian and Croatian kingdoms were counted officially among the vassals of the Empire; but, except with regard to Serbia, the claim was seldom justified. Further north, at the head of the Adriatic, was the republic of Venice, counted also among the vassals, and very assiduous at so formally acknowledging itself; but the vassaldom, though it moulded Venetian culture, had only the slightest effect on Venetian policy.

In Southern Italy the Empire claimed all the territory south of a line drawn roughly from Termoli on the Adriatic to Terracina on the Tyrrhenian Sea. Within these limits were the Lombard principalities of Capua-Benevento and Salerno, and the maritime republics of Amalfi, Naples and Gaeta. These States, though still overawed by the recent memory of Nicephorus Phocas, who had reconquered Southern Italy for Basil I, were by no means constant in their obedience to Constantinople. It was only the Greek-speaking theme of Sicily (Calabria) and the Latin-speaking theme of Longobardia (Apulia) that were directly administered by Byzantine officials. The island of Sardinia was also included among the Empire's vassals; but its history is very obscure. The island of Sicily had been finally given up to the Arabs by the fall of Taormina in 902; the one or two remaining Greek forts were negligible and could no longer be kept in touch with Byzantium.[2]

The islands of the Ionian and Aegean Seas were all Byzantine possessions, with the terrible exception of Crete, a permanent

1 *D.T.* p. 51. *Vita S. Lucae Minoris,* in *M.P.G.* cxi, p. 449.
2 See Chapter ix.

thorn in the imperial flesh and already for over a century the base of Saracen raids on the Aegean coasts.

Finally, isolated away to the north, was the semi-independent but jealously retained province of the Crimea, Cherson, valuable for its trade and its espionage on the great tribes of the Steppes.[1]

This large territory was administered, with considerably varying detail, from the Imperial Court of Constantinople, and was under the autocratic and undisputed control of the Emperor, the Basileus. This is not the place to tell the long story of how the old Roman oligarchy had merged into this absolutism. Ever since the days of Augustus, the dyarchy of Imperator and Senate had been little more than nominal; and by the tenth century the Senate, in its Byzantine disguise of οἱ σύγκλητοι, as a political force had vanished, appearing only as a respectable witness of the Emperor's acts, quite without constitutional power.[2] The Byzantine Basileus, as heir-general of the Roman Imperator, was commander-in-chief of the imperial forces. He also inherited an even more significant tradition, carefully fostered by the early Roman Emperors, that made the Imperator the source of all law. As against this, there still lingered the theory that the Senate elected the Emperor and so were indirectly supreme; but the Emperors had rendered it comfortably void by habitually co-opting partners (a right always permitted them) before the vacancy occurred, whose succession was then unchallenged. The position of the Basileus and the centralization of his government had further been strengthened by the reforms of the sixth and seventh centuries, subordinating the civil to the military authorities: which made a return to the old régime impossible. By Leo VI's reign it was possible for the Emperor to declare as an established fact his absolute supremacy. In the place of the old

1 See Chapter VI.
2 Its last public appearances as a body had been when the Empress Theodora, at the close of her regency, opened the Treasury in its presence to show its fulness, and when the Emperor Basil on his accession did likewise to show its emptiness (Theoph. Cont. pp. 171, 255); Leo the Wise on his deathbed commended his son to its care (Cedrenus, II, p. 273); and we are also told that it witnessed from the city walls the interview between Romanus and Symeon in 924 (Theoph. Cont. p. 407). As these examples show, its functions were purely formal—as a body it took no part in the regency of the young Constantine.

dyarchy we have a complicated, chiefly militarist, bureaucracy, subordinate through its various grades to the Emperor alone. And over the vast ecclesiastical hierarchy his authority, owing to the careful work of Constantine the Great and his successors, was equally supreme.

The Emperor was thus the pivot round which the Empire swung, the supreme autocrat, head of the civil government, the army and navy, and the Church, responsible to God alone, whose deputy he was on earth. As such his time was fully occupied. The Byzantines delighted in gorgeous pageantry; almost daily there was some splendid festival or ceremony, in which the Emperor played chief part. But more than aesthetic delight lay behind this magnificence; it was designed to surround God's representative with a halo of glory, a mist of sacrosanctity that removed him from being a mere person, turning him rather into a Presence, or a symbol of the Empire itself. An autocrat, the Byzantines well knew, must not resemble the common type of his subjects; otherwise they all will think themselves as good as him, and the ambitious will even hope to supersede him. From his birth in the Purple Chamber to his funeral service in St Sophia, he should be treated rather as a god than as a man. It was for this that the Emperor had mechanically raised thrones set between roaring golden lions, and heavily jewelled garments perpetually changed: that prostration was necessary before his face, and that a thousand rules of etiquette were drawn up to be obeyed. This policy had been given new vitality some eighty years before by the magnificence of the Emperor Theophilus, who, coming after three decades of dynastic chaos, had found and utilized the willingness of the people, even in the height of the iconoclastic controversy, to accept and respect any dynasty that should establish itself firmly. It was now being tested. The first test seemed unfavourable; Theophilus's son Michael, though he survived his minority, was, in middle age, lawlessly murdered. But we must remember that Michael was a notorious debauchee, who wore his crown with a quite remarkable lack of dignity, and that Basil, the usurping murderer, had, unscrupulously perhaps, but legally, already reached the rank of co-Emperor. During Basil's reign all went well, and his son succeeded without question; the new dynasty had inherited the sacrosanctity. But on Leo VI's death, a new test was to take place. To that, we shall come later.

This ceremonial life must have taken up much of the Emperor's time; but in addition he had the whole business of the government of the Empire in his hands. It was he that appointed and dismissed the ministers and generals, constantly interviewing them and supervising their actions, besides taking unofficial advice from trusted friends. The heads of the great departments of the bureaucracy and the great military officials reported to him alone; there was no grand vizier to whom he could deputize his control. Consequently the amount of work that he had to superintend was terrific; and he could not afford to neglect even the Church, lest the Patriarch should assume too great powers for himself. As commander-in-chief of the imperial forces he would often lead his troops himself on their campaigns; but at the moment such an action was not fashionable; for nearly a century after Basil I's eastern campaigns no Emperor commanded in person on the field of battle. It is impossible to assign the reason for this fashion. Perhaps it was due to the psychology of the Emperors concerned, perhaps to the pressure of business; the only reason for supposing the latter is that it was after the absentee government of the later great warrior Emperors that the machine showed signs of breaking down.

Thus there was very little time left over for the Emperor's personal recreations. To attend the circus was an official duty, whether he liked it or not; but his private pleasures had to be reduced. Michael III, who managed to live a life of dissipation on the throne, had only staved off chaos by relying all his lifetime on the capable regency first of his mother then of his uncle Bardas and finally of Basil. Leo VI found time during his reign to write books; but they were for the most part semi-official compilations; and writing is less arduous for an Emperor than for those who are without secretaries, and Leo would have been a better Emperor had he kept closer watch on his ministers.

Beside the Senior Emperor, the supreme authority, there were the co-Emperors. They had come into being owing to the Emperor's practice of crowning his heir to ensure the succession.

The co-Emperor need not necessarily be a son; Michael III had crowned his favourite, Basil. At first there seems to have been only one co-Emperor; the heir alone was crowned. But Basil I, in his desire to consolidate his parvenu dynasty, crowned three of his sons; and on his death (the eldest having died) both Leo and Alexander were there to succeed him, but Leo as the elder took over the supreme power. On Leo's death, leaving a son Constantine, who though crowned Emperor was a minor, Alexander became Senior Emperor. There are, however, no means of judging whether, had Constantine been adult, Alexander would still have become the senior, in the right of having been Emperor of an older creation, or whether Constantine as his father's son would have therefore been considered his father's full heir. Legally probably Alexander's claims would have triumphed, but their general acceptance would be doubtful. But fortunately for the Empire such a situation never arose. The co-Emperors probably had little work to do except on ceremonial occasions, accompanying the Senior Emperor or deputizing for him; but except in the case of an actual regency, there is no record of them having taken over any part of the administration.

The Empress, the Augusta, was a more important figure. Here again there might be more than one; but the co-Empresses can be disregarded as the still more shadowy counterparts of the co-Emperors.[1] The Senior Empress, however, was almost as powerful as the Emperor. Though usually she was the Emperor's wife or mother, it was not marriage with an Emperor that created her Empress; she had specially to be so crowned. Leo VI, when a widower for the second time, crowned his daughter Augusta to fill the vacancy. That there should always be an Augusta was desirable, as without her many of the Court ceremonies could not be held. The Empress was surrounded by her own court over which her authority was unquestioned; she had absolute control of her vast revenues. Far from living immured all her life in the gynaeceum, she would appear alongside of the Emperor at many of the official receptions and at the

---

[1] I do not, however, know of more than two ever having existed in the Palace at the same time.

circus; and she would frequently make journeys of her own, for some ceremony, for business or for pleasure. In the event of her son's minority, the Empress Dowager was expected by precedent as well as by sentiment to assume the regency,[1] and as regent she would see to the government and interview her ministers herself. The Empress Irene had even dispensed with an Emperor altogether, taking to herself his nomenclature and attributes; and though the army was dissatisfied by such conduct (but largely because Irene tended to be a pacifist) public feeling did not appear particularly outraged, and she fell eventually through a subtle *coup d'état* planned from the depths of the Palace. Thus the Empress was always inevitably a figure of supreme importance; and so we find trailing through Byzantine history an endless procession of magnificent powerful princesses, giving it in uncomprehending manly western eyes a strange appearance that they took for vice.

The other members of the imperial family need not be noticed. As such, the only power that they enjoyed lay in the influence that they might wield over their relatives. They might, however, occupy some official post and thus share in the government.

Round the Emperor and the Empress were grouped the high officials of the Court and the government, the Sovereign's intimate counsellors and the heads of the State departments that administered the Empire. These officials all had their important circumscribed duties and were arranged in the strictest precedence; they were appointed and dismissed by the Emperor himself. It is difficult to assign to each one member of this bureaucracy his functions,[2] which probably varied greatly from time to time. All the higher members had a title[3] as well as his official post; and, as in England to-day, precedence was given

1 During every minority from the Empire's early days to its fall, with the sole exception of the sixty years of the Nicene Empire, the Empress-mother was regent during some part if not all of her son's minority. For a short summary of the position and power of the Empress, see Diehl, *Figures Byzantines*, I, chap. I.

2 Bury assigns the functions in so far as it is possible to do so in his *Imperial Administration in the Ninth Century*, which also embodies Philotheus's list of precedence drawn up for Leo VI.

3 Such as Protospatharius, Patrician, etc.

for the most part according to the title, but certain posts carried with them a definite high rank. In the early tenth century the minister who appears to have enjoyed the most power was the Paracoemomene, officially merely a high chamberlain attached to the person of the Emperor, but actually chief adviser, an agent to whom many of the most important affairs of State were entrusted; it seems to have been in abeyance when there was no worthy candidate. From the time of Michael III onward the post was held by the most distinguished of the Emperor's intimate councillors, till in the latter half of the tenth century the Paracoemomene Basil in power and wealth rivalled the Emperors themselves.[1]

In this bureaucracy posts were open to all; birth counted for very little indeed. Influential relatives, in Byzantium as everywhere, helped on advancement; but it is remarkable how few of the great officials of the tenth century appear to have belonged by birth to the landed aristocracy that was beginning now to set itself apart; almost all rose on their own merits. Once they had risen, they would form cliques among themselves and seal their alliances with marriages; but it was seldom their children that enjoyed the power in the next generation. This openness, which was the great strength of the Byzantine administration, was largely due to the employment of eunuchs in the government—an ideal class in that they had no family life, left no descendants, and never could aspire to be Emperor. Indeed, for the ambitious, excepting those few who dreamed of the throne, it was wiser to be castrated. But, for the very ambitious, the throne itself was not out of reach.

The aristocracy, such as it was, confined itself chiefly to the army, where the highest posts, provincial governorships and viceroyalties, were more congenial to those with a pride in their birth. This aristocracy was still in its infancy; any *nouveau riche* could join its ranks. Its distinguishing mark was its great landed estates; the rich were finding that land was by far the safest investment, and were buying up their poorer neighbour's pro-

---

1 Under Michael the Paracoemomene was Basil; Basil appointed none; under Leo there was first the sinister figure of Samonas, then the eunuch Constantine, who will figure largely in this story.

perty as fast as they could—to the vain distress of the government, who neither desired the small peasant proprietors to disappear nor powerful hereditary landlords to take their place. As yet few of the great families had emerged into history, and only in the more settled themes of Asia. But their numbers were rapidly increasing and their predilection with the army gave them a sinister strength.

But even in the army the poorest could rise on their merits to the top. This lack of snobbishness was characteristic of the whole of Byzantine society. It is true that later chroniclers, wishing to insult Theophano, called her an innkeeper's daughter; but society would have to be very democratic where such a past would not be thought a little undignified for an Empress; while the fact that an innkeeper's daughter could become Empress shows a certain elasticity in the social divisions. It was lack of education rather than lack of birth that was considered a subject for mockery. The Byzantines prided themselves on their culture. Every self-respecting citizen could recognize a quotation from Homer or the Bible, and was well acquainted with the works of the Fathers and many of the masterpieces of the Classics. The University, recently refounded by Bardas Caesar and stimulated by the restless mind of Photius, radiated intellectual activity throughout Constantinople; and the Court prided itself on its patronage of literature and the arts.

The imperial provinces were governed on a military basis, a government that had been necessitated by the perpetual presence of active enemies on every frontier. The Empire, at Leo VI's death, was divided into twenty-seven themes, fifteen in Asia and twelve in Europe,[1] in each of which a regiment was kept, whose commander, the Stratege, was also the head of the civil administration. The whole administration was extremely diverse, varying according to the past history and present needs of each locality; and besides the government of their own provinces, the Strateges often had external duties to perform. Life in the various provinces was inevitably very different. The European themes, troubled incessantly with Bulgarian invasions

1 Including Cherson, but excluding Dalmatia, which was really a collection of small vassal cities.

or Slav insurrections had very little settled life outside the towns. The Asiatic frontier was even more lawless, subject perpetually to the raids and arbitrary rule of the great uncontrolled border barons, Christian and Saracen alike. But further from the frontier Asia Minor was still one of the most fertile countries of the world, and the busy peasants and farmers of its valleys formed the great backbone of the Empire—the classes from which the best portion of the army was drawn, and which provided a sturdy solid ground for Greek and Armenian versatility to work upon. But already things were changing for the worse. Peasants were on the whole bound to the soil, in a vain attempt to put out of their reach the attractions of town life; and the slave-worked estates of the magnates were swallowing up the countryside.[1]

For the towns were the magnet that drew all that was most enterprising in the Empire; and of the towns the only one that really counted was Constantinople, ἡ Πόλις, the city, the great metropolis of the whole Mediterranean world. Its population during these years has been estimated at about 800,000;[2] but it must have been steadily on the increase. Like every mediaeval city, Constantinople had its filthy side-streets, filled with a rabble which seemed to have no occupation other than to live parasitically on charity and the doles, to pander to vice, to attend the circus and to form the crowds that now and then changed the destiny of the Empire. At the other extreme it contained the palaces of the nobles and merchant princes, imitating as far as their owners' riches would allow, the Imperial Palace itself—a network of halls and galleries and sumptuous side-chambers, where amid marbles and mosaics and brocaded coverings, on tiled or carpeted floors, the Emperor and his consort led their ceremonious lives. It contained the Patriarchal Court and its entourage: innumerable churches and monasteries: the University: the law courts, where the litigation of the Empire was centred: public baths and public hostelries: and the circus and its vast organization, financed and controlled by the government to provide recreation for the citizens of the Empire. But the

1 For the details of rural life see Chapter XI.
2 Macri, *L'Economie Urbaine*, p. 7.

bulk of the city was occupied by the houses and the shops of the
trading bourgeoisie.

Constantinople was the centre of the commerce of the early
Middle Ages. Caravans from Bagdad and Syria drove over the
hills of Asia Minor to meet there the caravans from Hungary
and the Balkans. It was the goal of the Russian traders carrying
in their small ships goods to and from the Russian forests and
the Baltic. In the harbour of the Golden Horn the Greek ships
collected, some trading with Cherson or Abasgia and Trebizond,
with goods from the Steppes, the Caucasus and the distant East,
some journeying to and fro, to Egypt, to Italy or to Spain. It
was the market and the clearing-house of the whole civilized
world. The bulk of the carrying trade was done in Greek ships,
but the number of foreign traders visiting or residing in the city
was always large; and for the more barbarous, such as the
Russians, special policing regulations had to be evolved. Besides
the traders, there were the busy Byzantine manufacturers, chiefly
of arts and luxuries, to be exported to every land that prided
itself on its civilization—such as the silk brocades, the cynosure
of Europe, or the works in enamel or metal, so eagerly prized
by foreigners and Byzantines alike. Moreover, there was the
local trade, and all the shops and retail houses that so great a city
required, and the large class, highly respected among the Greeks,
of moneylenders and bankers.

Of the merchant firms far the greatest was the Imperial Court.
Not only did the Court keep a strict monopoly of the ore of the
Empire in its jealous regard of the mint; but also the silk industry
was almost entirely in its hands—the silk cloth being manu-
factured largely in the gynaeceum of the Palace and being sold
by the Court for the silk corporation to retail. Still more remarkable were the Court deals in food. The officials would buy up
immense quantities of corn and sell it cheaply to the corporations
concerned. Beside its wholesale deals the Court had also its
own retail houses under its own control, quite opposed to the
merchant houses of the city.[1] But the city firms were under
an almost equally strict control; the network of monopolies,

1 Macri, op. cit. pp. 16, 18, 23.

measures for protection and detailed regulations, dictated by both the economic and the religious theories then in vogue, has never since been equalled. Wages, prices, hours of work—all were fixed; and even special laws were made for Lent. Under Leo VI's instructions, a handbook of these rules was drawn up for the guidance of the Prefect of the City, which gives a full and bewildering account of them all.[1] It shows the great preoccupation of the government to be that the city should have an abundant and regular supply of all the necessities of life, and in this anxiety the export trade was deliberately neglected.[2]

The official in charge of the local government of Constantinople was the Prefect of the City, the ἔπαρχος, one of the highest dignitaries of the State, ranking in precedence next below the strateges of Asia. His duties were enormous and necessitated a huge department of clerks and secretaries to assist him. He kept the city registers, named assessors, appointed the presidents of the corporations, judged infractions of the rules, and was minister of trade, through whom the Emperor would enact any commercial legislation. He had also to superintend the policing of the city, that is to say, to ensure tranquillity and order, to approve or forbid the opening of new shops, to fix prices and weights, to watch exports, to see to the proper observance of Sunday, and to take precautions against fires.[2] Thus his position was extremely arduous, and needed a very capable and respected man to fill it; it was one of the only posts (along with those of quaestor and the various domestics) that a eunuch could not hold. It is curious therefore that the names of remarkably few prefects should have survived; probably they were too busy to spare the time for political intrigue—Byzantine officials were like women in ancient Athens; it was a good sign if they were not talked about.

Of the plan of the city[3] little can be said. Within the limits of its great walls it had grown up unmethodically, and its hills

---

1 *Le Livre du Préfet* (ed. Nicole). I give a fuller account of these rules, and of the fixed rates of interest, etc., in Appendix III.

2 Macri, *op. cit.* pp. 66–67, 79: *D.C.* p. 725: Philotheus's list in Bury, *op. cit.* p. 145.

3 See map.

helped the jumble. Palaces and hovels seem to have been built side by side, and the various districts had no particular social status. The eastern end was devoted to the citadel, St Sophia and the Patriarchal Court, and the vast precincts of the Palace, with the circus attached to it. The shops and bazaars were situated for the most part according to their categories on either side of the street called Mese, that ran from the Palace gates right through the heart of the city. Of the suburbs none were particularly important, except for Chrysopolis and Chalcedon across the Bosphorus, the terminus of the great roads of Asia.

No other city of the Empire could in any way rival the capital. The most important in Europe, and, till the recapture of Antioch, in the whole Empire, was Thessalonica. It was the main port of Western Bulgaria, at the end of the great trade route that entered the Balkans at Belgrade and ran up the Morava and down the Vardar to the sea; and since the last decade of the ninth century it had dealt with almost all the Bulgar trade. John Cameniates gives a picture of it in the plenitude of its power, before the Moslem sack of 904,[1] a great commercial city with a considerable intellectual life; and the number of old churches, till recently still standing in its midst, is witness to its prosperity. The Moslem sack had been a serious setback; but the city's fine position ensured a quick recovery. Throughout history Thessalonica has remained inevitably one of the most vital and busy cities of Eastern Europe. Of the other seaports, Trebizond probably ranked next, as the port of Armenia and Iberia; and Smyrna, at the end of a time-honoured trade route, never lost its activity. Mesembria (for Eastern Bulgaria), Dyrrhachium (for Albania), Cilician Seleucia, and Bari in Italy, though all ports of importance, were too near to a frontier to have an uninterrupted commercial life. The inland cities such as Ancyra and Iconium were chiefly mere market towns: though some, such as Nicaea or Athens, hallowed in history, enjoyed a certain prestige and probably certain privileges, while others, such as Thebes,[2] were the centres of famous local industries. Then there

---

1 Cameniates, *De Excidio*, pp. 490 *et seq.*
2 It is unknown when the famous Theban silk industry started—probably not till the eleventh century.

were the great garrisoned fortress cities, such as Adrianople in
Europe or Colonea and Caesarea in Asia, commanding the roads
that led abroad. But even in the smallest, pettiest towns, the
presence of the Greeks and ubiquitous Armenians made a certain
business activity inevitable.

Commerce affected the majority of the Empire's citizens, but
religion affected them all. In an age when religion everywhere
dominated its rivals, philosophy and science, the superstition and
passion for theological intricacies that characterized the Greeks
and their neighbours gave it a supremacy unequalled in history.
The cities were crammed with churches; everywhere there were
relics and icons to worship; continually there were ceremonies
to perform. And on every side you saw the teeming monasteries
—havens of rest and gateways to Heaven. The non-monastic
Church was organized on lines roughly parallel to the secular
administration—the provincial metropolitans and bishops playing the parts of strateges and turmarchs, and the Patriarch acting
as Emperor over it all. But there was one important difference;
though supreme over the hierarchy the Patriarch himself was
under the supremacy of the Emperor; the Emperor, not he, was
the Viceroy of God—an exact reversal of the Hildebrandine
theory of the Western Church. Officially the Patriarch was elected
by the Church, but actually the Emperor not only appointed him
but also could, by the device of packing a synod, easily depose
him. However, the Patriarchs perpetually rebelled against this
mastery; and when the imperial commands clashed with the
patriarchal conscience, victory was not always with the Emperor
—the religious sentiments of the populace were greater even
than its respect for the Basileus, and on them the Patriarch could
usually fall back. If his personality were strong enough, he
would win. Therefore wise Emperors tended to elevate either
unworldly saints or their own dutiful sons on to the patriarchal
chair; and, curiously enough, so long as the Patriarch conducted
himself in a seemly and dignified manner, such cynical appointments aroused no horrified complaints, and even were made by
the most pious Emperors. The same friction existed in the provinces; metropolitans continually quarrelled with the local strateges and the Patriarch would intervene heavily on the side of

his servants.[1] The Church was extremely rich; the Patriarch was possessed of enormous revenues, and the metropolitans even in the poorest districts ranked as wealthy—the wealthiest—personages.[2]

The monasteries were an even more outstanding feature of Byzantine life. After the turmoil and troubles of the world, it was pleasant to retire into seclusion, to prepare for the other world that no one doubted was to come. And, for the government, they were an invaluable political expedient, providing reputable and philanthropic imprisonment for opponents—ensuring present detention and future salvation: while the dangerously prominent, disappointed in ambition or fearful of disgrace, found in them a safe inviolable refuge. In them you would find fallen statesmen or unwanted princes together with scholars and holy recluses who had never known the world: or, among the women, Empresses whose sun had set, through widowhood or defeat in the Palace, alongside of weary housewives and girls for whom no dowry could be found. Such a retirement was usually final; but where the vows were forced unwillingly on victims whom popular sentiment could regard as wronged, there might be a return, though only among the highest; occasionally an Emperor or an Empress came back to the world and the Palace. The monks as a class were well liked and respected, and many of them consulted as prophets; and a means of acquiring popularity was to show a taste for their company. As a result of this fashionable piety the monasteries became extremely powerful and rich; Emperors and magnates would found and handsomely endow them, and the pious in all stations of life would send them gifts or would enter their walls bringing all their worldly goods with them, or would bequeath them legacies at their deaths. In consequence the monasteries ranked among the greatest landowners and wealthiest capitalists in the Empire. In addition they were allowed a third part of the property of those that died without close heirs, and they raised more money by the monks' work, by business deals, or by such petty means as the sale of holy

---

1 See Nicholas Mysticus's *Letters*, e.g. Ep. CXLVI.
2 In 934 the Metropolitans of Corinth and Patras could afford to send four fully equipped horsemen to the wars—more than anyone else (*D.C.* p. 243).

objects.[1] The monasteries were under seven various forms of control; there were the free or autodespotic, owing allegiance to no one, founded by a special charter from the Emperor (such as the monasteries of Athos, of which the earlier received their charters during the tenth century): the imperial monasteries, founded on the imperial domain and under imperial control: those similarly under the Patriarch, the metropolitans, and the bishops: those that were daughter-houses of another monastery: and finally those under private persons, who endowed and controlled them and had certain obligations towards them—a monastery unfinished at the founder's death could claim a share in his estate equal to that of each of his children.[2]

Besides the monasteries there were also the lauras, in which the monks lived separated from one another—as it were, a collection of hermits; and finally there were the hermits dwelling quite alone, especially common in Calabria and Greece. Many of these rose to the status of Saint, and exerted an influence that made them a real power in provincial politics.

Advancement in the Church was quite democratic; the humblest priest could aspire to be a bishop, an archimandrite or the Patriarch himself. The high ecclesiastical officials were consequently men of exceptional merit, save only when the Emperor was deliberately placing nonentities or princes in command.[3]

It is impossible to insist too much on the dominion of religion over Byzantium. At its best it could be seen in the tenacity with which so many Byzantines abode by the dictates of their conscience, at its worst by the scenes of riot that would accompany the deposition of a patriarch and the triumph of his enemies. Party politics were religious politics; the great political schisms

---

1 Ferradou, *Les Biens des Monastères en Byzance*, pp. 26 *et seq.* A man who entered a monastery usually disposed of his goods beforehand, and at the time of his entry his wife could reclaim her dowry and his children could receive gifts.

2 *Ibid.* pp. 72, 91 *et seq.*

3 Of the nine men that occupied the patriarchal throne in the century 860–960, two were princes (Stephen and Theophylact), two were deliberate nonentities (Stephen of Amasea and Tryphon), Anthony Cauleas, a rather dim figure, showed considerable character, Euthymius was a saint of great distinction, and Photius, Nicholas Mysticus and Polyeuct were all three men of very remarkable brilliance and forcefulness.

that rent the State were based on religious differences—you have iconoclast fighting iconodule, Nicholaan fighting Euthymian and bringing the whole Empire into the lists. Even the impious and irreverent could not escape from this dominion, and self-consciously indulged in orgies of mock religion and the Black Mass. For superstition enjoyed an almost equal power. Omens were eagerly watched for, soothsayers consulted, respected and obeyed; and everyone believed that he had a στοιχεῖον, an inanimate double or genius, such as a statue or a pillar, with which his life and fate were inextricably bound up.

The place of women in Byzantine life is less easy to gauge. It has been customary to regard the gynaeceum as a prison from which Byzantine women never emerged—an exact equivalent of the Russian terem, which most historians say derived from it, forgetting Russia's two and a half centuries of Mongol rule. Certainly in the houses of the well-to-do, the women lived apart surrounded by eunuchs, and in the churches they worshipped from their special galleries; yet they clearly could wield enormous power not merely restricted to the influence of feminine wiles on doting husbands. I have spoken above of the Empress, whose position no one could call servile or tightly circumscribed. In less exalted society we have for an example the widow Danielis, Basil I's benefactress, probably the greatest landowner and slave-owner of her day, who led a life of remarkable independence, indulging her every whim and fancy.[1] Among the poorest classes the drudgery of cottage life keeps women to the fore in much the same extent throughout the whole world. But among the bourgeoisie there were such women as Psellus's mother whom his eulogy of her shows to have dominated and managed the whole life of the family, acknowledged as the moral and mental superior of her husband;[2] and she is not regarded as anything so remarkably unique. The whole attitude towards women was different from that of Western Europe, but certainly no more degrading. In the West, women were the frail sex set apart by chivalry and owing their privileges to their frailty; but

1 *Vita Basilii*, pp. 227 *et seq.*
2 In vol. x of Sathas's Μεσαιωνίκη βιβλιοθήκη, and quoted in Diehl's *Figures Byzantines*, I.

in Byzantium women were men's intellectual equals. Girls usually received the same education as their brothers; and Byzantine history can point to several authoresses of distinction. This made family life very close; the chroniclers give a charming picture of Constantine Porphyrogennetus's affection for his cultured daughters, particularly the Princess Agatha, his private secretary;[1] and, in the romance of Digenis Akritas, the Ducas brothers showed for their sister (subsequently the hero's mother) a loving pride that would seem justified only by poetic licence: though, on the other hand, another Ducas lady, the hero's bride, was kept immured by her father to a degree as close as any Moslem contemporary; but the wildness of life on the eastern frontier and the sensational adventures of her mother-in-law make such precautions not surprising.[2] It was however difficult for women to carve out a career of their own, save as prostitutes —a class as powerful in Byzantium as anywhere—; in the Church they could only attain prominence as abbesses—though the abbesses of the greater houses were figures of real importance. The only secular public appointments that they could hold were those of autocrat and regent and various posts in the Empress's Court. Of these latter the highest, that of Zoste Patricia, gave its bearer one of the highest ranks in the imperial hierarchy, counting her as a member of the imperial family. Indeed, she seems often to have been the Empress's mother.[3]

Whatever was the influence of women in Byzantine life, it certainly did not equal that of the eunuchs, whose significance has never, I think, been properly realized. In the West, eunuchs never played nor were to play a rôle of any importance save as sopranos; in oriental countries—the lands of the Califate, Persia or China, they were primarily domestic servants who could be safely trusted with the harem: though occasionally, especially under the Califate during these centuries, an able eunuch might rise to high distinction. It was only in Byzantium that they

1 Theoph. Cont. p. 459.

2 *Les Exploits de Digénis Akritas* (ed. Le Grand), pp. 4–5 (esp. lines 108–112), 52 *et seq.*

3 *D.C.* pp. 726–7. Along with the Patriarch, Caesar, Nobilissimus, Curopalates and the Basileopator she could eat at the imperial table. Theodora's mother, Theoctiste Florina, was created Zoste Patricia.

became practically the government of the Empire. Their rise almost coincided with the genesis of the Empire at Constantinople; already by the sixth century one of the greatest of Byzantine generals was a eunuch. By the tenth century eunuchs took precedence of non-eunuchs: that is to say, patricians who were eunuchs ranked above the strateges and military commanders, while ordinary patricians ranked below them.[1] Throughout the tenth century many of the most prominent men in the Church and the State were eunuchs; indeed, so far from castration being a stigma in after-life, parents would castrate their sons to secure their advancement; the younger sons of even the Emperor himself might be so treated.[2] The only posts that a eunuch could not occupy were those of Prefect of the City, Quaestor, Domestic of the four imperial regiments, and the imperial throne itself. And in this last restriction lay the secret of their power. The Emperor, surrounded by eunuchs, knew that none of his entourage could hope to supersede him—even rival claimants to the throne could by this simple device be used safely in the service of the State. Moreover, the eunuchs left no sons, and had no family life; they were the weapon that kept feudalism at bay. In the West, as in Japan, an empire that once much resembled the Byzantine in its form, great posts tended to become more and more hereditary, until either devolution followed or Mayors of the Palace swamped out the lawful line of monarchs. But the Byzantine Emperors, with eunuchs for their great officers of State, need not fear. In the army the nobility might hand on high commands as though they were heirlooms, but the Empire was Constantinople and the Court; if that were kept pure all would be well. It was only in the late eleventh century when the extinction of the dynasty coincided with the dangers of foreign invasions all round that the army captured the government, and the Empire had to taste the rule of feudal families—a taste that was poison. Eunuchs might intrigue for their brothers and nephews, but collaterals never have the same appeal to the instincts as descendants, and so such intrigues were fitful and

1 Philotheus in Bury, *Social Administration*, p. 145.
2 Theophylact Lecapenus was said to be a eunuch (Maçoudi, *V.P.* p. 35; but Maçoudi was not very well-informed about the imperial family).

without much force. Thus the eunuch system was of immense value to Byzantium, enabling the Emperor to keep a firm control over the government and to give posts according to merit. Castration may be degraded and disgusting, but it certainly had its uses.

Of the effect of these many eunuchs on Byzantine society little need be said. It is not the place here to discuss the psychological results of castration, but one or two comments must be made. It has long been the custom to talk of eunuchs as always having a demoralizing influence all round, and historians that seem otherwise sane[1] talk Gibbonesque cant about the intrigues and cowardice rampant in a life so full of eunuchs and women. When we read this, we should remember that, in the first half of the tenth century, the only period during which the Byzantine government pursued a bold and straightforward policy—a policy which failed largely through these 'masculine' qualities—was that during which it was controlled by the Empress Zoe Carbopsina and her eunuch minister the Paracoemomene Constantine. Such generalizations are a disgrace to the historians that make them. You cannot interpret history if you create three inelastic types, man, woman, and eunuch.

Finally, mention must be made of the many different races that composed the Empire. In no Empire were so many different nationalities gathered together, speaking one language, following one religion and obeying one government. In the Byzantine army there was hardly a tribe unrepresented—Saracens, Armenians, Caucasians, Chazars, Russians, Hungarians, Southern Slavs, Bulgars, Dalmatians and Italians all were to be found there, besides strange Syrian tribes such as the Mardaites, long domiciled within the Empire but ethnologically unadulterated. Among the upper classes the ingredients were already mixed; families might be of definite racial origins, but intermarriage soon modified the purity of their blood. The majority of the citizens of Constantinople were Greek or of the indigenous inhabitants of Asia Minor,[2] but many, especially among the

---

1 E.g. Professor Diehl (*Camb. Med. Hist.* IV, p. 756).

2 I use the word 'indigenous' in the full consciousness that it is incorrect, merely as a simple *façon de parler*. The inhabitants of Asia Minor were a

richer classes, were Slavs and still more Armenian—the imperial family itself (the so-called Macedonian house) claimed royal Armenian descent—and occasionally even Saracen converts joined up with the nobility. In the provinces there were even more ingredients—the original inhabitants and the tribes introduced by the various barbarian invasions or by the Byzantine habit of transporting whole peoples, either to remove them from a place where they might create trouble or to use them as a peaceful leaven in districts already too troublesome. The effect of these peaceful penetrators was very beneficial. The Empire had had too overpowering a personality not to absorb them, but the constant influx perpetually brought in new ideas, new blood and new vigour; and coming in as it did on all sides it did not weigh the Empire too far down on any one side. Even all the Armenians, the most numerous of these invaders, though their Sassanid heritage deeply moulded the imperial art of the capital and still more the art of the provinces, never could make Byzantium an Asiatic land. The conception of the Roman Empire was too strong.

Rambaud, whose summary of the Empire as a universal Empire with its cosmopolitan character created and conserved by Constantine, is the best that has been written,[1] gives, I think, one ruinous misconception in denying it nationality, in saying that Greek had the *spurious* air of a national language. It may seem paradoxical to urge the nationality of the Empire while insisting on its cosmopolitan nature; certainly, if nationality implies a common ethnological past the Byzantines had none. But such a past is not necessary, as to-day the United States of America is witness; and in Byzantium the tradition inherited from the world-empire of Rome combined with the tradition of orthodox Christianity, embodied in the holy person of the Emperor and expressed in the common Greek language, did give the Byzantines a national unity that overpowered ethno-

muddled mixture of innumerable races. Phrygians, Hittites, Lydians, Scythians, Greeks, Romans, Gauls, Jews, Armenians and Arabs, to mention a few ingredients. The noble Asiatic families, such as the Comneni, usually claimed a Roman ancestry—always quite untraceable.

1 Rambaud, *L'Empire Grec*, pp. 531–540.

logical divergencies—a national unity far more real than any
that was to exist in Western Europe till the days of the Reforma-
tion. Every Byzantine citizen, were his blood Greek or Armenian
or Slav, was proudly and patriotically conscious that he was
'Ρωμαῖος, belonging to the universal everlasting Empire of Rome
and to the one orthodox faith, despising foreigners and heretics
alike. This nationality even tended to mould its people according
to one fixed form; and it is as possible to talk of Byzantine
characteristics as to talk of Roman or British characteristics.

Of these characteristics little need be said. The Byzantine love
of art and culture and splendour is amply proved. Better known
are their superstitious piety and their intriguing subtleties. A
passion for theological discussion and for politics characterized
the Byzantines; and under an autocracy the latter can only be
expressed in intrigues. Moreover, the lack of a fixed hereditary
principle in the imperial succession, together with the small
families that chance perpetually reserved for the imperial house,
resulted in an alarming paucity of Emperors that died a natural
death on the throne.[1] The commercial genius of the Byzantines,
that gave Constantinople her wealth, has lasted among the
Greeks and Armenians to this day, though the organizing ability
shown by so many of the great statesmen of the Empire seems
to be lost. There are constant proofs of the resilient vitality of
the Byzantines—the ease with which they recovered from disaster,
either overmastering it or adapting themselves to new conditions.
Less easy to gauge is the atmosphere of cruelty in Byzantine life.
It has long been fashionable to talk of Byzantinism as a by-word
for decadent cruelty. Certainly the Byzantines were masters of
the art of torture, certainly they were callous to an extreme in
their treatment of enemy prisoners, certainly religious disagreements would rouse them to frenzies which killed all humani-
tarianism, and certainly they experienced a large number of
crimes passionnels in high places; but, on the other hand, we
must remember that the mutilations, which seem to us such an
unpleasant feature of Byzantine life, were adopted as being more

---

1 The proportion is however very misleading. The violent depositions usually
occurred in a swift succession over a short period of time, and the ample
interstices were filled by long peacefully terminated reigns.

humane punishments than the death that Roman and western law prescribed for offences of an equal degree. For political offenders the customary punishment was nothing more barbarous than seclusion in a monastery, though occasionally scourging might be attached: while an act of real severity among citizens of the Empire might excite disapproval enough to wreck the government that ordered it.[1] On the whole, Byzantium compares well with the contemporary West.

This, then, is a rough picture of Byzantine society as it was at the beginning of the tenth century—a passionate prejudiced society, but sensitive and intelligent, consciously the one legitimate heir of classical refinement and Christian truth in a dark and ignorant world. On such a stage, in such a setting, with its high lights and its shadows, the grand dramas were played out, on whose intricate plots were hanging the fate of millions.

1 Such as the punishment of the Ducas conspiracy in 913.

CHAPTER II

The Legacy of the Emperor Leo the Wise

IN Lent, 912, the Emperor Leo the Wise lay dying, racked
with pain and fearful for his country and his son. His reign
had not been very successful; abroad and at home there were
problems still unsolved; his life had been one of trouble and
sorrow, and his death meant trouble to come. The renascence
brought about by his predecessor, Basil the Macedonian, was
hesitating—was being tried in the balance.

Most of the Empire's foreign problems had been more or less
unchanged for the last two centuries. On the eastern frontier
there were always Saracen raids to meet and there was always
a watchful eye to be kept on the key country Armenia. In Italy
there were similar Saracen raids, and there always might be
trouble from the Lombard princes or the Western Emperors.
For the last century the Aegean coasts had needed special care
owing to the Saracens' occupation of Crete and use of it as a
pirate base. In the north there was Cherson to guard; in the
Balkans there was the perpetual danger of barbarian invasions.
With regard to these permanent factors Leo's legacy did not
promise to be a great liability. There had been defeats and
disasters, especially by sea. The Byzantines could claim a great
victory under the Admiral Himerius in 906, but already they had
suffered in 902 and 904 the sack by the renegade Leo of Tripoli
of Demetrias and of the great city of Thessalonica itself; and in
911 Himerius's huge expedition against Crete had been annihilated by this same Leo off Samos. In the West, Sicily had been
finally lost; but that was according to the policy of Basil, that it
was better to reconquer Southern Italy than to retain the island.
In the East there had been a terrible series of Arab raids from
Tarsus; but further north Leo had increased and consolidated
Basil's conquests on the Upper Euphrates and had further made
an alliance with the Bagratid King of Armenia. Moreover, the
Califate was in an obvious decline; the Calif himself (al-Mokta-

dir) was a minor, round whom plotted viziers, generals, and his
Turkish bodyguard, while in the provinces revolt was seething
and local dynasties emerging. There was, however, danger in
Armenia; for as Leo lay on his deathbed, the Arabs under the
powerful Emir of Aderbaijan and Northern Persia were planning
and setting out on the conquest of the whole of the country.[1]
Finally, in the Balkans there had been no barbarian invasions of
any significance;[2] but the reason for this lay in the greatest
foreign problem that Byzantium had had to face for two centuries, a new unprecedented problem. Right along the northern
frontier stretched a strong semi-civilized and ambitious Empire,
the Empire of Bulgaria.

The Slavs had crossed the Danube during the sixth century;
and, though they had formally submitted to the Empire, it was
only from isolated fortresses that the imperial government could
control the Balkans. During the seventh century a new tribe
had pushed across into the Balkans from Bessarabia and was
proceeding to occupy the old province of Lower Moesia. This
was the Bulgars, a Turkish tribe organized in a militarist system
in clans the chief of whose leaders was the Prince, the Sublime
Khan. During the eighth and ninth centuries various developments had been taking place. Externally, the Bulgar Empire had
increased its dominion, stretching down to the mountains of
Rhodope and into Macedonia. Internally, the Sublime Khan
was engaged in establishing his supremacy over the other clan
leaders and in organizing his realm on centralized autocratic
lines, the Bulgars were rapidly blending with the Slavs and
adopting their language, and the whole civilization of the nation
was proceeding apace. The ninth century saw the crowning of
these achievements. In its early years the Khan Krum had in
his fierce wars, despite occasional imperial victories, broken down
the old imperial prestige and shown the menace that lay in his
country. He had captured the last fortresses of the Empire north
of the mountains, he had raided to the very walls of the capital,
and he had slain in battle an Emperor himself. It had been

1 See Chapter VII.
2 I regard Oleg's invasion as almost certainly apocryphal; and the Magyar
invasions in the neighbourhood of Thessalonica were of small importance.

disquieting for the government at Constantinople; but after all Krum was only a barbarian raider. The next generation, however, could not be dismissed so lightly.

The great event of Bulgarian history in the ninth century was the conversion of the Bulgars to Christianity about the year 865. This had been chiefly the work of the Byzantine government, who had even gone to war to secure it. But though such a missionary triumph reflected glory on all concerned, the work had not been entirely voluntary. The Byzantines had had their hands forced; for the Western Emperor, eager for support against Moravia, was planning to bring Bulgaria into the sphere of the Latin Church. The chief gainer by the conversion was the Prince Boris.[1] By taking his religion from the Caesaropapist East, he became more than ever autocrat of his people, while the new religion with its Slavonic liturgy more than ever blended the two races; and the unwillingness of his nobles, which they expressed in an insurrection, enabled him to indulge in a wholesale massacre and silence them for two generations. Moreover, negotiations with the Latin Church had taught him how to put his soul up to auction; Rome and Constantinople outbid each other in concessions in order to obtain his spiritual allegiance. Constantinople won; but it was to Boris's advantage that it should.[2]

The Byzantines had come out of a difficult situation as well as they could. The Bulgar prince was the Emperor's godson; the Archbishop of Bulgaria was under the authority of the Patriarch, to whom he ranked second in ecclesiastical precedence. Stimulated by their religion, fashionable Bulgarians hastened to Constantinople for their education, and copied with wondering enthusiasm the refinements of the capital. All seemed well and amicable. Peace outlasted Boris's reign, giving a false fair promise for the future.

It is at such a stage that a nation is most dependent on the character of its autocrat; a great king can make a great people.

1 The 'Sublime Khan' had already become the 'Kniaz', the Slav Prince.
2 For the best easily obtainable account of the effects of the conversion see Prof. Zlatarsky's articles on 'The Making of Bulgaria' in the *Slavonic Review*, IV (1925-6).

Boris was such a king; and now a greater was to come. Boris abdicated in 889 in favour of his elder son Vladimir. But after four years, during which Vladimir showed himself to be both incompetent and anti-Christian, Boris returned from his cloister to depose and do away with him, placing instead his younger son Symeon on the throne.[1] He then retired with confidence. Symeon had been intended for the Church; he had been educated at Constantinople, where he had studied not only the Holy Fathers but also Demosthenes and Aristotle, and had further seen the methods of Byzantine government, and learnt their lesson. From this education he was known as Hemiargus, the half-Greek;[2] and once on the throne he showed his tastes by everywhere patronizing culture and the priests who were its main exponents, ordering sacred writings and secular romances to be translated into the Slavonic, and by adorning the new capital of Preslav with a magnificence that was the cynosure of all his countrymen.[3] Less obviously, he must also have improved the organization of his country; during his long, sensational and exhausting reign, he was never, it seems, disturbed by the slightest rebellion or unrest [though this was probably due chiefly to the force of his personality. After his death the organization broke down]. In addition, he showed an aptitude for war.

He had tasted blood early in his reign. In the year 896 a war broke out owing to a trade dispute. Jobbery at the Byzantine Court had caused the removal of the Bulgarian counters from Constantinople to Thessalonica, thus upsetting the whole Bulgarian commerce. Symeon, watchful of his country's interests, protested to the Emperor, and, finding his protests unheeded, took to arms. The Emperor Leo countered by calling in the Magyars, a fierce Finnish tribe then settled in Bessarabia, to attack the Bulgars in the rear. The device was at first successful, and Symeon appeared to submit; but meanwhile, having learnt the device, he called in against the Magyars the still fiercer tribe

1 Zlatarsky, *Istoriya*, I, 2, pp. 246 *et seq.*
2 Liudprand, *Antapodosis*, p. 87.
3 John the Exarch, Gregory the Presbyter and the Monk Chrabr, all wrote at Symeon's command. John the Exarch describes Preslav at the time of its glory (pp. 46, 47).

that lay beyond, the Petchenegs. Then, with the Magyars occupied, he turned on the unsuspecting Byzantines and routed
them at the battle of Bulgarophygum (897), thus winning the
war.[1] At the ensuing peace, though it seems that the Bulgar
trade still was diverted to Thessalonica,[2] and though there is no
evidence of Symeon having made any territorial annexations,
Symeon certainly was able to demand and receive a yearly tribute
from the Imperial Court. It was a triumph for Bulgar prestige.[3]
The further results of the war, the tribal migrations that altered
the fate of Central Europe, need not concern us here, except in
that through them Symeon lost the vast but vaguely governed
Trans-Danubian Empire (Wallachia and Transylvania) that he
had inherited from his fathers. It was not a serious loss; and it
made him all the more eager to turn his attention to the south.

Since then there had been peace; and Bulgaria had grown in
prosperity and culture, and Symeon in ambition. Careless politicians at Byzantium might notice no danger, but Symeon was
evolving a grandiose idea. He would aim at nothing less than
placing himself on the throne of the Emperors, founding a new
Bulgaro-Byzantine Empire on the ruins of the Second Rome.
The idea, which has tormented the dreams of every Balkan
monarch since his day, seemed feasible enough, given an opportunity to strike the necessary blow. And now, after fifteen years'
vigil since his first victories, the opportunity was coming. For
the Empire was sick at its heart, tormented by schism in the
Church and dissension in the Palace, the outcome of the cruel
fate that dogged the Emperor Leo the Wise.

Had Leo been able to leave as his legacy to his son perfect
peace at home, in the Church and in the State, the Bulgarian
menace would not have been so very hard to face. But disasters,
incalculable and unforeseen, had left him and his heir in a
position of complex difficulty and had roused up all the latent
hostilities between the Imperial and the Patriarchal Courts. We

---

1 Theoph. Cont. pp. 357 et seq.; Zlatarsky, op. cit. pp. 283 et seq.; Bury, The
Treatise De Administrando Imperio, pp. 565–6.
2 In Constantine Porphyrogennetus's day, the Western Bulgarian trade certainly was carried through Thessalonica (D.A.I. p. 177).
3 The tribute that Alexander refused to pay (Theoph. Cont. p. 380) dates
clearly from now. See Zlatarsky, op. cit. pp. 320 et seq.

must go back to the founder of the Macedonian house, the
Emperor Basil I. Basil, when he first entered the Palace as the
favourite of Michael III, was already the father of a boy, Constantine; but almost at once, with better tact than taste, he had
divorced the boy's mother, the rustic bride of his youth, and
married the Emperor's chief mistress, Eudocia Ingerina. Eudocia
bore three sons, the eldest, Leo, during Michael's lifetime, the
others, Alexander and Stephen, after his murder and her husband's accession. Thus from the outset of his life Leo's position
was difficult; no one knew which was his father, Basil who
officially recognized him or Michael whom everyone suspected.
Nor can we tell to-day; all that is clear is that Basil and Leo
always regarded each other with a cold suspicious enmity. At
first it did not matter; Basil had for his heir his beloved Constantine. But in 880 Constantine died, and Leo became heir to
the throne.

Basil's first care was to provide a bride for his successor; and
in about 885[1] Leo was married to a relative of his mother's by
name Theophano. The marriage was unsuccessful from the first;
Theophano, unlike Eudocia Ingerina, was of a devout, austere
temperament, and Leo, amorous and passionate, began to look
elsewhere. In 888 Basil died, leaving his throne to Leo and to
Alexander—but there was no love between the brothers: so that
Alexander enjoyed no power nor influence during Leo's lifetime.
Deprived of her father-in-law's support, Theophano passed into
miserable neglect. She had only borne one child to Leo, a
daughter Eudocia, who was not enough to bind them together.
Meanwhile, Leo carried on an open liaison with a young married
woman of very bad repute, Zoe, wife of Theodore Guzuniates
and daughter of the chief minister Stylianus Zaützes. Things
reached so shameless a pitch that Zoe would accompany Leo on
his journeys, while Stylianus was honoured with the specially
created title of Basileopator, father of the Emperor. The child
princess died late in 892, and the Empress, after one more year
of even lonelier wretchedness, followed her to the grave. Very
shortly afterwards Zoe's husband also died. Leo was overjoyed.

---

1 de Boor says 882–3; all that we know is that it was before 888.

As a pious penitent gesture he caused the dead Theophano to be created a saint; but then the world was scandalized by the sight of a saint's widower promptly marrying his mistress, and crowning her with the imperial crown. The Patriarch felt sufficiently strongly on the subject to suspend the officiating priest. Providence however punished the guilty pair more effectively. Zoe, after her long waiting, had only a short triumph. After twenty months she died, leaving behind her one daughter alone, Anna, born before her parents' marriage. Repentant at the end she had carved on her coffin the words: "The miserable daughter of Babylon".

In his *Novellae* Leo had expressed himself very strongly not only against concubinage but also against third marriages,[1] proving himself in this an orthodox son of the Church. Already, on the first of these rules, his practice had not come up to his precepts; and now he was to be tested on the second. He hesitated, but his position was urgent. He himself was delicate; he had no son; his only surviving brother, Alexander, was childless and debauched. For the sake of the dynasty and the Empire surely indulgence would be allowed. In the meantime he crowned his daughter Anna Augusta, as without an Augusta so many ceremonies could not be performed; and perhaps if the worst were to happen it would indicate her as his successor. But by 898 he was negotiating for her marriage with Louis of Provence, the most promising candidate for the Western Empire. By 899 he considered himself, and was, it seems, generally considered, justified in marrying once more, and took as his bride a young Phrygian girl, Eudocia Baiana.

Within a year Eudocia was dead and her infant son Basil dead with her. Leo was worse off than before. A third marriage had been pardoned, but a fourth was unthinkable. Leo must resign himself to his cruel fate, the stern punishment for the criminal love of his youth. His daughter Anna stayed with him; her marriage to the western prince never took place; but she soon fades out of history, claimed no doubt by death[2]. There was a

1 Leo, *Novellae*, Const. xc, p. 604.
2 It seems that Alexander's wife never enjoyed the position of Empress. Probably Alexander did not marry until after Zoe Carbopsina was already crowned.

pause; then a new factor suddenly arose to intensify the situation; the Emperor fell once again in love. His choice was a second Zoe, surnamed Carbopsina from her dark eyes, a girl of noble birth, niece of St Theophanes the celebrated chronicler, and of high ambitions and a proud temper, determined to sit on the Empress's throne. At first Leo did not dare to marry her: though he took her to the Palace as an acknowledged *maîtresse en titre*: and marriage was the obvious aim of both. He had hopes now of ecclesiastical support; in 902 he had placed in the patriarchal chair his intimate friend Nicholas Mysticus. Late in 905 the question became desperately acute. In the Purple Chamber of the Augustas Zoe gave birth to a boy, Constantine, called Porphyrogennetus. Leo had a son at last. Now, more than ever, his parents must be married to remove from him the stigma of bastardy that would hamper his succession to the Empire. But on this the Patriarch openly declared himself. He had long disapproved of the liaison, and in January, 906, he announced that he would baptize the child, but on the one definite condition that Zoe left the Court for ever.

Had the ultimatum been accepted, Constantine might indeed have reached the throne, but existing thus admittedly only on patriarchal tolerance, he would probably never have survived his troubled minority; or if he had, the power of the Church would have been increased to be a terrible menace to the Emperors and the whole State. However, neither Leo nor Zoe dreamed of accepting. The child was baptized, indeed; but three days later a complacent priest married the Emperor to his concubine, and Zoe was crowned Augusta.

The Church was scandalized. For several months Nicholas alternately pleaded with and fulminated against the Emperor, and finally forbade him to enter St Sophia. It was a direct challenge; but Leo saw his way to victory. With an air of conciliation he appealed to the Pope of Rome, whom all recognized as the world's premier bishop, and who, he knew, was still smarting under the taunts of Photius and was eager to reassert his authority, and to the other Patriarchs of the East, equally jealous of Constantinople. These would certainly be on his side. But Nicholas remained inflexible; and finally, on Christmas Day

(906) he closed the great gates of the cathedral in the Emperor's face. Leo could stand no more; when the Roman pontiff's written support arrived, he replied to the insult by arresting Nicholas in the midst of a festival and sending him over the February snows to an exile at Galacreni. With him were deposed all his leading followers. Ingeniously Leo found a saint to take his place; the gentle monk Euthymius the Syncellus was willing to condone much in the interests of peace, and was fortified, men said, by a revelation. And it was equally simple to find equally willing if less virtuous clerics to fill the other empty places. An appearance of concord was restored; and Leo could worship freely at his cathedral with his beloved Augusta. But it was only an appearance; Nicholas kept his supporters, and added to them by his sufferings.[1]

Leo had won the first battle; but the war was not yet over. It had involved issues too deep to be settled so simply. The first point was the succession to the throne; for that Leo's victory had achieved its purpose. His son was accepted as the heir and, when in 911 the child was crowned co-Emperor, his succession was assured. Constantine was an Emperor himself, his father was the Basileus, his mother the Augusta; and, however immoral was their union, it had been, rightly or wrongly, legalized. Indeed, so firmly were his rights embedded in the minds of the people that not only did Alexander never dare to harm him in his childhood but also the house of Lecapenus even after keeping him in the shadow for twenty-five years could not ultimately shake him from the throne. Some inexplicable sentiment surrounded the Porphyrogennetus, a sentiment that his personal attributes never can have caused, that gave to him and his dynasty a loyalty hitherto unknown in Byzantine history. Leo, by his matrimonial perseverance, established an acknowledged legitimate succession, and gave its greatest dynasty to Byzantium. Despite long minorities and rulers as preposterous as the Porphyrogenneta Zoe, no one could displace the Macedonian house till it died out in the withered figure of the Empress Theodora.

1 For the references for these events (known as the Tetrogamia) see Theoph. Cont. pp. 360 *et seq. passim*; Nich. Myst. Ep. XXXII, pp. 197 *et seq.*; and, most important of all, *Vita Euthymii* (ed. de Boor), *passim*.

But the war had raised another question—the whole question of the relations between Church and State. Leo had been an autocratic Emperor; early in his reign, angry at the power and insubordination of Photius, he had deposed the proud Patriarch, and set up his own brother Stephen in his place. This device failed owing to Stephen's early death; and Anthony Cauleas, his successor, showed independence enough to protest against Leo's second marriage, though his protests were overruled. But in Nicholas Leo had met his match. Leo triumphed by the sheer weight of the imperial authority; but he split the Church and, with the Church, the State. On his side he kept those who, like Euthymius, took the legal view of regarding the Emperor as supreme; spiritual advisers might protest unofficially, but the Emperor's public decisions were law. Opposed to him, allied with his political enemies, were Nicholas and his followers, who set the laws of God above the laws of the Empire, regarding the Patriarch and the Church as the exponent of the former and as the keeper of the imperial conscience. The Nicholaans were out of power at the moment, but they were by no means dead. Constantine Porphyrogennetus might succeed to the throne; but it was very uncertain what authority that throne would have—whether the Patriarch might not establish himself as God's deputy, with the Emperor merely a secular underling—might not be an earlier, oriental Hildebrand. Leo's son was a little child, his brother the Emperor Alexander his enemy, the ally of this opposition. The world might well doubt the result.

The Bulgarian king in all his power was watching on the frontier; the Empire at home was rent in twain. Leo on his agonized deathbed saw the future black before his Empress and his son. After thirteen months, he said, an evil time was coming. Only, though he prophesied accurately the length of Alexander's reign, for the rest he made a mistake. Lent passed, and Easter; then on Tuesday, May 11th, he died and that day the evil time was on Byzantium.

CHAPTER III

The Regency: Alexander, Nicholas and Zoe

AT once the Emperor Alexander stepped into his brother's place. He had been crowned co-Emperor in his childhood, some forty years before; and ever since he had waited in impotent obscurity. Byzantine society merely knew of him as being fond of hunting and debauchery, and a passionate opponent of his brother. Indeed, his complicity in certain plots had been punished, on one occasion, by the removal of his wife; and it seems that in 904 he had for some time lost the rank of co-Emperor.[1] Nevertheless there was no question now of anyone else taking over the government. He was by far the senior co-Emperor and his nephew and colleague was only a child of six. The friends of the little Constantine had to resign themselves to fate, and wait, hoping for the best, till in his turn the childless debauchee should die.

Alexander's reign was to be a cruel test of the Empire. His policy was governed by one simple motive—to overturn everything that his brother had ever done. Beyond that he did not care. First he turned his attention to the lay administration. The Empress Zoe was ejected from the Palace, followed by all her friends such as the Paracoemomene Constantine; her cousin, the Admiral Himerius, was disgraced and died after six months' agony in prison.[2] A régime of new favourites came in. Then he could deal with the Church, where a common opposition to Leo had allied him to Nicholas. Nicholas himself, in his apologia to the Pope, claimed that he had been reinstalled by Leo, repentant on his deathbed.[3] That made a prettier and more creditable story. The truth was less palatable. A council was held in the Magnaura, packed with Nicholaan supporters and attended by Alexander. There the gentle Euthymius was declared de-

1 *Vita Euthymii*, p. 29; Lampros in *Byz. Zeitschrift*, 1895, p. 92.
2 Theoph. Cont. p. 379; *D.C.* p. 230.
3 Nich. Myst. Ep. XXXII, p. 217.

posed and covered with insults (though to the pious joy of the righteous the cleric who plucked his beard returned home to find a burnt house and a paralysed daughter) and was sent to an imprisonment at the monastery of Agathon. With him fell his friends and followers; and Nicholas reigned triumphant in the Church[1]. But now the Euthymians too had the asset of a prominent martyr.

Having paid these debts to his fraternal hatred, Alexander settled down to enjoy himself. He removed his wife and his mother-in-law from the Palace, to make way for his more amiable concubine.[2] And he saw with especial care to the enrichment of his two young Slavonian favourites, Gabrielopulus and Basilitzes. The latter he even intended for the imperial throne, planning to put his young nephew out of the question by castration; but Zoe's friends could persuade him that it was dangerous and unnecessary thus to outrage public opinion; the child was sickly, it would be wiser to await his early death. Meanwhile, Alexander and his favourites spent their time in drinking-bouts or in acts of awful impiety; he thought that a bronze boar in the circus was his double, his στοιχεῖον, and not only did he provide it with a set of teeth, but he paid it solemn worship, setting around it hangings and candelabra stolen from the churches. And all Constantinople was alarmed by a sudden swordlike comet, the inevitable herald of disaster.[3]

Foreign politics did not trouble Alexander's mind. For the most part he did nothing. But it was after one of his drinking-bouts that an embassy arrived from Symeon of Bulgaria to greet the new Emperor and demand the yearly tribute. Alexander received the envoys with insults and threats and sent them back tributeless to Bulgaria. Symeon was not displeased. The financial loss might be irritating; but he had an admirable pretext for declaring war, and he knew now that the Empire was governed by a fool. Carefully, at his leisure, he prepared his forces to march upon the capital.[4] The Greek chroniclers say that Alex-

1 Theoph. Cont. pp. 377 et seq.; Vita Euthymii, pp. 61 et seq.
2 Vita Euthymii, p. 68.
3 Theoph. Cont. p. 379. The comet was Halley's comet.
4 Ibid. p. 380.

ander did nothing worthy of mention on the throne.[1] It is untrue; he embittered the religious quarrel into a further frenzy, and he provoked a Bulgar war when the Empire could least afford to meet it.

But now the thirteen months were nearly done. On Friday, June 4th, after dining and drinking too well, Alexander went out to play his favourite ball game. In the midst of the play he was struck down by a serious fit, and it became apparent that he would not recover. The news sent a tremor through the city. The Empress Zoe forced her way into the Palace, to be in at the death. The Patriarch Nicholas, fearful for his position, looked round for a candidate of his own to push on to the throne, and thought of Constantine Ducas, Domestic of the Schools,[2] by birth a foe to the Macedonian house; and secret messages began to pass between the Patriarchate and the army headquarters in Thrace. But the dying Alexander recovered consciousness and conscience enough to acknowledge his nephew as successor and to nominate his council of regency, determined to the last to oust his sister-in-law from power. Then, on the Sunday, he died.[3]

Constantine Porphyrogennetus was left sole Emperor, a sickly child, seven years old, and the last scion of his house. No one could expect the dynasty to last, and on all sides there was a scramble for power—and power sufficiently well established to outlast the probable death of the crowned child. The Regents left by Alexander numbered seven, chosen, in a curious combination, out of reputable statesmen and disreputable favourites. They were the Patriarch Nicholas, Stephen the Magister, John Eladas the Magister, John the Rector, Euthymius (not the ex-Patriarch), Basilitzes and Gabrielopulus.[4] Of these Euthymius is only a name—the later chroniclers even forget to mention him[5]. Basilitzes and Gabrielopulus and John Lazanes the

1 Theoph. Cont. p. 378.
2 I.e. Commander-in-chief.
3 Theoph. Cont. p. 380; *Vita Euthymii*, pp. 69, 70.
4 Theoph. Cont. p. 380. The Slavonic version of the Logothete (p. 125) leaves out John Eladas, but refers to him as Regent on the next page.
5 E.g. Cedrenus, II, p. 279.

Rector—an athletic and dissolute priest—were Alexander's creatures and without him were negligible. The two Magistri were more distinguished, and the chroniclers treat them with respect. John Eladas's past is unknown, but he was clearly of some position and ability when he entered the council. Stephen, son of Calomaria, the sister of the Empress Theodora, had come into prominence at the beginning of Leo's reign as an enemy of Photius, and so perhaps held anti-ecclesiastical views.[1] Certainly he and John Eladas formed an opposition to the dominant figure on the council, the Patriarch Nicholas.

It was easy for Nicholas to dominate the council. His prestige as Patriarch and as the man who had defied the Emperor for his conscience's sake set him far above the other members of the regency. Moreover, though on the verge of old age, his energy was unabated, and his character too proud to endure a second place. He kept a vast correspondence, that showed both culture and individuality, on every conceivable matter of State; he watched every possible channel for intrigue with an unscrupulousness that fitted ill with his stern theological conscience. He was passionately ambitious, but not, probably, so much for himself as for his office, for the Patriarchate; it was his religion to serve its interests; he justified anything done in its service and would fight implacably to enhance its power. Such a character aroused hatred in many quarters but respect in all. Yet it had its suaver side. To enemies that were safely defeated he could be generous, even charming, and his letters could show at times a remarkable delicacy and sympathy. And, for all his faults, he had a genuine love of his country and his faith. Now, as chief Regent, he reached the height of his ambitions and took over the government of the Empire.

With Nicholas in supreme power, his party seemed to triumph. But Alexander's death greatly improved the Euthymian party's position, and it gave Nicholas some awkward problems. Nicholas was in power, but he was in power as the Regent for Constantine; and Constantine, according to the Nicholaan party, both was a bastard and had been crowned by an illegal patriarch. Nicholas had therefore not only to suppress the Euthymian party

1 Theoph. Cont. pp. 175, 354.

but also to protect himself from his own too logical supporters. Against the former he tried direct action, against the latter ingenious intrigue.

The Euthymians were by no means negligible. Alexander's martyrdom of their saintly patriarch, especially when followed by his sacrilegious orgies, could only discredit their enemies; and though Euthymius himself was too gentle, old and ill to lead them, they had as impressive a leader in the Empress Zoe. She alone in the Empire held a position that challenged that of Nicholas. Whether rightly or wrongly, she was the crowned Augusta; she was the mother of the Emperor; and according to all precedents she had the first claim on the regency. And now she was back again in the Palace by her son's side; and there, in all the romance of her beauty and her past, she was waiting.

Nicholas lost no time. His politics saw in her an immoral woman, his sense his greatest rival. She was promptly arrested and sent into a monastery, where with shorn hair she was to repent at leisure under the name of Sister Anna, forgotten by the world. Her health failed under the hardship; and Nicholas was given the delightful opportunity of allowing her with paternal benignance to dispense with the observance of fasts.[1]

This swift stroke disabled the Euthymians; and Nicholas now could dabble in more dangerous intrigues. As Alexander lay dying we saw that messengers began to pass between the patriarchal palace and the army headquarters just outside the walls, where Constantine Ducas lay with his regiments, waiting to fight the Bulgars. The chroniclers say that Nicholas only encouraged him before he was certain of the regency; but Nicholas probably was playing a deeper game. He was Regent, it is true, but Regent for a delicate child whom legally he could not recognize and whose mother was his bitterest enemy. His position would be quite as powerful and far more secure if instead of this hostile moribund child he could place on the throne a sturdy candidate of his own who in gratitude would agree to terms that should ensure the triumph of the Patriarchate. Constantine Ducas was admirable for the rôle; with his aristocratic connections and the support of the army his chance of success was

1 *Vita Euthymii*, p. 71.

large. Moreover, eager as he was to avenge the ill-treatment that the Emperor Leo had dealt to his father, he would gladly crown the downfall of Leo's heirs and followers. He would be a second Alexander, only far more respectable and in the Patriarch's debt. And, in the event of failure, nothing would be lost, provided only that secrecy was kept. The cleric who carried the messages to and fro had a curiously brilliant rise in the hierarchy.

Unfortunately for Nicholas, Constantine Ducas's *coup d'état* failed, owing to the vigilant energy of John Eladas. Constantine let himself into the city by night with a small company, and his partisans joined him at his father-in-law's house. They attempted to storm the circus, but were repulsed by the guards, and turned instead to attack the great bronze gate of the Palace. There they met the militia hastily collected by John Eladas, who had been warned. In the skirmish several of Ducas's followers were killed, including his son Gregory; and he himself, when trying to escape, was fatally thrown from his horse. The leader dead, the revolt faded out, and the chief accomplices fled out of the city or to the churches, as best they could.

The Regents proceeded to punish with a severity that shocked Constantinople. It was Nicholas's method of proclaiming to the world his innocence from all complicity; and his colleagues, knowing how easily such a revolt might recur, welcomed a deterrent. Officers and their companies involved were butchered and impaled. Others were blinded and exiled or scourged; the refugees in St Sophia were dragged out and shorn as monks. Ducas's only surviving son was made a eunuch; his widow was shorn and sent to a gloomy life on her estates in Paphlagonia. Even more would have been done in punishment, but the row of corpses along the Asian side of the Bosphorus outraged public opinion; and the Empress's friends took advantage of it.[1]

It was at this unfortunate moment that the Bulgarians, let loose by Alexander's inebriety, marched into the Empire. In August, having met no opposition on the way—none could be organized amid such chaos—Symeon appeared with a huge army

[1] Theoph. Cont. pp. 381–5: *Vita Euthymii*, pp. 70–71—placing Zoe's expulsion after Ducas's revolt, and connecting the two. Whenever Zoe may have been expelled (and that must have been soon after Alexander's death) certainly she cannot have been implicated in the revolt, even falsely.

before Constantinople. The walls of the city daunted him, but he sat down to wait, with his troops stretching the whole four miles between the Golden Horn and the Marmora.[1]

Nicholas approached the Bulgarian problem with a definite pre-conceived policy, a policy of peace. Throughout all the wars he remained in close correspondence with the Bulgar Court and eagerly preached moderation on both sides, till in extreme old age he realized the true character of the monarch whose heart he thought Christianity could soften, and in two bitter letters washed his hands of the incorrigible barbarian. The motive underlying his policy is easy to see. The Bulgarian Church was still under the Patriarchate of Constantinople, of whose rights Nicholas was always a jealous guardian. A war must mean, sooner or later, a rupture between the Churches; Bulgaria would at least declare its spiritual independence, and might very probably come under the dominion of the pontiff of Rome. By peace alone Nicholas thought to avoid such disasters, not seeing that to avoid the Roman danger the Patriarch would have to yield a part of his control and bribe the Bulgars with Cyrillism and its essential idea of a national Church. But Nicholas would never thus betray the trust placed in his hands by God.

Symeon, being unable to capture the city, sent envoys to suggest peace terms. The Regents were delighted, and welcomed Symeon's two sons inside the walls, where they were feasted; and Nicholas went out to interview Symeon, who to his gratification received him with the deepest respect. But Symeon was not so blind as actually to make peace with an Empire so feeble and ill-led; and so having received a great many presents and even the offer of the Emperor as his son-in-law, and having committed himself in return to nothing but vague promises, he withdrew to his own country.[2]

1 Theoph. Cont. p. 385.
2 *Ibid. loc. cit.* It is difficult to say when actually the proposals for a Bulgar-imperial marriage alliance were put forward. Nicholas's letter No. XVI (p. 112) gives a definite impression that Symeon had been promised a marriage and considered himself cheated. If any promise had been made, it must have been made now, as Zoe certainly would not hear of such a thing; and she would not have considered herself bound by a promise of Nicholas. Eutychius of Alexandria (*V.P.* p. 22) says that Symeon wanted Constantine's sister for his son. That must be due to misinformation. Constantine's only

The regency council barely survived his departure. The Empress Zoe had no intention of remaining Sister Anna for the rest of her days; the general public had been shocked by Nicholas's cruelty both to Euthymius and to the Ducae and their friends; on the Council the Magistri John Eladas and Stephen, were tired of the domination of Nicholas; and in the Palace there was the touching spectacle of the little Emperor calling for his mother. The details of the intrigue are unknown; it seems that the Magistri precipitated the crisis and summoned Zoe back to the Palace. Once there, she took full possession of the government, with John Eladas at her right hand. The revolution was complete; the Nicholaan partisans were superseded and replaced by friends of the Empress and her late husband—the Paracoemomene Constantine who recovered his old post, the Gongylii brothers, and Domenicus who became Hetaeriarch[1] (but soon fell before the jealousy of the Paracoemomene and was succeeded by John Garidas). Alexander's creatures, John the Rector, Basilitzes and Gabrielopulus, were removed and died in obscurity. Nicholas was a greater problem. Zoe invited Euthymius to return to the Patriarchate; but the weary old man declined. His previous experience of patriarchates and princes had not been encouraging; he preferred to live on in retirement. The Empress had no other choice than to put up with Nicholas. She did so with a bad grace, angrily telling him to mind his own business—the Church.[2]

The new government was certainly a change for the better. The Magistri however reaped little benefit from it. Almost at once John Eladas fell ill and died: while Stephen seems never to have enjoyed the Empress's confidence. After John's death the functions of chief minister devolved on Constantine the Paracoemomene, with whom, eunuch though he was, even in Leo's lifetime court gossip had connected the Empress too closely. His influence now was certainly paramount: though Zoe herself kept the initiative and decided on the policy to be

sister who survived infancy was the Augusta Anna, now almost certainly dead; and such an alliance would be much less effective for Symeon's purposes.

1 The Hetaeriarch commanded the Palace bodyguard.
2 Theoph. Cont. pp. 381 *et seq.*; *Vita Euthymii*, p. 73.

pursued. She soon found it necessary to come to some sort of a concordat with Nicholas, and even would utilize his eloquence and experience in diplomatic despatches, though it was her views rather than his own that he was obliged to express; and a superficial peace reigned in the Church. Nicholas went so far as to have one or two friendly interviews with Euthymius (who died early in 917); and, though he and the Paracoemomene were enemies of long standing, when the Paracoemomene's sister died he condescended to write him a charming letter of condolence.[1]

The improvement in the government was quickly reflected in the provinces. On the Saracen frontiers, in Asia and Italy, the summer of 913 had been a season of triumphs for the enemy; but in 914 the yearly Arab land raid from Tarsus was a failure, and the sea raid of the Emir Damian ruined by his death at Strobyle. The heir to the throne of Armenia, then overrun by the Arabs, was invited to Constantinople and sent back next year with a Byzantine army that penetrated as far as Dovin. In Italy the government achieved a still more sensational victory. In 915 the Empress's nominee, Nicholas Picingli, Stratege of Longobardia, brought about a Pan-Italian alliance and turned the Saracens out of their formidable fortress on the Garigliano; and the triumph raised Byzantine prestige to an unprecedented pitch throughout the country.[2] Even Symeon of Bulgaria was temporarily checked. Forgetting his promises of peace and ignoring the reproachful letters of Nicholas he had invaded Thrace and captured Adrianople; but the Empress's prompt despatch of troops and money to recapture it made his victory short-lived. And she took further steps to meet the danger. Bogas, Stratege of Cherson, agreed to incite the Petchenegs against the Bulgars; and, though Symeon was also negotiating with the Petchenegs, Bogas's bribes and persistency won.[3] Meanwhile Zoe also cultivated the alliance of Peter, Prince of Serbia and vassal to the Empire.

But the Empress's successes did not last. In 915 the Bulgars

1 Theoph. Cont. *loc. cit.*; *Vita Euthymii*, pp. 73 *et seq.*; Nich. Myst. Ep. XLVII, p. 236.
2 For references see below, Chapters VII, VIII and IX.
3 Theoph. Cont. p. 387.

reinvaded the Empire, and probably also in 916. By 917 Zoe decided that the time had come to deal directly with the problem, to declare a concentrated aggressive war against Bulgaria and to crush it for ever.[1] She chose her time well. Concord was at last established at home; in Italy subjects, vassals and neighbours alike were overawed by the recent memory of the Garigliano; in the east the situation had been vastly improved by the Byzantine re-establishment of the Bagratids of Armenia. Still, it was necessary to come to terms with the Arabs on both frontiers; for their raids enforced the presence of more troops than the Empire now wished to afford, and the main Byzantine army was still occupied in Armenia.[2] On the west the Fatimid Calif of Africa, fully occupied in reconquering the independent Emirate of Palermo, gladly signed a treaty with the Stratege Eustathius of Calabria, who promised him a yearly tribute of 22,000 gold pieces.[3] Meanwhile ambassadors were sent to Bagdad, and, after a delay of two months while a sufficiently spectacular reception was prepared, were received there in June. In the peace treaty that ensued, the success of Zoe's eastern policy can be gauged by the fact that at the exchange of prisoners in the autumn the Moslems had 120,000 dinars' worth more of prisoners to buy back than the Greeks.[4] And from the north came the news that John Bogas had worked up the Petchenegs to a promise to cross the Danube[5]. By the summer everything was ready; it was now for the army and navy to play their part.

The commander-in-chief of the army, the Domestic of the Schools, was Leo Phocas, son of the celebrated Nicephorus who had reconquered Italy. Though his many personal attractions included great bravery, his ability was generally doubted; but his high aristocratic connections and the fact of being brother-in-law to the all-powerful Paracoemomene kept him in his position, and recently he had commanded with some success in the east. Under him served many others of the nobility, his brother Bardas, a Caesar in years to come and father of an emperor, the Argyri brothers, Romanus and Leo, and all the generals of the

1 Theoph. Cont. p. 388.   2 Ibn-al-Asir (*V.P.* p. 105).
3 Cedrenus, II, p. 355.   4 Ibn-al-Asir, *loc. cit.*
5 Theoph. Cont. p. 387.

themes.[1] The navy was under a much less distinguished command; the Grand Admiral, the Drungarius of the Fleets, was an Armenian peasant's son, who by painstaking merit and a few scraps of imperial favour had worked his way up until on Himerius's disgrace he had succeeded to the naval command. He was called Romanus Lecapenus, and everyone ignored him as being an excellent officer and no more.[2]

The doles were given to the troops. The fleet set sail from the Bosphorus; and the great armies crossed over to Thrace.[3] Fortified by oaths to live or die together, and blessed by the Holy Cross, the soldiers marched northwards into Bulgaria along the Black Sea coast.

Καὶ οἷα τὰ τοῦ Θεοῦ κρίματα, ὡς ἀνεξερεύνητα καὶ ἀνεξιχνίαστα. On the Danube, where the Byzantine ships were to carry the Petchenegs across, Romanus quarrelled with John Bogas; neither would accept the other's command, and neither could act alone. The Petchenegs soon grew weary of the delay and returned to their homes. All John Bogas's work and money were wasted. Romanus and his fleet sailed uselessly back to join the army as it marched along the shores of the Gulf of Burgas. And Symeon, free of the Petcheneg danger, watching from the hills saw that his time had come. On August 20th, the imperial troops lay at the Achelous, close to Anchialus;[4] and there the Bulgars fell on them. What exactly happened is unknown. There were later stories in which Romanus the admiral appeared as villain (but his villainy had been done already) and others in which Leo Phocas's horse, accidentally riderless, caused a panic among the soldiers. Whatever the reason, the Greeks were overwhelmingly routed. The slaughter was colossal; bones lay bleaching on the

1 Theoph. Cont. *loc. cit. et seq.* We are told that Romanus Argyrus ἐστρατήγευσε. Probably this means that he was Stratege of the Anatolic theme, i.e. the most important Stratege.

2 For Romanus's early history, see the beginning of the next chapter.

3 The fleet must have set out some time before the army.

4 Some historians (e.g. Bânescu in his review of Zlatarsky's *History of Bulgaria* in *B.Z.* xxvi, p. 114) pour scorn on those that declare that this battle took place on a river Achelous, attempting instead to prove that Achelous was another name for Anchialus. But the fact of a river in Western Greece being called the Achelous does not necessarily mean that the name can belong to no other river nor force us to follow Gibbon's error in placing the battle in Western Greece.

field for over half a century. Many of the highest generals were amongst the slain. Leo Phocas himself with difficulty fled north to the safety of Mesembria, and thence with the remnant of the army returned by sea to Constantinople. Romanus Lecapenus, who should have stayed to rescue the fugitives, set sail at once for the Bosphorus.[1]

Zoe had staked the Empire on a victory over the Bulgars; and now she had lost. Her situation was desperate, but with feverish energy she attempted to repair the disaster. At once suspicious of Romanus Lecapenus, she held an inquiry to examine his conduct; and he was sentenced to be blinded. But Constantine Gongylius and Stephen the Magister used their influence in his favour and answered for his future good behaviour; and so, feeling too insecure to risk making enemies in the Palace, she agreed to let him be. Against the Bulgars, the Stratege of Dyrrhachium was ordered to incite Prince Peter of Serbia to invade Bulgaria, and to bring in the Hungarians behind him. Meanwhile a new army was scraped together for Leo Phocas, and he was sent out to fight once more. The Bulgars were overrunning Thrace unopposed, to the very suburbs of the city. Leo took his new troops out to Catasyrtae. As he lay there by night, the Bulgars attacked and took the army by surprise. The Stratege Nicholas Ducas was killed, with the bulk of the soldiers; Leo and the Hetaeriarch John Garidas, with the scanty remainder took refuge behind the walls of Constantinople. It was now well on in the winter of 917 or early 918.[2]

This second disaster destroyed the last hopes of the government. Zoe could never conquer Bulgaria now; and in the meantime her army had vanished, and the populace was alienated by her failure. She thought of making peace with Symeon, and Nicholas wrote sad letters to the Bulgar Court justifying his country and pleading for moderation. But Symeon's only peace terms involved, it seems, the marriage of his daughter to the Emperor; for he knew how useful a stepping-stone such a connection

---

1 Theoph. Cont. pp. 388 et seq.; Cedrenus, II, p. 286; Zonaras, III, p. 465.
2 Theoph. Cont. p. 390. The chroniclers provide us with no dates from August 20th, 917 (Achelous), to March 24th, 919 (Romanus's entry into the Bucoleon harbour).

might be. This was more than Zoe could stand, and she refused the proposal with scorn.[1] Symeon contented himself throughout the year 918 in raiding the European themes at his will, and in punishing the Prince of Serbia for his imperial alliance, replacing him by a cousin. Zoe could send no troops out to oppose him, though, mercifully for the Empire, her peace treaties with the Saracens held firm, and she could thus once again laboriously try to rebuild the army. In Constantinople the year passed in a maze of intrigue. Zoe searched frantically for a prop to support her tottering throne; and Nicholas dreamed of recovering the regency. But they both were discredited as rulers and neither possessed any positive power. The power lay in other hands, in the hands of the martial commanders; and men's eyes turned to the Bosphorus. On the far side Leo Phocas was encamped with his army—half defeated veterans and half raw recruits; and between them and the city the fleet rode at anchor round the flagship of Romanus Lecapenus. The great unscathed warships were a disquieting sight; but who, after all, was this admiral? an unconnected parvenu, distinguished only for his misdeeds in the recent fighting. Leo Phocas, with his aristocratic relatives, was a far more formidable figure; he was brother-in-law to the Paracoemomene.

Zoe agreed with the popular view. Realizing her shaking position and the precarious health of her child, she saw that she must act; and she came down on Leo Phocas's side. It was according to the desires of her dear Paracoemomene; but there was a further reason, at which the chroniclers hint. Leo Phocas was a widower, a very eligible widower; she would marry him, and bring, as Augustas had done in the past, the imperial crown to her spouse. His elevation need not prejudice her son's future, but even if the worst befel the child, her own position would be assured; and the Empire would have once more an adult Emperor, with the army at his back. It was an admirable solution for her troubles.[2]

1 See above, p. 51, n. 2. Nicholas implies and Eutychius (an unreliable guide, however) states definitely that Zoe refused the overtures for a marriage.

2 This projected marriage is nowhere stated definitely, but my reasons for assuming it are as follows: (1) We know that a sister of the Paracoemomene's had recently died (Nich. Myst. Ep. XLVII); this may well have been the wife

In many quarters of the Palace the Augusta's decision aroused alarm. The young Emperor had a tutor, called Theodore, blindly devoted to his pupil's welfare. Theodore, terrified that the rule of Leo Phocas would mean the suppression of the rights of the Porphyrogennetus, suddenly thought of invoking as a counter-stroke the protection of Romanus Lecapenus. In Constantine's name he wrote a letter to Romanus appointing him the Emperor's knight-errant. Rumours of this letter reached the Palace; and the Paracoemomene Constantine sent angrily to Romanus, ordering him to pay off his sailors and disband the fleet. Romanus politely invited him to come down and superintend the business himself. Constantine fell into the trap. He came with a small attendance on board the admiral's ship; there he was suddenly seized and put under arrest: while his suite fled away in terror, to tell the Augusta.

It was a terrible shock to Zoe. The fall of her one trusted servant foreboded the very worst. She summoned the Patriarch and the high officials of State to meet her, and she sent envoys to Romanus to demand his reasons. The envoys were stoned by the populace, and they brought back no answer; she had lost the favour of the city. Next morning she met the ministers at the clock of the Bucoleon. Wildly she complained of the rebellion, but she only saw hostile glances around her; Theodore the tutor coldly answered that it was to save the Palace from the Paracoemomene and the Empire from Phocas. Then he brought forward the young Emperor and made him announce that his mother's regency was over and that the Patriarch and the Magister Stephen were in control of the government. To her horror

of Leo Phocas. (2) Liudprand, whose father was shortly afterwards in Constantinople, quite clearly considers the title of Basileopator to mean step-father to the Emperor, not father-in-law; and to justify Romanus's possession of the title he invents a liaison between Romanus and Zoe. He then says that Leo Phocas also wished to be Basileopator (*Antapodosis*, p. 87). (3) Theodore's precipitate action and subsequent behaviour make it clear that he was seriously alarmed and that his enmity was directed against Zoe as well as against the Paracoemomene and Leo. But Zoe's interests were obviously bound up with her son's, unless she could keep the title of Augusta by becoming the wife of the new Emperor. Some forty-five years later a similar situation arose, and Zoe's granddaughter-in-law, the Empress-Regent Theophano, solved the problem by marrying Leo Phocas's nephew, the Domestic Nicephorus Phocas. This intended marriage of Zoe seems to me to provide the key for the complicated politics of this crisis.

Zoe saw that her day was done. On the morrow, men were sent
to remove her from the Palace; but this was more than the boy,
in whose name it all was done, could bear. Before his pleading
they let her be; and she lingered on, powerless and neglected,
in the shadows of the gynaeceum, to watch the sceptre slowly
slipping from her child's helpless hands.

Nicholas was once again triumphant; but it was a barren
triumph. He could not stand alone and he did not know on
whom to lean. First he deposed Leo Phocas and appointed John
Garidas Domestic of the Schools. Then when Leo came to protest, nervously compromising he appointed Leo's brother-in-
law and nephew, Theodore and Symeon Zuphinezer, Hetaeri-
archs. Solemn oaths were sworn and Leo retired satisfied.
Promptly Nicholas set a patriarchal example of perjury and
deposed Leo's relatives. Leo, in despair, tried a final move;
like so many others before him, he could not believe that Romanus
Lecapenus would presume to have ambitions for the supreme
power, and he tried to draw him over to his side by proposing
a family marriage bond. Romanus met his proposals politely;
and the rivals swore oaths of alliance. Leo then returned across
to Chrysopolis, to his still faithful army.[1]

Romanus kept faith as honourably as Nicholas. On March
24th, 919,[2] he sent his devoted friends, John the Presbyter and
Theodore Matzuces, to the Palace with an apologia, in which he
declared that he was acting solely through fear of Phocas's plots,
and asked to be allowed to come into the Palace. Nicholas was
too wily to be caught thus and firmly refused; but Theodore the
tutor, in the blind panic into which the mention of Phocas
always threw him, invited Romanus to bring his fleet round to
the private palace harbour of Bucoleon. On March 25th, by

1 Theoph. Cont. pp. 291 et seq.
2 Some justification is necessary for the date 919. Some historians counting
seven years (as Theophanes's Continuator gives) for Constantine's first reign
from 913 (Alexander's death) give the year 920. But the Continuator also
says that Romanus's reign lasted for twenty-six years, whereas we know that he
fell in December, 944. It is therefore better to assume that he was a year out in
both reigns, especially as he definitely tells us that Romanus's wife Theodora
was crowned Empress in January, Indiction 8 (920), and Romanus had been
crowned in the previous December. It is hard to believe that Zoe's government could have tottered on till 920.

Theodore's contrivance, Romanus appeared there, fully armed, and took possession of the Marine Gate. From there he could command the Palace. The government fell; on Romanus's arrival, the Magister Stephen left the Palace, in fear or in disgust, and Nicholas was forcibly removed by Romanus's friend, the Patrician Nicetas. Romanus himself, swearing oaths of allegiance on the Holy Cross at the church by the lighthouse, was appointed Magister and Chief Hetaeriarch, and took over the government. Constantinople had been taken by surprise; the peasant-born parvenu was on the steps of the throne.

Once supreme, Romanus acted mildly. His first move was to establish an understanding with Nicholas, whose help he felt he needed. It was not difficult, for Nicholas too needed an ally, and in Romanus Lecapenus saw the useful friendly usurper that he had failed to find, six years ago, in Constantine Ducas. He was only too delighted to act as adviser to the newcomer; and the friendship matured. Leo Phocas received letters courteously ordering him in the Emperor's name not to revolt. The unhappy Paracoemomene was, on swearing oaths of submission, allowed to retire in peace to his home. Romanus's ambitions, however, rose higher than the rank of Chief Hetaeriarch. In April the engagement was announced of the young Emperor (now just over thirteen years old) and Helena Lecapena, Romanus's beautiful young daughter. When a few days later the marriage was celebrated and the bride crowned Augusta, Romanus took the title of Basileopator, invented by Leo the Wise for Stylianus; and his son Christopher was appointed Hetaeriarch in his stead.

This was too much for Leo Phocas. From his headquarters at Chrysopolis he got into touch with the Paracoemomene Constantine and Zoe's friends the Gongylii brothers; and all together they planned a revolution in the name of the Emperor Constantine. Romanus adopted a curious device to counter this. He wrote letters in his son-in-law's name, which he gave to a cleric called Michael and a prostitute Anna to disseminate among the troops. Michael was caught by Leo and punished; but Anna's work bore excellent fruit in wholesale desertions to Romanus. Leo promptly drew up his remaining regiments in fighting array along the Asian shore. Romanus then sent another

letter, in which the Emperor was made to deplore Leo's continued bad behaviour and to praise Romanus as his defender.
This letter in spite of Leo was read out to the soldiers and
apparently appealed to their loyalty; for Leo could only think
now of flight. He was repulsed when trying to enter the castle
of Ateus (in Bithynia), and was finally captured at a village called
Goeleon. John Tubaces and John's relative Leo were sent to
bring him under arrest to Constantinople. On the way they put
out his eyes, at which Romanus professed to be very angry.[1]

His great rival blinded, Romanus was now securely entrenched.
The remaining plots and revolts against his domination were
feeble, and easy to put down. In August some friends of Phocas,
including the curator of the arsenal, were discovered in a conspiracy; they were blinded and exiled, and the miserable Phocas
was dragged round the forum on a mule. Romanus then decided
to rid himself of two remaining dangers. The Empress Zoe still
lived in the Palace, and she never had borne misfortune and
powerlessness willingly. So now the charge was brought against
her of attempting to poison the Basileopator. It may have been
true—for her position was desperate—and at any rate it served
Romanus's purposes. Her hair was shorn once more; once more
she was Sister Anna, and the gates of St Euphemia-in-Petrium
closed behind her. This time it was for ever; her son could cry
in vain. The romance and the glory were over; the world where
she had played so spectacular a part, and played it not un-
worthily, would never know her again, until her marble coffin
passed by, to join its imperial fellows in the oratory of St John.
His mother was taken from him; but the child Emperor had yet
one more faithful friend, his tutor Theodore. At Romanus's
orders, the Patrician Theophylact, Count of the Stables, gave a
feast, to which Theodore and his brother Symeon were invited.
In the midst of it they were arrested by the Drungarius of the
Watch, John Curcuas, and hastily deported, as conspirators, to
their country house in the Opsician theme; and from that dreary
distance Theodore could realize and reflect upon the pass to
which his meddling folly had brought his dear imperial pupil.

Mother and tutor gone and all the Palace servants changed

[1] Theoph. Cont. pp. 392 *et seq.* for the whole narrative.

Constantine had no one left to protect him from his father-in-law. Romanus had no care now to remember his oaths and the Holy Cross. On September 24th, 919, he was appointed Caesar by the powerless child. It was only a step to the higher honour. On December 17th, the Octave before Christmas, the Emperor Constantine and Nicholas the Patriarch crowned Romanus Lecapenus with the imperial crown.[1]

1 Theoph. Cont. pp. 397–8.

CHAPTER IV

Romanus Lecapenus and his Government at Home

So, with little bloodshed and much perjury, Romanus Lecapenus climbed to the summit of mortal ambition. He had sprung from the depths, and his whole past was lost in obscurity[1]—unlike Basil the Macedonian he had no pious and literary grandson to give him a romantic history and a royal pedigree. His father, Theophylact, unattractively surnamed Abestactus, the Unbearable, an Armenian peasant, had been adroit enough to rescue Basil I from hostile Saracens at Tephrice, and as a reward was allowed a place in the imperial guard.[2] This must have taken place in about the year 871. We do not know if Theophylact's opportunism lifted him any higher; certainly his son Romanus, who was born somewhere about 870, did not receive the ordinary education of a Byzantine gentleman.[3] Romanus had made his name as a naval officer, under Leo VI. Stories attributed his success to a brilliant single combat with a lion;[4] be that as it may, by the time of Himerius's defeat by the Saracens in 911 Romanus occupied the important naval post of Stratege of the Samian theme;[5] and shortly afterwards—it is said before Leo's death, but more probably it was actually on the fall of Himerius under Alexander—he was appointed Grand Admiral, Drungarius of the Fleets.[6]

1 I can find no convincing derivation for the surname Lecapenus (or Lacapenus)—both forms occur. Possibly it is of Armenian origin. The South Italian chronicles call Romanus 'de Eliopolim' (*Annales Cavenses*, p. 188) or 'Heliopolitanus' (*Chron. Vulturnense*, p. 332). So presumably he was born at some town called Heliopolis. As they would not hear of him till he was Emperor they would know him by his birthplace rather than by his previous surname.

2 Georgius Monachus, p. 841.

3 *D.A.I.* p. 88. Constantine Porphyrogennetus was very scornful of his lack of education.

4 Liudprand, *Antapodosis*, pp. 83 et seq.   5 Theoph. Cont. p. 377.

6 Liudprand, *loc. cit.* Probably he preferred it to be said that he had been appointed by Leo, just as Nicholas pretended to have been reinstated by Leo. To be connected with the dissolute and impious Alexander was bad for one's reputation.

He brought a large family with him to the Palace. Of his wife
Theodora, we only know the dates of her coronation and her
death, the place of her burial, and the fact that he loved her
dearly. He had four sons and (it seems) four daughters. Of his
sons the eldest, Christopher, was already married and now was
chief Hetaeriarch. The other three were still children, born
probably after 912;[1] one of them, Theophylact, almost certainly
the youngest, was a eunuch, intended for the Church; the others,
Stephen and Constantine, were given imperial rôles to play later
on. Of his daughters, besides the Empress Helena there was her
younger sister Agatha, who soon was married to Romanus,
son of Leo Argyrus, in an attempt to win the alliance of that
powerful family: and two others (we do not know their names)
probably older, one of whom married a wealthy and cautious
nobleman called Romanus Saronites, the other was the wife of a
member of the distinguished house of the Musele.[2] Connected
with the Lecapeni was the patrician Nicetas, a *nouveau riche* Slav
from the Peloponnese, about whom Constantine Porphyrogennetus has left a very obscure joke;[3] his daughter Sophia was the
wife of Christopher Lecapenus. And with Romanus rose many
of his friends, particularly Armenians, as, for example, John
Curcuas.

Romanus's model was Basil the Macedonian; like him, he
aimed at founding a dynasty. But the murder of a child of fourteen was a very different thing to the murder of a middle-aged
debauchee verging on insanity: moreover, Romanus had a kind-
lier nature than his prototype. So, instead of making a corpse
of his rival, he had to be content with turning him into a son-
in-law: which is less satisfactory. But undoubtedly, like Alexander before him, he daily expected the delicate boy's death, and
daily was disappointed. For that happy day he prepared by

1 Liudprand (*Antapodosis*, p. 91) says that they were born after Romanus's
accession; but he imagined Romanus as immediately following Alexander.
Theophylact was almost certainly born early in 917 (Cedrenus, II, p. 332).
The other sons are nowhere called Porphyrogennete, as they should have
been, if their mother was already Empress. Moreover, Theodora died two
years after her elevation.
2 Theoph. Cont. p. 399; Cedrenus, II, pp. 342–3.
3 *D.T.* p. 54. Bury explains it in *Eng. Hist. Review*, IV (1891), p. 152.

imperializing his family. He had been crowned Emperor on December 17th, 919. On January 6th, Epiphany, 920, he crowned his wife Theodora Augusta.[1] Next year, on Whitsunday, May 20th, he took a more decisive step; he crowned his son Christopher Emperor.[2] It showed the world that he did not intend to remain an Emperor-guardian, the father-in-law of Emperors, but aimed at being their father.

To strengthen himself further against the legitimate line, Romanus had recourse to the Church. As the enemy of Zoe, he was a natural ally to Nicholas, and he cultivated the alliance with care. Once more the Nicholaans triumphed over the Euthymians. Together Romanus and Nicholas held their victorious peace congress. In July, 920, a synod was held to unite the Church. After the death, in voluntary retirement, of Euthymius and the fall of their political props the Euthymian clergy were feeble: they were contented by the vindication of their patriarch's memory. It was the house of Macedonia that paid the price of the defeat. Nicholas and Romanus were able to blacken Leo VI's memory at their pleasure, the one for revenge and self-justification, the other to discredit the rival dynasty. In the Tomus Unionis, their peace-treaty, published that month, Leo's last two marriages were condemned in the severest terms and Constantine Porphyrogennetus declared legitimate only on sufferance; and every year, on the anniversary of the day, the unhappy Emperor had to hear these articles, so humiliating to his house, read out in the great cathedral. The Empire, weary of schism, accepted the Union willingly, and Romanus thus secured the support of the united Church. Meanwhile, careful for his diplomacy, he induced Nicholas to write a long apologia to Rome and to attempt to renew relations with the Papacy.[3]

Romanus was entrenching himself well; but there were still points of danger. Plot after plot was discovered close at hand, all in the name of Constantine. It was necessary to weed steadily

1 Theoph. Cont. p. 398.
2 *Ibid. loc. cit.* The chroniclers treat of the two coronations together, but actually while Theodora's was definitely in Indiction 8 (920) a year elapsed before Christopher's; Whitsunday fell on May 20th in 921. It is natural that Romanus would wait a year before taking the decisive step of crowning his son.
3 *Ibid.* p. 398; *D.C.* p. 186; Nich. Myst. Ep. xxxii, pp. 186 *et seq.*

from the Palace and the city the remaining friends of Leo and
Zoe. Constantine sadly records the fall of such as the Proto-
carabus Theodotus and the Protospatharius Theophylact; and
with them fell many of the other State officials.[1] In February,
921, Stephen, son of Calomaria, Magister and ex-Regent, who
in his time had saved Romanus's eyes, was sent with his house-
hold to a monastery in the island of Antigoni.[2] About the same
time John Garidas, Domestic of the Schools, was superseded by
an obscure general called Adralestes.[3] By such gradual work,
and by the patience, the watchfulness and the judgment of men
that Romanus showed throughout his whole life, his position
grew more and more unassailable; he had the navy at his back,
he was master of the Palace and the legitimate Emperor's person,
he was father of the legitimate Augusta and himself crowned
Emperor, ally of Nicholas and peace-maker to the Church. It
was a position that no one else could rival.

In the eyes of contemporary and subsequent historians, the
first eight years of Romanus's reign were dominated by the
Bulgarian War. But Romanus's negative policy with regard to
the war enabled him not only to interest himself on the other
frontiers, but also to establish himself even more firmly at home,
to work out at his leisure his method of government and to
choose by experience his most valuable ministers. The con-
solidation of his dynasty did not seem difficult. Constantine
Porphyrogennetus was the only remaining member of the old
imperial house; and the wan boy could have little chance against
the numerous exuberant family into which he had married. We
have seen how in May, 921, Romanus took the decisive step of
crowning his son Christopher. Already he had prepared for it
gradually by giving himself precedence over the Porphyrogennetus.[4] It became clear that Constantine was to be elbowed out

1 *D.A.I.* p. 241; Theoph. Cont. p. 400.
2 Theoph. Cont. p. 398.
3 *Ibid.* p. 400.
4 *Ibid.* p. 400. The evidence of the coins of the reign (see Regling, *Ein Goldsolidus des Romanus*, I, pp. 280 *et seq.* and Wroth, *Imperial Byzantine Coins in
the British Museum*, II, pp. 453 *et seq.*) shows that first he placed his figure in
the prominent place on the coin, though still leaving Constantine's name to
precede his; then, some time before Christopher was crowned, he definitely
placed his name also first.

into obscurity by the pushful Lecapeni; in 921, probably at the time of Christopher's significant coronation, his friends made their last plot against Romanus. It was soon discovered, and made an excuse for ridding Palace and city of the last remaining enemies of the upstarts. Henceforward there was no one left to intrigue for the rightful Emperor.[1]

The Lecapeni steadily advanced. In February, 922, Romanus's wife, the Augusta Theodora, died; and Romanus's deep genuine sorrow did not distract him from crowning next month his daughter-in-law Sophia, Christopher's wife, to take her place —his daughter, the Augusta Helena, derived her title from her husband the Porphyrogennetus.[2] His next step was on Christmas Day, 924, when he crowned his younger sons Stephen and Constantine Emperors.[3] It was already known that—following the model set by Basil I and Leo VI—he intended to elevate his remaining son Theophylact to the patriarchal throne. On this same Christmas the child, at the age of seven, was created, by the Patriarch Nicholas, Syncellus, or patriarchal secretary, with the understanding that he should succeed to the chair, though, as it turned out, Nicholas died next spring while he was still too young to step at once into the vacancy.[4] In 927 Romanus used the excuse of his granddaughter's wedding to the Bulgarian Tsar to give her father the Emperor Christopher precedence over the Porphyrogennetus. This, it was said, was done on the demand of the Bulgars; but the demand was a fine piece of tactful diplomacy.[5] The Court had long since been entirely devoted to Romanus, and no one there troubled themselves about the lawful Emperor. The lonely youth grew up hopeless and apparently forgotten, spending his days in painting, in studying etiquette, or in collecting information about the distant world.

By 927 Romanus had also found an ideal minister. Till his

---

1 *Ibid.* p. 400. The plotters were Anastasius the Sacellarius, master of the mint, Theodoretus the chamberlain, Demetrius the imperial notary, and Nicholas Cubatzes. Theodotus, whose name is also given probably had already fallen.

2 *Ibid.* p. 402; Nich. Myst. Ep. CLVI, p. 384.

3 Theoph. Cont. p. 409.

4 *Ibid. loc. cit.* and p. 410.

5 *Ibid.* p. 414.

death in 925 the Patriarch Nicholas had practically occupied the position of Foreign Secretary: which meant, in a time when foreign politics were the prime concern of the government, that he was chief minister. The only other minister of whom we hear during these years was John the Rector, one of the officials responsible for the defeat at Pegae; but by 924 he was already in disgrace and had retired, pleading ill-health, to be a monk at Galaereni.[1] By the spring of 925 Nicholas's health finally began to fail, and his dominant place was taken by John the Rector's successor, John Mysticus.

The career of John Mysticus made a considerable sensation at the time; to us, however, it is very obscure. His rise was sudden. He first emerges into history in 924 as Nicholas's companion on his visit to the Bulgar Symeon. On April 19th, 925, at a time when Nicholas must have been quite incapacitated by illness (he died next month), he was created Patrician and Anthypatus. Of his policy we know nothing. Romanus certainly valued his judgment, and perhaps we should attribute to his influence the successful diplomacy of the year 925 onward. His position, however, caused great jealousy, and soon tales were brought to the Emperor of plots between John and his father-in-law, the Patrician Cosmas the Logothete. In October (presumably still in 925) John was removed from the Court, but the Emperor continued to see him and to ask his advice on public affairs. But at last his enemies provided damning evidence, and Romanus made up his mind that he must be examined. John in terror proved his guilt by fleeing to the monastery at Monocastanus, and his friend Constantine Boelas followed his example. Cosmas was left to face the trouble, and suffered deposition and scourging.[2] John's post as chief adviser was taken by the Protovestarius Theophanes.[3] Here Romanus found what he had

---

1 Theoph. Cont. pp. 401, 406 *et seq.* This John the Rector is certainly not the same as John Lazanes the Rector, with whom Rambaud (*L'Empire Grec*, p. 19) and Bury (*Imp. Adm.* p. 115) identify him. John Lazanes, Alexander's creature and subsequently Regent, died soon after Alexander's death, playing ball (Theoph. Cont. p. 379). This John was a far more reputable figure, and subsequently reappeared in public life as a diplomatic agent with regard to Prince John of Bulgaria (*ibid.* p. 419).

2 *Ibid.* pp. 406, 410–411.

3 *Ibid.* p. 411.

wanted. Theophanes (whose birth and early history are unknown to us) showed himself to have remarkable ability, in diplomacy and even in naval warfare; and he combined it with a gift still more invaluable in Byzantium, unswerving loyalty that disaster could not kill. Henceforward for nearly nineteen years, while the reign lasted, he was, after the Emperor, the most important figure in the government, and during that long period he did nothing save what his contemporaries could chronicle with admiration. At this great distance it is impossible to tell how much the policy of the reign was inspired by his advice or by Romanus himself. Earlier, the letters of Nicholas indicate clearly, despite the patriarchal pride, that it was Romanus's ideas that controlled the imperial policy, and it seems probable that this control never passed from him. However, it is more commendable to be a good servant than a good master, and as such Theophanes is worthy of superlative respect.

Romanus had already been equally, or, rather, even more, successful in his choice of a military commander. His first Domestic of the Schools, after the removal of John Garidas, whose loyalty to Constantine had ruined his career, had been an obscure general called Adralestes, who died in 921, very shortly after his appointment. His successor was Pothus Argyrus, senior member of that important family. Unfortunately his talents did not correspond to his birth, and he shared the responsibility for the disaster at Pegae in 922.[1] Perhaps, after that, Romanus removed him—he was sufficiently allied to the Argyri through his daughter Agatha's marriage—or perhaps his timely death intervened. Certainly in 923[2] there was a new Domestic, an old Armenian friend of the Emperor's, called John Curcuas. Curcuas had been Drungarius of the Watch, and had helped Romanus in his earlier intrigues, and this was his reward. The choice was amply justified. To his admiring contemporaries Curcuas seemed a giant from the age of Justinian,[3] and his genius brought in a new dawn on the eastern border. Moreover, like Theophanes, he was loyal to the end.

1 *Ibid.* p. 400.
2 At the time of the Chaldian revolt, *ibid.* p. 404.
3 *Ibid.* p. 428. One of them (Manuel the Protospatharius) wrote his life in eight volumes, now all lost.

In 925 Romanus acquired complete control over the Church. Nicholas while he lived was too formidable a figure to be entirely dominated; his past showed an alarming independence. By steady wooing the Emperor had established a firm alliance with him, and could employ him with profit as Foreign Secretary; but still his personal and spiritual influence barred the way to many of Romanus's foreign projects,[1] and, in spite of the present amity, was always a potential source of danger at home. So Romanus settled down to wait in patience. It was not long. Nicholas was growing very old, and could not busy himself in every direction as once he used to do. At last in the spring of 925 his health broke down utterly, and on May 15th he died. Luckier than Euthymius, he died still Patriarch, triumphant over the corpse of Leo and over his immoral Empress, with his partisans in high places and a friend on the throne. Nevertheless, in the end he lost his battle; the Church, for whose independence he had so firmly fought, passed as he died straight into the hands of the Emperor. The patience of Romanus succeeded where Leo's rough usages had failed; Caesaropapism once more emerged victorious. At the time of Nicholas's death the Prince Theophylact was too young to take his place, and Romanus had to find a stop-gap. He chose an inoffensive eunuch, Stephen of Amasea, who appears, from the lack of information about him, to have been satisfactorily subordinate and quiet.[2]

Apart from these elevations and appointments few events of importance occurred in the internal history during these first years. The chroniclers find little to record beyond a *cause célèbre* of attempted parricide in high society,[3] and Romanus's decoration of his monastery of the Myrelaeum, where his wife was buried.[4] After 921 Constantine's friends conducted no more plots in the capital, but in the provinces there was one serious revolt. In 923 Bardas Boelas, Stratege of Chaldia (and therefore

---

1 I refer to the entente with Rome and the recognition of the spiritual independence of Bulgaria; see Chapters V and VIII.

2 Theoph. Cont. p. 410.

3 The case of Rentacius: Theoph. Cont. p. 399.

4 *Ibid.* pp. 403–4.

one of the greatest military officials) with two friends, Adrian
the Chaldian and a rich Armenian, Tatzaces, turned against the
Emperor and held out for some time in the citadel of Paiperte.
Eventually the town and they were captured by John Curcuas,
but they were punished without particular severity. Bardas,
whose former friendship with the Emperor gave him no worse
a prison than a monastery, was succeeded in his post by Curcuas's
brother Theophilus, a general with his full share of the family
ability.[1] This revolt does not seem to have been an attempt to
overthrow the central government, but rather, taking advantage
of the central government's weakness in the Bulgarian war, an
essay in devolution, an unsuccessful anticipation by three
centuries of the Empire of Trebizond.

The Bulgarian peace of 927 removed the likelihood of such
a danger recurring; but, though it utterly altered the foreign
affairs of the Empire and released the European themes from
the bondage of everlasting invasion, it did not otherwise interrupt the quiet sequence of things at home. The capital was now
well reconciled to Romanus's rule. He had, however, one more
plot there with which to deal—one of a new significant type.
He had fortified himself against the legitimate house by raising
his own family; but now the members of his own family, too
large to be manageable, were suffering from ambition and longing for the hegemony. In 928 a great sensation was caused by
the sudden removal from the Palace to a provincial monastery
of the Patrician Nicetas, one of Romanus's oldest and most
intimate friends and the father of the Augusta Sophia. It was
said that he was instigating his son-in-law Christopher against
Romanus.[2] How well the instigation succeeded is unknown.
Probably Christopher's health was poor—he died young, three
years later—and Sophia and her father, fearing and foreseeing
their insignificance should the Porphyrogennetus or the younger
Lecapeni succeed Romanus, tried to guard against it in the only
possible way—to induce Christopher to take possession of his
heritage while he still lived to do so. Romanus never lost his
affection for Christopher, so probably Nicetas had not gone

1 *Ibid.* p. 404.
2 *Ibid.* p. 417.

far in his plotting. It is however possible that he had implicated his granddaughter's husband, the Tsar of Bulgaria.[1] This stillborn conspiracy was the last that troubled Romanus till the very close of his reign.

In the provinces there was just one more slight personal revolt. In 932 a Macedonian, claiming to be that Constantine Ducas whose rebellion had failed in 913 appeared in the Opsician theme, and, attracting around him a body of lawless malcontents, began to ravage those districts. After some time he was captured and sent to Constantinople, where he was imprisoned and suffered the loss of a hand. But he soon escaped and returned to his company wearing a brass hand and still declaring that he was Ducas. He even succeeded in taking a fort on the Platia Petra; but there, with all his band, he was eventually recaptured. He was tortured and burnt, but not before he had from sheer malice named as his accomplices numbers of the innocent nobility. His accusations were not, however, believed.[2]

Of tribal, as opposed to personal, revolts Romanus, like every Byzantine Emperor, had his share. The Asiatic populations had long since been welded into a harmonious whole; but in Europe there were still undigested masses, tribes consciously distinct from, and hostile to, their neighbours and resentful of the imperial government. With the Lombards in Italy, the most extreme instance, I deal in a later chapter. Apart from them the only bad disturbances came from the Slavs of the Peloponnese, the Milengi and the Ezerites of Mt Taygetus. The history of the Peloponnese, since the arrival of the Slavs, was a long series of petty fighting; the Milengi and the Ezerites, like their neighbours in the inaccessible mountains, the pure Greek Mainotes, had never been completely conquered; but during Michael III's reign they had been forced to pay tribute by the Stratege Theoctistus Broeenius, the Milengi paying 60 nomismata yearly and the Ezerites 300. This arrangement lasted till about the year 934, when the province was ruled by an incompetent stratege, called John the Protospatharius. Under his rule the Milengi and

---

1 This may be a solution for the mysterious deprivation from Tsar Peter of the imperial title, granted by the peace of 927. See below, p. 100.
2 Theoph. Cont. p. 421.

the Ezerites refused blankly to accept the archon that he sent them, to take service in the imperial armies or to pay their tribute at all. However, the government at Constantinople had already discovered John's incompetence as a stratege, and before his letters arrived at Court announcing this rebellion, it had been decided to replace him by the Protospatharius Crinites Arotras, an official distinguished for his diplomatic work in Armenia and now on the point of retiring from the post of Stratege of Hellas (Northern Greece). When the news at last reached the capital, Crinites had already set out for the Peloponnese. A message was hastily sent after him, telling him to meet any delinquencies by arms. Accordingly, from March to November of the next year (935?) there was incessant guerilla warfare, at the close of which, despite the impenetrability of Taygetus, Crinites succeeded in extracting humble submission from the tribes. To punish them their tribute was increased; each tribe had now to pay 600 nomismata yearly. His work accomplished, Crinites was re-appointed to the theme of Hellas. Unfortunately, his successor in the Peloponnese, the Protospatharius Bardas Platypus, was a cantankerous man who quarrelled with his subordinates in so public a manner that the Slavesians from across the Gulf of Corinth thought it an excellent opportunity to raid the Peloponnese. The Milengi and the Ezerites took advantage of these raids to send to Constantinople to demand a reduction of their tribute. The Emperor knew that a refusal would make them join the Slavesians and so sent them a Golden Bull restoring the former rate of payment—60 nomismata for the Milengi and 300 for the Ezerites. It was probably an economy in the long run; to secure the larger tribute it would be necessary to have permanently in the province a stratege of such character and with such an array of troops behind him as to keep the Slav tribes in a state of constant fear.[1]

---

1 *D.A.I.* pp. 220 *et seq.*; *Vita S. Lucae Minoris*, pp. 465 *et seq.* I have given the date 934–5 in order to connect it with the unwillingness of the Peloponnesians to go to fight abroad (see next note), but to fix a date with certainty is impossible. Diehl in his essay on St Luke in *Choses et Gens de Byzance* (pp. 4–5) dates the revolt about 943 to fit in his chronology of St Luke's life. But it does not seem to me that St Luke's history necessitates so late a date; in the account in the *De Administrando* it clearly took place earlier in the reign, as some time certainly elapsed between the suppression of the revolt

It was due to such troubles that the Peloponnesians in 934–5 were unwilling to fight in person in Lombardy, and asked to be allowed instead to supply 1000 horses and the sum of one centenarium. Their request was granted. Certainly, to denude the province of its fighting population, and thus to leave it open to the raids of the unruly Slavs, would not make for the comfort of Peloponnesian life.[1]

These provincial incidents are without great importance in the central history of the Empire, but they are of great significance in showing the sort of problem with which the Emperor had continually to grapple. Throughout the provinces there were these far from homogeneous ingredients, kept together only by the most careful control. A stratege like John the Protospatharius could upset everything, and therefore the government at Constantinople had to keep perpetual watch—to be ready to recall its officers or to pour in troops at the very shortest notice. If the central government was weak or slow, the local population, even in the most civilized themes, would take the law into its own hands: as when, under Zoe, the unpopular Stratege Chases met a violent death in the very cathedral of Athens. On such cases a long inquiry would have to be held and the offenders suitably punished, to re-establish the imperial majesty.[2]

and the tribes' demand, yet Romanus was still Emperor. There are two curious points about the story: first, the Life of St Luke only refers to Crinites being transferred from Hellas to the Peloponnese and the *De Administrando* from the Peloponnese to Hellas. But both are logical in their context, so it must be that Crinites was given the Peloponnesian strategia solely as a temporary post—particularly as ordinarily the post of Stratege of Hellas ranked higher than that of Stratege of the Peloponnese. Secondly (and this is harder to explain), in the *De Administrando* story the Milengi were forced as a punishment to pay ten times their former tribute, while the Ezerites had only to pay twice. Constantine is too positive about the figures to admit of a misprint. He must have merely been misinformed.

1 *D.A.I.* p. 243. The expeditions in question must be those of Cosmas and Epiphanius. The unwillingness of the Peloponnesians to fight abroad has been usually explained as being due to a distaste for war—cowardice or laziness. It seems to me that troubles at home are an infinitely more probable excuse. It is unlikely that the home government would have acceded to the request had it been based on the former reason.

2 Theoph. Cont. p. 388. In Chases's case there is no record of an inquiry being held after; but Chases was one of Alexander's appointments and the Empress had therefore no interest in upholding him. Calabria in 920 provides a less remarkable (Calabria tended to be lawless from its position) but more fully documented instance (see Chapter IX).

The raids to which the frontier provinces were continually subjected belong more properly to the foreign history of the Empire.
But they deserve mention here, as they and the unruliness that
usually followed them interrupted the tranquillity of many of
even the most loyal districts. The Asiatic frontier was notoriously
lawless, and large tracts were under the undisciplined control of
the great border barons: while almost all the European themes,
at any rate up till the peace of 927, were perpetually liable to
looting, slave hunting or murder. The Slav brigands that Liudprand's father met and overcame near Thessalonica in 926[1] were
probably by no means an isolated phenomenon. Provincial history is seldom well documented; but it is foolish to suppose that
therefore it is a history of quiet.

Nevertheless, there seems really to have been remarkable
quiet during the greater part of Romanus's reign. We can
return from this excursus to the provinces with nothing further
untoward to relate except for one episode due solely to the hand
of God. This was the remarkable severity of the winter of 928–9.
With the grave economic consequences of this winter and the
ensuing famine in the provinces I deal in a later chapter. In the
capital the whole affair resulted in little else except the growth
of Romanus's popularity, owing to the efficient government
relief system which he organized and personally helped.[2] It was,
indeed, in philanthropy that Romanus now spent most of his
time. Like all his predecessors he was a great builder, and his
subjects noted with satisfaction his generous construction of
almshouses and of hostels for litigants from the provinces and
of public recreation grounds.[3] His control over State and Church
alike was now complete. With the latter he had had to exercise
a little additional patience, but by 931 he was rewarded. Nicholas,
the great stumbling-block to his ecclesiastical control, had died
in May, 925, when his destined successor, the Prince Theophy-

---

1 Liudprand, *Antapodosis*, p. 83. See also Chapter VI.
2 Theoph. Cont. p. 417; see Chapter XI.
3 *Ibid.* p. 430. The only building of his that is still standing is the
Boudroum Djami—the Church of the Myrelaeum (identified by Ebersolt
and Thiers, *Les Églises de Constantinople*, pp. 145–6). He also built a palace
at Bonus (Cedrenus II, p. 343) and an oratory at Chalce.

lact, was only eight years old.[1] Boy-bishops, such as were
common in the West, shocked the more civilized sentiment of
the East; and so Romanus had had to choose Stephen of Amasea.
To be a patriarch then was a task requiring tact; but Stephen
did his duty, lived insignificantly and died well in time—too
well, in fact, for in July, 928, the date of his death, Theophylact
was still impossibly young. Another stop-gap patriarch had to
be found; and in December, 928, Tryphon of Opsicium, a monk
of well-known virtue, ascended the patriarchal throne, but, it
seems, on the clear understanding that he was to resign if he
lived too long. Unfortunately, Tryphon found that he enjoyed
being patriarch, and it was only by ingenious trickery that he was
removed. The chroniclers are vague about the reason of his
removal. Their story that it was because his time was up cannot
be true, as Romanus waited another fourteen months before
proclaiming Theophylact, simply owing to the boy's youth. The
truth must be that Tryphon, with the obstinacy of the righteous,
was putting up a resistance to the imperial control, and menacing
Caesaropapism. He was declared deposed in August, 930, when
Theophylact was still only thirteen; and for more than a year
there was an interregnum.[2]

Eventually in October, 931, when Theophylact was nearly
fifteen years old, his father appointed him Patriarch. However,
for the glory of the Lecapeni and for the justification of his
appointment, it was decided to install him in style, and legates
were summoned from Rome to attend with the Pope's blessing.
In 932 when the Byzantine request arrived at the papal court,
Rome was in a state of disorder; the stage was set for the drama
of Marozia and her last wedding, but by the end of the year her
son Alberic was firmly established, and eager to improve his
position by an alliance with the Basileus. He induced his half-

1 Cedrenus, II, p. 332, supplies Theophylact's age (see above, p. 64),
saying that he died in the 14th Indiction (956) having been patriarch twenty-
three years, since he was sixteen—i.e. counting from the official installation
in 933.
2 Theoph. Cont. pp. 421–2 (who merely says that Tryphon's time was up)
Cedrenus, II, p. 313, who also offers no better reason, but gives further details
of the deposition, saying that owing to a taunt of illiteracy Tryphon was induced to sign his name on a blank sheet, which Romanus filled up with a
promise of resignation.

brother, Pope John XI, whom he kept conveniently in prison, to send the papal blessing and approval for the new Patriarch. The legates arrived at Constantinople, well supplied with gifts, early in 933, and on February 2nd, in the presence of the Emperor, they led Theophylact, with high pomp, into the patriarchal chair.[1]

So impressive an installation gave Theophylact a prestige that compensated for his youth and doubtful qualifications. Nevertheless his patriarchate was very uneventful. As a good son he never questioned his father's imperial authority; and his only important action was to get into touch in 937, undoubtedly at his father's dictation, with the Patriarchs of Antioch and Alexandria, and to inform them of the changes in the Liturgy that had taken place since the time of the Ommayids. The two Patriarchs concurred with the newer practices, and thus a closer and politically important bond was made between the Empire and the Christian subjects of the decaying Califate.[2] Theophylact himself was a good-natured youth who could not learn to take his position seriously. His interests were elsewhere; he kept 2000 horses, which he fed on fruits and spices and wine, and he would interrupt the celebration of the Holy Mysteries to be present at the accouchements of his mares. He made one brave attempt to reconcile pleasure with piety by brightening up divine service on the lines of a pantomime; but it met with disapproval, though some of the turns lasted to shock the righteous more than a century later.[3] Among the Byzantines, to whom pious correctitude ranked among the highest virtues, his memory was handed down with execration; but it seems unreasonable to expect a high-spirited, probably spoilt boy of fifteen to turn at once into a dignified and respectable ecclesiastic. And Theophylact had one good quality lacking in all his brothers—unbroken filial loyalty and gratitude to his father.

Thus the family advancement of the Lecapeni was completed. There had however been a disaster that had far-reaching effects

---

1 Theoph. Cont. p. 422; Liudprand, *Legatio*, p. 209. With the diplomatic significance of the Roman blessing I deal later (see pp. 192, 201).

2 Eutychius of Alexandria, *V.P.* p. 22.

3 Theoph. Cont. p. 444; Cedrenus, II, p. 332.

on the dynasty's fate. In August, 931, the Emperor Christopher died, and Romanus wept "more than the Egyptians" for his firstborn son.[1] Christopher is a shadowy figure, only emerging, in a doubtful light, in connection with his father-in-law Nicetas's conspiracy. Nevertheless he was clearly his father's favourite, and had been by his precedence indicated as the heir apparent. Had he survived, the dynasty might also have survived, but his death altered the whole situation. He left three children; his daughter Maria was the Tsaritsa of Bulgaria, his elder son Romanus, whom the old Emperor loved and thought of raising to his father's place, was still a child and died as a child at some unknown date soon after,[2] his younger son Michael was in his earliest infancy. Their mother, the Augusta Sophia, soon retired from the Court and died in the monastery of the House of Canicleus.[3] A further consequence of the death was the loosening of the connection between Constantinople and Preslav. The Tsaritsa, who before had often paid visits to her old home, came only once again in all her long life.[4] The fabric of the family was torn.

Christopher's death gave a new importance to his younger brothers, the Emperors Stephen and Constantine Lecapenus. It was on them that Romanus would have to concentrate now, to preserve his dynasty. In 933 Stephen was married to a lady called Anna, daughter of Gabalas, and she was at the same time crowned Augusta.[4] A few years later (939?) Constantine married an Armeniac, Helena, daughter of the Patrician Adrian; she died next February, and her widower was promptly remarried to a member of the Mamas family called Theophano.[5] Stephen was childless, but Constantine soon had a son, Romanus, born to him. Unfortunately, it became dreadfully apparent that the two young Emperors werè debauched, unbridled and undesirable. Even Romanus, it seems, came to realize their worthlessness; for he never altered the order of precedence that placed them

1 Theoph. Cont. p. 420: πολλὰ κοψαμένου καὶ θρηνήσαντος αὐτὸν τοῦ πατρός, μεῖζον ἢ κατ᾽ Αἰγυπτίους.
2 Zonaras, III, p. 474, who says that Romanus intended to give him too, had he lived, precedence over the Porphyrogennetus.
3 Theoph. Cont. p. 471.   4 Ibid. p. 422.
5 Ibid. p. 423.

after the Porphyrogennetus, thus making it clear that it was to be the latter who would succeed him.[1] It is possible that the Augusta Helena, a lady of undoubted force of character, had influence enough over her loving father to secure justice for her husband; nevertheless, though patriotism or his conscience restrained him from giving the young Emperors the supreme power, he was too fond of them not to indulge their every lesser whim and caprice even to the detriment of the State. He himself, as he grew older and his health began to fail, lost the old unscrupulousness that he had shown; he sought more and more the company of monks, and wilted beneath the long-suppressed hammering of his conscience.

To the world outside the Palace it would have seemed that Romanus, long since established as a pious philanthropist in his subjects' affections, would reign on in peace till his death; though what might follow then, none could be certain. But those in the Court itself would prophesy trouble sooner. Romanus was in the hands of holy confessors, monopolised by his anguished sense of guilt. The gentle Porphyrogennetus wandered between his studio and the churches, or pestered foreign envoys for bits of information. Such quiet was too tempting for the young imperial brothers; their ambition grew restless, but in their unrestrained folly they outraged the sentiment of the city. Their sister Helena, wife of the Porphyrogennetus, was equally ambitious, and less unwise. The air was heavy with a coming storm, and, as the year 944 drew near, men whispered of strange omens.

1 Zonaras alone of all the chroniclers says that he gave them the precedence (III, p. 474). But we know of no coins on which they are given precedence; and official acts (e.g. the Land Act of 934) run in the names of Romanus, Constantine, Stephen and Constantine. As Stephen Lecapenus was older than Constantine, the former Constantine must be the Porphyrogennetus. Theoph. Cont. p. 435, says that Romanus in his will gave the Porphyrogennetus the precedence, as a mode of repentance.

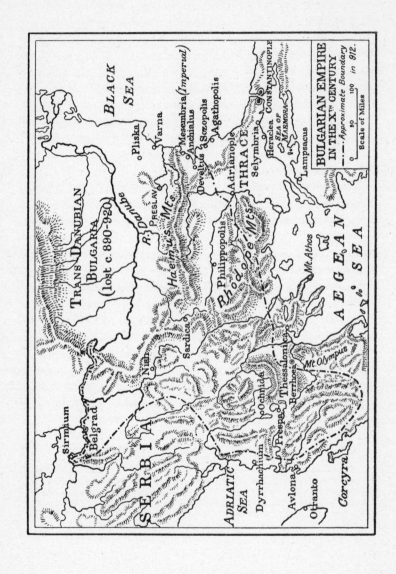

BLACK SEA

TRANS DANUBIAN BULGARA
(lost c. 890-920)

o Pliska

Varna

PRESLAV

R. Danube

Haemus Mts.

Mesembria (imperial)
Anchialus
Develtus o Sozopolis
Agathopolis

Adrianople

THRACE

Selymbria

CONSTANTINOPLE

Heraclea

SEA OF MARMORA

Lampsacus

Philippopolis

Rhodope Mts.

Mt. Athos

AEGEAN SEA

Sardica

Nish

Belgrad

Sirmium

SERBIA

Ochrida
Prespa
Berrhoe o

Thessalonica

Mt. Olympus

Dyrrhachium

ADRIATIC SEA

Avlona

Otranto

Corcyra

BULGARIAN EMPIRE
IN THE Xᵗʰ CENTURY
--- Approximate Boundary
in 912.

0   50   100
Scale of Miles

CHAPTER V

The Bulgarian War

THE lurid politics of the regency, from which Romanus emerged as Emperor, and the early events of Romanus's own reign, were all played out against the unchanging background of the Bulgarian war. At times it had even dominated the whole stage and had decided the fate of the Palace; and during all these years it was a factor of the most ominous importance in the history of the Empire. It is therefore worth while, at the risk of repetition, to follow the whole history of the war in its external aspect, apart from its influence on the palace politics of Constantinople.

At once we come against the usual difficulty, the lack of clear information. The chief and most valuable source is the correspondence of the Patriarch Nicholas with the Bulgarian Court. These letters, over twenty in number, show the varying hopes and temper of the Byzantine government whose spokesman the Patriarch was; but they tell very seldom of actual events, and in them we have to discount the fact that Nicholas had his own reasons (a desire to keep the Bulgarian Church under his control) for being as conciliatory as possible with the Bulgars. The Greek chroniclers deal only, with rare exceptions, with events in the close neighbourhood of the capital. For the rest we have only casual allusions in provincial writings or in Constantine Porphyrogennetus's brief history of the Serbs. There is nothing to tell us the Bulgarian point of view, except what we can gather by implication and deduction from the Byzantine writers, particularly Nicholas.

It was Alexander's insulting refusal to pay the customary tribute to the Bulgars that provided the opening for the war. But what was at stake was not merely tribute; Symeon of Bulgaria soon showed that he aimed higher—that he meant to crown himself with the imperial crown as Emperor of the Romans and the Bulgars alike.¹ In consequence, Symeon did not interest himself in conquering outlying provinces of the Empire—a task that could not have been difficult, considering the state of the Byzantine government—but, hoping thereby to possess himself of the whole Empire, he concentrated on attacks on the capital. Though Bulgar raids often troubled Greece and Macedonia, and Byzantine diplomacy involved Symeon in Serbia, the real seat of the warfare was Thrace, the country between Adrianople, the Gulf of Burgas and the capital.

The great main road from Constantinople into Bulgaria ran through Thrace to Adrianople; there it forked, one branch going up the Maritza to Philippopolis and Western Bulgaria, the other up the Tundja over the frontier by the heights of Bakadzhik (Meleona) to Jambol (Diampolis), there turning east to Karnabad and so over the Balkans to Preslav. This was a time-honoured route and had been fortified by the Bulgars in their earliest days with huge stone forts:² on the imperial side, the great fortress was Adrianople. There seems, however, to have been a second road, running close along the Black Sea coast to the Bulgarian port of Develtus and then striking inland north to Preslav. This road would be preferable for invading Greeks, as it would enable them to keep their flank protected by the sea and their fleet, and to avoid the dangerous, well-guarded mountains.³ Symeon, on the other hand, would prefer the inland route, but to control it properly he would need to be in possession of Adrianople.

We have seen how in the summer of 913, as the regency council was tottering, Symeon invaded the Empire and encamped in full

1 Abundant evidence for Symeon's ambition is provided (i) by his refusal to be contented with tribute (in 913); (ii) by his desire to marry the young Basileus to his daughter—a fine stepping-stone to the Throne, as Romanus proved; (iii) by the fact that after Romanus's accession, the only peace terms that he would offer involved the deposition of Romanus; (iv) by his assumption of that very title. His concentration on Thrace points to the same conclusion.

2 Bury, *History of the Eastern Roman Empire*, pp. 338–9.

3 In the absence of any detailed map of the country or of a personal survey, it is impossible to place the road accurately. That it existed seems to be certain from the fact that in many campaigns the Byzantine army and fleet worked in conjunction: while Develtus, from its frequent recurrence in the narrative, was certainly on some important road.

force outside the walls of the city. He could not force an entry into the city, and after negotiations retired. This abortive campaign was really the most significant in the whole war. Nicholas had attempted to prevent the invasion by offering to send to Develtus the arrears of the tribute;[1] but Symeon had refused, showing that it was not tribute that he wanted. The sight of the city walls taught Symeon a new lesson: that Constantinople by land alone was practically impregnable. Failing sea-power, he would have to rely on negotiation. That Symeon was content with rather vague negotiations is easily explained. He did not realize the precariousness of Nicholas's government; but he did realize how much Nicholas's interests were bound up with his own. Nicholas had no affection for the Macedonian house; on the other hand, he was very anxious to keep the Bulgarian Church under his supremacy. Symeon desired to supersede the Macedonian house; and as he intended to rule both Bulgaria and the Empire, the independence of the Bulgarian Church was a thing of no importance to him; he could promise as he pleased; it all was to come to the same thing in the end. So Symeon, after receiving many presents and the arrears of the tribute and having been promised the Emperor as his son-in-law, returned to his own country, confident that he could put pressure on Nicholas to carry out the promise.

Symeon's expectations were rudely shattered by Nicholas's fall and the accession to power of the Empress Zoe. She had no interest in the Bulgarian Church, but she was a determined guardian of the rights of her son and her dynasty; the marriage trick would not deceive her. Symeon considered the truce at an end and had recourse again to arms, ignoring Nicholas's reproaches and warnings against those that break their oaths. In September, 914, treachery on the part of its Armenian governor put Adrianople into his hands and thus gave him a safe entry into Thrace; but the Empress hastily sent money and troops which effectively recaptured the fortress. The next two years are clouded in obscurity. Symeon never apparently campaigned

---

1 Nich. Myst. Epp. v, vi, vii, pp. 45–60, esp. pp. 53, 57. Develtus, as the seaport of Bulgaria, was the natural place to which the Byzantines would send tribute. It seems, however, that Symeon was at Develtus himself, and therefore probably invaded Thrace by the coast route.

in the winter, but in these summers he cannot have been inactive.
Thrace was left in peace; probably the Empress's government
seemed too well-established at the moment and too active for
invasions there to be worth while, and Symeon, temporarily
despairing of the imperial throne, turned his attention to the
ill-guarded provinces further west. Certainly during these years
the Strateges of Dyrrhachium and of Thessalonica reported to
the capital acts of Bulgar aggression and those of Thrace and
Macedonia told of new Bulgar preparations:[1] while in Greece
itself Bulgarian troops penetrated, probably in 916, as far as the
gulf of Corinth and intermittently occupied the intervening districts till Symeon's death, making life there too unpleasant even
for a saint.[2] Meanwhile both Bulgars and Byzantines alike
intrigued wildly for the support of the Petchenegs[3].

In 917 the Empress decided to launch a grand offensive
against Bulgaria. Partly this must have been due to dangerous
activities on the part of Symeon; but she had other reasons for
her decision. Her wars in Asia Minor and in Italy were successfully finished, and thus she could afford a new war; and particularly, in view of her doubtful position at home, she wished to
establish herself firmly in the love and gratitude of her people
by crowning it all with a greater, more sensational triumph.
Moreover, her Petcheneg intrigues had resulted at last in definite
promises. There followed the dramatic tragedy of the Achelous
campaign. We have seen in an earlier chapter how the Admiral
Romanus quarrelled with John Bogas, the guide of the Petchenegs, so that the barbarians never crossed the Danube, and how
a little later the great Byzantine armies were annihilated by the
Bulgars near Anchialus.[4] It is however worth while to look at

1 Nich. Myst. Ep. IX, pp. 72, 76.
2 *Vita S. Lucae Minoris, M.P.G.* CXI, p. 449. Diehl in *Choses et Gens de
Byzance*, pp. 3–4, dates Symeon's invasion of Northern Greece after the
Achelous, placing it ten years exactly before Symeon's death, as we are told
that St Luke lived ten years in Patras to avoid the Bulgars and only returned
after Symeon's death. But surely the ten years need not be strictly accurate.
In 917 Symeon would not have had time to invade Greece; in 918 the Bulgars
were probably engaged in Serbia. It seems therefore better to connect this
invasion with the attacks reported from Thessalonica before the Achelous.
3 See above, p. 53–4.
4 See above, p. 55.

the campaign for a moment from the Bulgarian point of view. At first it must have been seriously alarming for Symeon, squeezed between the Petchenegs and the imperial forces. He was saved by the quarrel on the Danube. The cause of that quarrel seems to have been merely the rivalry between Bogas and Romanus Lecapenus; but it is just possible that bribery from Symeon affected Romanus's actions.[1] Once Symeon was free of the Petcheneg danger, he could wait confidently for the Byzantine army. Leo Phocas, who had been marching up the coast, on the receipt of the bad news from the Danube did not strike inland to Preslav, but clung to the shores of the Gulf of Burgas, probably intending to go north to relieve the isolated peninsula fort of Mesembria; at Mesembria the army would be in close touch with Constantinople and the fleet. But Symeon intervened, and Leo Phocas never reached Mesembria, save as the leader of a few fugitives. From Mesembria the defeated army could only return to Constantinople by sea. The land was all in Symeon's hands.[2]

The victory of the Achelous not only freed Symeon from any further fear of invasion, but enabled him to penetrate once more to the walls of Constantinople. The Empress-Regent did not however lose her energy. In the hope that she might yet save her government and the Empire, she launched on diplomatic intrigues with the Prince of Serbia, and she scraped together a new army for her generals. The latter work was wasted through their carelessness. A surprise night attack by the Bulgars at Catasyrtae, just outside the walls, destroyed this second army, and the Empire was left with no more defence than the walls.[3] But, though her armies had been routed, Zoe's diplomacy was successful and saved her country but not her government. In the year 918, which was passed in Constantinople in the most frantic intrigues, it is hard not to believe that had Symeon been at hand he would have fished successfully in those troubled

---

1 The chroniclers all imply that Romanus rather than Bogas behaved badly in the quarrel, and that his conduct needed an inquiry. Romanus at this stage in his career was not over-scrupulous.

2 See above, pp. 55–6.

3 Theoph. Cont. pp. 389–90. Catasyrtae followed soon after the Achelous, probably in October, 917.

waters—that somehow he would have made his way into Constantinople. But he was unable to be at hand. His movements during the whole year are very obscure. After Catasyrtae he probably retired, as he seems to have done every year, to winter in Bulgaria. In 918 the Bulgarian armies under Symeon's generals Marmaëm and Sigritze, were occupied in Serbia: where Prince Peter had been induced by Zoe's intrigues and by his natural fear of a greater Bulgaria, to threaten Symeon's western frontier. The Bulgars had little difficulty in overrunning Serbia and replacing Peter by his cousin Paul, a prince of professed Bulgar leanings[1]; but while they were so occupied, Byzantium weathered the storm. When, in 919, Symeon was free to turn his attention once again to Thrace, the crisis in the Palace was over and the imperial government firmly in the hands of Romanus Lecapenus.

The whole complexion of the war was changed. While the young Emperor was an unmarried child under the uncertain tutelage of his mother or of the Patriarch, there always might be hope of a Bulgar princess on the Augusta's throne and her father following her into the Palace and eventually assuming control. But now an Augusta was provided, and, worse, the Emperor had an active and experienced father-in-law, himself stretching his hands out for the crown. Romanus, Basileopator, Caesar and Emperor, was eager to secure a peace with Bulgaria; he was ready to pay tribute, to cede territory and even to sacrifice a relative on the marriage altar.[2] But Symeon, in his baffled fury, would hear of nothing. In vain throughout the years 919 and 920 Nicholas wrote conciliatory letters to the Bulgar Court, offering to come and interview Symeon if his health permitted,[3]

---

1 *D.A.I.* p. 157. The war is undated; we only know that the intrigues of the Byzantines with Prince Peter came to a successful head about the time of the Achelous. As the Bulgar armies were in Thrace till the winter of 917–918, it seems certain that the Serbian campaign took place next season—it is the only reasonable explanation for Symeon's abstention from reinvading Thrace that year. Possibly Symeon had other troubles. Nicholas's letter (No. IX, p. 69), written just after the Achelous, is pathetically apologetic; the next (No. X, p. 80) is much more confident, even triumphant in tone.

2 Nich. Myst. Ep. XVIII, pp. 121 *et seq.*

3 *Ibid.* Ep. XI, p. 84, written probably when the Bulgars were in Thrace in the autumn of 919.

announcing to Symeon the union of the Church[1] (news which cannot have pleased Symeon as much as Nicholas piously supposed), exonerating himself and the present government from the policy and aggressions of Zoe's government—a government, he says, of eunuchs[2]—and announcing the generous concessions that Romanus was prepared to make. But Symeon's answers, though they announced his longing for peace, rang with no sincerity; he made it quite clear that his only terms involved the deposition of Romanus—terms which, obviously, Romanus's government could not accept.[3] And so the war went on, more vindictively and desperately than before.

In the late summer of 919 the Bulgars invaded Thrace as far as the Dardanelles, where they encamped opposite to Lampsacus.[4] In 920 there is no record of them in Thrace; it is probable that in that year they were fully occupied in Serbia where Romanus had organized a revolt of a Serbian Prince Zacharias against the reigning Bulgar nominee, Paul. The revolt was a failure and Zacharias was carried off to a Bulgar prison; but it had distracted Symeon's attention.[5] During that same year, while Symeon was so engaged, Romanus contemplated himself leading an expedition into Bulgaria; but nothing came of it.[6]

In 921 Symeon reinvaded Thrace, and advanced as far as the site of his former victory at Catasyrtae. The new Domestic, Pothus Argyrus (Adralestes had just died) went out to meet him, and one of his lieutenants, Michael, son of Moroleon, the governor of Adrianople, made a successful surprise attack on the Bulgars.[7] In the course of it Michael himself was killed, but as a result Symeon moved back to the neighbourhood of Heraclea and

1 *Ibid.* Ep. xiv, p. 100.
2 *Ibid.* Ep. xviii, p. 124.
3 *Ibid.* Ep. xviii, pp. 121 *et seq.*
4 *Ibid.* Ep. xcv, p. 301, written to Romanus when he was Caesar (Sept. to Dec. 919).
5 *D.A.I.* p. 157. Constantine dates it three years after Peter's fall; but as all his intervals in Serbian history are of three years, some latitude is probably allowable.
6 Nich. Myst. Ep. xvii, pp. 113 *et seq.*
7 Theoph. Cont. p. 400.

Selymbria. There Nicholas offered to go to interview him; but
Symeon's answers showed that any discussion of peace would
only be a farce.[1]

In 922 there was a fresh Bulgarian invasion to the walls of the
capital. The Bulgars overran the European bank of the Bosphorus; and Romanus, anxious about a small palace that he had
at Pegae, prepared an army to save it, under the Argyri brothers
(Pothus was still Domestic), John the Rector, and the Admiral
Musele. The imperial troops foolishly encamped in the narrow
valley at Pegae. The Bulgars suddenly appeared on the hills
above and swooped down. They met with barely any resistance;
the whole Greek army fled. The Admiral was drowned, trying
to reach his ships; John the Rector just escaped into a light boat;
the Argyri fled to a neighbouring fort; the bulk of the army was
captured or killed. The palace of Pegae was burnt, and the
whole district of Stenum devastated.[2] Yet this victory, like so
many others, brought Symeon no nearer to his goal inside the
walls of Constantinople.

The Bulgars stayed in Thrace throughout the summer, and
later in the year reappeared in the suburbs of the city, reaching
the Palace of Saint Theodora. Romanus, fearful lest the disaster
of Pegae should be repeated, invited all his generals to lunch and
delivered them a stirring harangue. Thus fortified, one of them,
a certain Sactices, next day triumphantly attacked the Bulgar
camp, with great slaughter; though while returning from the
sortie he was fatally wounded, and died at Blachernae.[3]

This victory heartened the Byzantines; and in the year 923
the situation was decidedly easier. Symeon attempted to invade
Thrace, down the Maritza, but was held up by the resistance of
Adrianople under its valiant governor Moroleon. At last famine
forced the garrison to surrender, and Moroleon was punished
for his resistance with the most terrible tortures and death. But
Symeon made no attempt to advance further; a sudden emergency forced him to turn back, and the troops that he left behind

1 Nich. Myst. Ep. XIX, pp. 125 *et seq.*
2 Theoph. Cont. pp. 401–2.
3 *Ibid.* pp. 402–3. No date is given, but from its place in the chronicles it
seems safe to place it in the autumn of 922.

to guard the fortress retired at the first approach of Byzantine armies.[1] The emergency that summoned the Bulgars back was the usual trouble; Serbia was on the warpath once more. Prince Paul had at last been induced by Byzantine diplomacy to break with his Bulgar benefactors. As before, Symeon had no difficulty in crushing the Serbs; Prince Paul was replaced by Prince Zacharias, the recent rebel and prisoner in Bulgaria;[2] but probably the summer was lost for campaigning in Thrace. Meanwhile Byzantine spirits had revived; the Emperor had been greatly cheered by the recent magnificent sea victory over the Saracen pirate Leo of Tripoli at Lemnos;[3] and he was satisfied with the progress of his anti-Bulgar intrigues among the Petchenegs, the Russians, the Magyars and even the Alans.[4] Indeed, so lightly did the war weigh on Byzantium now, that the new Domestic was with the main armies on the eastern frontier, where he suppressed the Chaldian rebellion[5]. In consequence Symeon began to consider the idea of peace, and twice asked the Patriarch to send an ambassador to discuss terms[6]. Nicholas gladly complied with the request; but his letter took on a new patronizing tone, and he carefully announced to Symeon the recent Byzantine triumphs in war and diplomacy; it was only, he said, in deference to his Patriarchal wishes that the Emperors would condescend to entertain any thoughts of withholding their attacks.[7] Symeon, however, when Serbia was crushed, thought better of it; he clung to his old outrageous demands, and nothing followed[8]. Nicholas climbed down a little; a few months later, in consequence of his attempt to reconcile himself with Rome, the Pope's envoys Theophylact and Carus arrived at Constantinople, and he sent them on to Preslav to do what they could with the stubborn Bulgar, writing to beg Symeon not to mock

1 *Ibid.* p. 404.
2 *D.A.I.* p. 157—three years after Zacharias's revolt. 923 seems therefore, all things considered, to be the certain date.
3 Theoph. Cont. p. 405; Nich. Myst. Ep. XXIII, p. 156.
4 Nich. Myst. Ep. XXIII. p. 149.
5 Theoph. Cont. p. 404.
6 Nich. Myst. Ep. XXIII, p. 149: Ep. XXVII, p. 176.
7 *Ibid.* Ep. XXIII, p. 152, Ep. XXVI, p. 169.
8 *Ibid.* Ep. XXVII, p. 173.

papal legates too[1]. He need not have troubled; the papal policy was to join with Symeon in mocking the Patriarch.

In 924[2] Symeon determined to make one more grand attempt against Constantinople. This time he would leave nothing undone. Experience had taught him that by land alone the city was impregnable; accordingly he looked round for a friendly sea-power from among the enemies of the Empire, and his choice fell on the Fatimid Al-Mahdi of Africa. His ambassadors reached the African Court and arranged an alliance; but on their return with the African mission they were captured by a squadron of Calabrian Greeks and sent to Constantinople. Romanus acted with great prudence; he detained the Bulgars but sent the Africans back with honour to Al-Mahdi with an offer to renew the peace and tribute arranged in 917 by the Calabrian Stratege Eustathius. The offer was accepted;[3] and so Symeon was baulked of his allies on the sea. Nevertheless Romanus was distinctly alarmed by all Symeon's preparations, and thought it wise to send an embassy to Bagdad to arrange a truce and an exchange of prisoners: which took place that same year.[4] He was thus free to summon his main legions over to Europe.

In the summer of 924 Symeon crossed the frontier and marched in full force through Macedonia and Thrace, ravaging as he went. In September he reached the walls of Constantinople; but there he stopped. Perhaps he only heard now of his failure with the Africans; perhaps he knew that the armies from Asia were at hand; perhaps, as before, the virgin towers and ramparts overawed him. Instead of ordering a general assault, he sent to the city and asked to see the Patriarch.[5]

It was an admission of defeat; and the Byzantines, secure

1 Nich. Myst. Ep. xxviii, p. 176. This probably took place in the spring of 924; see Chapter ix, p. 200.

2 I give my reasons for choosing this date for the famous interview between Symeon and Romanus below in Appendix i, p. 246.

3 Cedrenus, ii, p. 356. He alone mentions it and gives no date; but it almost certainly took place in 923. See below, Chapter ix, p. 189. Prof. Vasiliev also sees Symeon having relations with the Arab Suml or Tarsus. (*Vizantiya i Arabyi*, ii, p. 222.) But he is confounding Balkan Bulgars with the Black Bulgars of the Volga; see below, Chapter vi, p. 117.

4 Ibn-al-Asir, *V.P.* p. 106. See below, Chapter vii, p. 136.

5 Theoph. Cont. pp. 405 *et seq.*

behind their walls, breathed again. But Symeon's behaviour was none the less distressingly arrogant. As he had required, after a suitable exchange of hostages, Nicholas and two high officials, the Patrician Michael Stypiotes and John Mysticus, ventured out to interview him. But Symeon, finding how obediently the Patriarch came, decided now that he would see the Emperor instead. Even this was granted, and with elaborate care, a pier was built out into the Golden Horn at Cosmidium, well fortified and with a wall across the middle; Symeon was to come on from the land and Romanus from his imperial yacht, and they were to talk to each other over the wall. While this was being built, Symeon, whose veneer of culture was always rather thin, had an attack of barbarism. He could not resist shocking and terrifying the Greeks by ravaging the countryside and burning one of their holiest sanctuaries, the church of the Virgin at Pegae, built by Justinian four centuries before.

At last, on Thursday, September 9th, all was ready for the interview. Symeon came with lines of glittering guards, ordering some, with insulting distrust, to look for treachery in the works of the Greeks, and taking others as interpreters—for Symeon, though an excellent Greek scholar, knew well the value and dignity of not understanding a foreign tongue. Romanus's behaviour was an exemplary contrast. He retired with Nicholas to pray at the church of the Virgin at Blachernae; then, arming himself with the Virgin's sacred cloak, he went fearlessly and humbly to the meeting-place: while all the dignitaries of Constantinople watched in admiration from the walls. He arrived first, for Symeon waited for the exchange of hostages before he would approach and dismount. The two monarchs then greeted each other and conversed.

During the interview Symeon made an irreverent joke about Nicholas's use of prayer, mocking him for not doing his patriarchal duty in stopping the war himself.[1] But the chief feature was Romanus's speech. Whether Romanus actually uttered the words attributed to him by the chroniclers is impossible to say; but all the versions are practically identical, word for word, and must be derived from a common, probably contemporary, source,

1 Nich. Myst. Ep. xxxi, p. 189.

and so represent the official report of what Romanus said. As such, and as an illustration of the Byzantine attitude with regard to semi-barbarians, it is worth quoting in full.

"I have heard", said Romanus to Symeon, "that you are a religious man and a devoted Christian; but I do not see your acts harmonizing with your words. A religious Christian welcomes peace and love, for God is love, as it is said; but it is a godless and unchristian man who rejoices in slaughter and the shedding of innocent blood. If then you are a true Christian, as we believe, cease from your unjust slaughter and shedding the blood of the guiltless, and make peace with us Christians—since you claim to be a Christian—and do not desire to stain Christian hands with the blood of fellow-Christians. You are a mortal; you await Death and Resurrection and Judgment. To-day you live and to-morrow you are dust; one fever will quench all your pride. What will you say, when you come before God, of your un-righteous slaughter? How will you face the terrible, just Judge? If it is for love of riches that you do this, I will grant your desires to excess; only hold out your hand. Welcome peace, love concord, that you yourself may live a peaceful, bloodless and untroubled life, and that Christians may end their woes and cease destroying Christians. For it is a sin to take up arms against fellow-believers."[1]

Symeon returned to his Bulgars deeply impressed. In every great battle he had been victorious, Serbia had been repeatedly crushed, and all the European thrones of the Empire were in his power; yet Romanus, instead of begging humbly for peace, reproved him as a schoolmaster might reprove a naughty pupil (though he skilfully inserted an offer to pay a larger tribute). Symeon had to realize that not only were the Byzantines pro-tected by their strong walls, but inside they were fortified by the traditions and memories and majesty of Rome and faith in their long-established orthodoxy; Constantinople, stretching far back into a past when the Bulgars were savages in Turkestan and the Slavs homeless nomads on the Steppes, stretching again far into the future, was something greater than he had thought; it would never be his. Romanus's speech was not mere bravado. With a thousand years of imperial rule behind him, he genuinely thought it apposite to remind the monarch of the mushroom Bulgaria that "to-morrow you are dust," and instead of suing for peace

---

1 The earlier chroniclers (e.g. Georgius Monachus, p. 901) leave out this last sentence.

to treat Symeon as a recalcitrant spiritual subordinate, and to talk to the old barbarian of death and of the Hell that awaits the wicked.[1] It never occurred to the Byzantines that the Emperor was actually a beaten man begging for the best terms that he could secure; and their serene attitude persuaded Symeon. He never invaded the Empire again.

Meanwhile two eagles met in the air high above the monarchs' heads; then one flew back to Constantinople and the other to the mountains of Thrace. Their tactful symbolism has been the theme of many a subsequent historian;[2] but it was not really so apt. It is true that two monarchs had met and were returning home; but that henceforward there were to be two empires in the Balkan peninsula is less true. Symeon's empire was even now on the point of crumbling, and Bulgaria was soon to relapse into two centuries of Byzantine rule. The message of the eagles was to Symeon alone; he never would be the only Emperor.

At the same time some sort of truce was arranged. It seems that Symeon was to cede back some of his territory, notably the Black Sea fortresses—Agathopolis and Sozopolis and perhaps the cities of the Gulf of Burgas. In return Romanus was to pay the yearly subsidy of 100 'scaramangia' that Leo had paid, and in addition a handsome indemnity of money and valuable gifts. The truce was only partially successful. As the impressive memory of the interview faded, Symeon recovered his insolence and refused to hand over the Black Sea fortresses, rudely telling Romanus to ask back his land from the Arabs and declaring that the Empire would not be able to afford the upkeep of the forts. Consequently, Romanus withheld the rich indemnity; he did, however, pay the yearly present of the 'scaramangia';[3] and that, it seems, was enough to keep Symeon from reinvading the Empire. There is no more record of fighting on the Thracian

1 Nicholas uses the same method, reminding Symeon of his age (over sixty) and of his imminent death. Symeon, with the superstition of a fairly recent convert, would probably be impressed by such warnings (Nich. Myst. Ep. XXIX, p. 181).

2 Theoph. Cont. p. 409, Rambaud, p. 337, builds up a sermon on it.

3 Ep. Rom., Sakk. I, pp. 658–664, II, pp. 40–45: Zlatarsky, *Pismata na Romana Lacapena*, pp. 8 et seq., 10 et seq. The Black Sea fortresses must be Agathopolis and Sozopolis, and possibly also Develtus and Anchialus: though these latter had been in Bulgar hands some eighty years. Mesembria was never captured by Symeon.

front.[1] Romanus had good reason to be satisfied with the result of the interview. Nicholas, however, was furious. The episode had shown him how little hold he had, as Patriarch or as friend, over Symeon's mind and soul; the barbarian had merely mocked at him. And probably a new dreadful rumour was reaching his ears. He wrote two more letters, bitter disillusioned letters, still talking of peace but in a different angrier way. When he wrote the second, his health was utterly broken, and with pathetic pride, he labelled it his last. Then on May 15th, 925, he died.[2]

The new rumour was that Bulgaria was about to declare her spiritual independence. Symeon was altering his policy. Hitherto, as an expectant Emperor, he had carefully respected the forms and institutions of the Empire, content to leave his Church under the ultimate jurisdiction of the Patriarch of Constantinople, and to take for himself the humble title of Kniaz or $\mathring{a}\rho\chi\omega\nu$. Now in his old age, he saw that he would never be legitimate Emperor; he therefore decided to take the title illegitimately. Sometime in 925 he proclaimed himself Basileus and, to make it more grandiose and insulting, added $\mathring{P}\omega\mu\alpha\acute{\iota}\omega\nu$ $\kappa\alpha\grave{\iota}$ $\text{Bov}\lambda\gamma\acute{a}\rho\omega\nu$. He would be Emperor of the Romans and the Bulgars. In vain Romanus wrote two angry letters to protest. Symeon looked elsewhere for support.[3] Next year an ambassador (Madalbert) came from Rome bearing the Pope's confirmation of the imperial title.[4] At the same time, probably with the Pope's authority, Symeon raised the head of the Bulgarian Church to the rank of Patriarch; though the autonomous independence with which he endowed the new Patriarchate must have been subsequent to Madalbert's departure.[5] There has survived no Byzantine pro-

1 According to the *Vita S. Lucae Minoris*, p. 453, the Bulgars stayed in Northern Greece till Symeon's death.

2 Nich. Myst. Epp. xxx and xxxi, pp. 185 *et seq.* Nicholas never refers to the establishment of the Bulgar Patriarchate, which must have taken place about a year after his death; but it is quite possible that he heard rumours of the intention: which explains his changed tone.

3 Ep. Rom. *ibid. loc. cit.* Zlatarsky, *loc. cit.* pp. 486 *et seq.*

4 Farlati, *Illyricum Sacrum*, III, p. 103. Madalbert, on his return from this task, held the second Synod of Spalato (927) and made peace between Croatia and Bulgaria. Šišić, *Priručnik*, pp. 221–2.

5 We do not know the date of the foundation of the Patriarchate, only that it was done by Symeon; see below, p. 96, n. 2. In view of Madalbert's visit, 926–7 seems the most likely date.

test against this; Nicholas was dead and with him the old inflexible policy of his Church. Romanus, it seems, was wise
enough to realize that ecclesiastical independence alone was the
sure means of keeping Bulgaria from the grasping arms of Rome.
And besides, in practice the Bulgarian Church had been free
long since, obedient only to the will of Symeon.

It was only by these abstract irritations that Symeon harmed
the Empire now. Romanus was able, without any hindrance
from the north, to turn his attention to the eastern frontier, and
plan and carry out great offensives against the Moslems. Symeon,
as a corollary of his new policy, was fully occupied in subjugating
the Balkans. In 925, Zacharias of Serbia, as inevitably as every
Serbian prince before him, turned against the Bulgars; and the
Serbians, with unwonted success, destroyed the first army that
Symeon sent against them. Symeon changed his policy; Serbia
had been a constant annoyance to him; now he had time to deal
with it properly, as befitted the Emperor of the Balkans. Next
year he triumphantly invaded the country, and reduced it, by
treacherous massacres, abductions and wholesale devastations,
into a desert province of Bulgaria, too lifeless now to be animated
by any intrigues from Byzantium.[1] But his evil genius tempted
him too far. Beyond Serbia lay the great militarist kingdom of
Croatia. Geographically, it was possible to hold Serbia without
controlling Croatia; politically there was no question of Croatia
being on too friendly terms with Byzantium, and the fact that
it was the retreat of dispossessed Serbian princes did not make
it so tremendous a menace; yet, whether from jealousy or insen-
sate love of conquest, Symeon determined on offensive action
against the Croatians. Following on the conquest of Serbia, he
sent a grand armament under his General Alogobatur into
Croatia. But the Bulgars met their match. Their army and
general were utterly destroyed; only one or two fugitives crept

1 Zlatarsky, *Ist.* I, 2, p. 500, talks of a Byzantine-Croatian alliance as the explanation of this war. But I do not believe that Tomislav of Croatia ever had
any diplomatic dealings with the Imperial Court; Constantine Porphyrogennetus never heard of him; see below, Chapter X, p. 210. Also, if there had
been an alliance, a power as strong as the Croatians would surely have taken
the offensive, not have waited till they were invaded. I believe Symeon's
megalomania to have been the main cause of the war.

back to tell the tale to Symeon.[1] Humbly and wisely the old
monarch made peace with Croatia,[2] but he was heartbroken; the
shock affected his health. He lasted bravely through the winter,
but on May 27th, 927, he died of heart disease.[3] The pious
Byzantines had however another theory; obeying an astrologer's
instructions, Romanus had decapitated a certain statue in the
Forum that was Symeon's στοιχεῖον: whereupon, at that very
moment, the arch-enemy expired.[4]

At once there was chaos in Bulgaria. The country had so long
been wholly dependent on the will of its tremendous autocrat
that his sudden disappearance meant the utter disorganization
of everything; while the neighbouring nations, sighing with
relief and expectation, crowded like carrion round the corpse.
Symeon, fearing what might happen, had left careful instructions
as to the succession to the throne; and the force of his personality
survived his death long enough for his wishes to be implicitly
obeyed. He had been married twice and had four sons. The
eldest, Michael, his first wife's son, for some reason he passed
over, preferring the second family, which consisted of Peter,
John and Benjamin, all three still children. Of these, Peter was
to be Tsar, with his mother's brother George Sursubul as
Regent. Michael was immured in a monastery, and John and
Benjamin kept in the background. They did not long remain
there; Michael determined to escape, John took to plotting, and
Benjamin to magic—he became the most exalted in precedence
of all the were-wolves of history.[5]

The Regent of Bulgaria had a difficult task. The country was
exhausted by its long war and had recently lost a great army in

---

1 *D.A.I.* p. 158; Georgius Monachus, p. 904. By the time of Theophanes
Continuatus the story had become muddled. There (p. 411) Symeon leads his
own expedition against the Croatians, is defeated on May 27th, 927, and dies
soon after.

2 Farlati, *loc. cit.* It seems therefore certain that Madalbert was in Bulgaria
giving Symeon the papal confirmation of his title at the time of the Croatian
disaster, as he made peace between the two nations on his return through
Croatia. 926 is the almost certain date. See also Zlatarsky, *Ist.* 1, 2, p. 501 and
Šišić, *Geschichte der Croaten*, pp. 132 *et seq.*

3 Georgius Monachus, *loc. cit.*

4 Theoph. Cont. pp. 411–412.

5 *Ibid. loc. cit.*; Liudprand, *Antapodosis*, p. 88.

Croatia. Now, on the news of Symeon's death, Croatians, Magyars and probably Petchenegs rushed to invade the frontiers.[1] His newly established prestige would not stand military disasters. In these circumstances peace with Constantinople was essential, particularly as the display of an army on the frontier was not sufficient to deter the Greeks from joining the birds of prey. Accordingly, the Regent sent secretly (there was probably still a powerful war party in Bulgaria) an Armenian monk to the city to suggest peace and a marriage alliance. The suggestion was accepted, and a peace conference was held at Mesembria, attended in the name of the Basileus by the monk Theodosius Abuces and the Imperial Secretary Constantine of Rhodes, the poet. Terms were discussed and settled, and the imperial ambassadors returned by land (they had gone by sea, there still being officially war), accompanied by Stephen the Bulgar, a relative of Peter's; and soon after followed the Bulgarian Regent with many of his nobles, including a half-brother of the Tsar. The Bulgar mission saw Maria Lecapena, the Emperor Christopher's daughter, and reported favourably on her to Peter, who at once set out for Constantinople. The Patrician Nicetas, grandfather of the princess, was sent to meet him with honour.

On October 8th, 927, with George Sursubul and Theophanes the Protovestiarius as witnesses of each side, Peter and Maria were married by the Patriarch Stephen in the church of the Virgin at Pegae (the successor of that church that, three years before, Symeon had so impiously burnt); and Maria was rechristened with the propitious name of Irene. After the marriage Maria returned to the city with Theophanes. Three days later they all met again at a sumptuous wedding feast at Pegae, and then the little bride had to follow her strange husband to a strange land, proud at the prospect of a throne, but weeping to leave her family, her home, and the comforts of Constantinople. Wisely, she took her furniture with her. Her parents went with her as far as Hebdomum, and there said goodbye.[2] Meanwhile,

---

1 Theoph. Cont. *loc. cit.*

2 *Ibid.* pp. 412 *et seq.* It is interesting that Peter was never allowed inside the city—just as Symeon had been left outside in 913, though his sons were entertained within.

less spectacularly, the peace treaty was signed, chiefly through the work of the Protovestiarius Theophanes.[1] The long war was over at last.

The magnificence of the wedding distracted the chroniclers' attentions, so we are not told of the clauses of the treaty. They seem to have been divided into three headings—territorial adjustments, financial arrangements, and titular concessions. With regard to the first there was probably little drastic change. In the neighbourhood of Thessalonica a few towns were ceded to Bulgaria, such as Berrhoea;[2] but in return it seems likely that the towns of the Gulf of Burgas, Develtus and Anchialus, returned to imperial hands. There had been talk of restoring all the Black Sea fortresses while Symeon was still living;[3] and soon afterwards Constantine Porphyrogennetus includes the two towns among the cities of the Thracian theme;[4] while a little later he implies that the Bulgarian frontier ended on the coast north of Mesembria, at a river that he calls the Ditzina.[5]

The financial arrangements are even harder to decipher. It seems that some yearly subsidy was to be sent from the Byzantine Court to the Bulgars—perhaps the 100 'scaramangia' that Romanus mentioned in his letters to Symeon. Some forty years later the Emperor Nicephorus Phocas, wishing to divert the Russians from Cherson, induced them to join with him in a war against Bulgaria. Leo Diaconus says that the *casus belli* was his

1 Theoph. Cont. p. 413.

2 Berrhoea was Greek in 904 (John Cameniates, p. 496) but a long-established Bulgar fort in Basil II's reign (Cedrenus, II, p. 452).

3 See above, p. 93.

4 *D.T.* p. 47. Constantine is apt to be careless and misinformed about the European themes, but it is hard to believe that he would make a mistake with regard to Thrace.

5 *D.A.I.* p. 79, talking of the Russians sailing down the coast on their way to Constantinople: καὶ ἀπὸ τοῦ Κωνοποῦ εἰς Κωνσταντίαν (Constanza), εἰς τὸν ποταμὸν Βάρνας (Varna), καὶ ἀπὸ Βάρνας ἔρχονται εἰς τὸν ποταμὸν Διτζίναν, ἅπερ πάντα εἰσὶ γῆς τῆς Βουλγαρίας, ἀπὸ δὲ τῆς Διτζίνας εἰς τὰ τῆς Μεσημβρίας μέρη καταλαμβάνουσι. It is possible that Develtus, up at the head of the Gulf of Burgas, and therefore missed by the Russians, might still be Bulgar, but it indicates that Mesembria was not now an isolated possession, but was set in a hinterland all imperial south of the Ditzina. Zlatarsky, *Ist.* I, 2, p. 525, says that the frontier remained the same as in Leo VI's time (at 896 and 904), only the Byzantines renounced Develtus, Sozopolis and Agathopolis. The statement is unproved, and seems to me unwarrantable. Finally, there is no record of the coast towns having later to be reconquered by the Byzantines.

refusal to pay the humiliating tribute to the Bulgars, thus making the whole war an arbitrary affair. During the war, it was the Russians, not the Byzantines, that did the fighting. Cedrenus, on the other hand, mentions no specific war, but says that Peter, *after his wife's death*, sent to renew the peace with Constantinople and provided his sons as hostages. By correlating these stories, the reasonable conclusion seems to be that the subsidy was only to be paid during the Tsaritsa's lifetime, that Peter put himself in the wrong by demanding it after her death, was punished by the Russians, and then attempted to re-ally himself with the Empire on much humbler terms. Viewed in this light, the subsidy becomes merely an income paid to the Bulgars in order that the imperial princess that shared their throne might live as befitted an imperial princess—or in other words, to pay for the titled ambassadress or spy that the Emperor kept at the Bulgarian Court.[1] At the same time, we are told, Romanus received back a large number of prisoners of war. It is not stated whether he had to pay for them; but it is implied that the honour of marrying the daughter of an Emperor was sufficient payment in the eyes of the Tsar.[2]

The concessions of title were clearer. The Byzantines agreed not only to recognize the independence of the Bulgarian Patriarchate,[3] but also the imperial title of the Bulgarian monarch,[4] and, as an additional honour, to give Bulgarian ambassadors for evermore precedence over all others.[5]

These then were the terms settled at Mesembria and confirmed at Constantinople. For a consistently defeated nation, Byzantium had done very well. In territory she had lost nothing of importance, but had probably made some very handsome recoveries; in money she was paying no more than before, and paying it now to a Court presided over by a Byzantine princess; and she redeemed all her captives. The concessions of titles might seem damaging to Byzantine prestige, but were harmless.

1 Leo Diaconus, pp. 61, 80; Cedrenus, II, p. 346.   2 *D.A.I.* p. 88.
3 See Golubinski (p. 33) who establishes this.
4 Theoph. Cont. p. 415, talking of Maria, χαίρουσα δὲ ἐν οἶς βασιλεῖ προσήρμοστο ἀνδρί....
5 Liudprand, *Legatio*, p. 186.

Indeed, the recognition of the independence of the Patriarchate, which was the recognition of a *fait accompli*, was, as Romanus no doubt saw, highly beneficial in that it finally took away from the Bulgars any desire to secede to Rome. The gift of the title of Basileus to the Bulgarian monarch, and the precedence consequently accorded to his ambassadors (for no other foreign potentate was allowed that high title) were more striking and provided happy sops to Bulgarian vanity. But it seems that Romanus took away the title at his will—whether as a punishment to Peter for some unfriendly act such as helping in the conspiracy of his grandfather-in-law, Nicetas, we do not know; but it certainly seems that Peter was still addressed as ἄρχων by the Byzantine Court, until the accession to power of Constantine Porphyrogennetus.[1] Thus even the peace terms won by the Bulgars after their long years of victory scarcely disguised the fact that actually Bulgaria had collapsed. Symeon's incessant energies had exhausted her and strained her heart; his army at last defeated and himself dead, she crumpled to the ground. And the Byzantines, to their delighted surprise, suddenly saw, instead of a monster power continually menacing on the north, a feeble, almost a client state, vast indeed but effete, over which foreign invaders roamed at their will. The peace was accepted without protest,

[1] Peter was certainly given the title of Basileus now (see reference above). But in the *De Ceremoniis* there are formulae in which the Emperor greets his spiritual *grandson*, the *Archon* of Bulgaria (*D.C.* p. 681—Canarti and Butias Tarcan must be hereditary Bulgar titles). This clearly refers to Romanus and his grandson-in-law, Peter. Bury (*The Ceremonial Book*, p. 226) says that this refers to Leo VI and the son of the Emperor's godson, i.e. Vladimir, son of Boris. But Boris's godfather was Michael, who was officially no relation to Leo, and it is absurd that the Emperor should always be considered the same person while with regard to the Bulgar prince generations were taken into account. Moreover Leo did not have sons who were Basileis, as are mentioned here in the formula with which the Bulgars were to reply. Basil I had such sons, but at the time of his death Boris was still reigning in Bulgaria. Romanus was the first Emperor after him to crown more than one son. Constantine (*D.C.* p. 690) goes on to say that lately (ἀρτίως) a new formula has come into use in which the ruler of Bulgaria is given the title of Basileus; but there is also a specific formula for Constantine and Romanus (II) to use, calling the Bulgar merely Archon. With regard to this, Bury (*loc. cit.*) says that the Emperor's names are probably interpolations. Rambaud (pp. 340 *et seq.*) and Zlatarsky (*Ist.* I, 2, p. 526) both discuss the question, but without reaching satisfactory conclusions. It is possible that Constantine Porphyrogennetus gave back the imperial title as a price for Peter's neutrality at the time of the fall of the Tsaritsa's Lecapene relatives.

and lasted for some forty years—a rare stillness in the turgid story of the Balkans.

Thus the Empire passed triumphantly through its greatest ordeal since the days of the Saracen sieges. We may look back now and realize that Byzantium was the stronger combatant, with its conscious prestige and carefully fashioned, well-matured organization; while Bulgaria had been built in a hurry, on sand. But at the time it must have seemed that only the walls of Constantinople stood between the Empire and its end, and chaos in the Palace brought the end daily nearer. And indeed had Symeon once entered the city, the shock would surely have been too much for Byzantium and such horrors would have fallen on it now as actually fell at the time of the Fourth Crusade. Nicholas had attempted to deal with the problem by negotiations and concessions, short-sightedly ready to give Symeon even an entrance into the Palace through a daughter's marriage, if only he could so keep the Bulgarian Church under his supremacy. Zoe saw the danger more clearly; she determined to meet arms by arms and staked all on a military triumph; but Symeon was the better soldier, and she lost. Romanus was wiser than his predecessors. He established himself firmly in Constantinople, and then waited there in patience. He knew that Symeon would never be able to storm the great land walls, were the city under good control, and that without sea power the capital was impregnable. He was therefore content to sacrifice the European provinces for the time being, till Symeon should exhaust himself in fruitless triumphs. Meanwhile, he hastened on that exhaustion by the traditional Byzantine weapon of diplomacy, of which he was a master. Continually Symeon was distracted in his rear; the great Steppe tribes threatened him, and every few years Serbia struck at him. He conquered, but grew steadily more weary: till at last there came the Croatian disaster (in which Romanus had no hand) and his death; and his work fell to pieces. Romanus then prudently made a moderate and satisfactory peace, and troubled himself very little about the Bulgars again. The danger was past; the great days of Bulgaria were over. To recover her glory now she needed a warrior and statesman far greater than Symeon or than Boris had been. Instead, she had Tsar Peter, who was only a saint.

CHAPTER VI

Byzantium and the Nations of the Steppes

THE collapse of Bulgaria entirely altered the foreign affairs
of the Empire. Even in Italy and in the East, where fighting could never long be interrupted, the menace in the
Balkans had kept the Greeks for many years in check. Now at
last the menace was gone, and Romanus could turn his un-
hampered attention to punishing rebel Lombards and to his
grander schemes of conquest on the Euphrates. But it was with
regard to the nations beyond Bulgaria, the nations of the Steppes,
that the revolution was most complete. Hitherto, during the
period of her greatness, Bulgaria had acted as a buffer between
these nations and the Empire; their raids could never penetrate
through to the imperial provinces. Consequently, the imperial
diplomacy with regard to them had been simple and straightforward, consisting entirely in persuasions and bribes to make
them attack the Bulgars in the rear. But now Bulgaria had fallen
low, and over her corpse the Empire found itself face to face
with these predatory tribes. They could raid now at ease right
to the imperial provinces. Moreover, the last fifty years had seen
great movements and changes on the Steppes. It was an entirely
new set of problems that Romanus had to meet—shifting complicated problems requiring subtle and adjustable solutions.

Bulgaria now no longer mattered. In her weariness she lay
inert, with a Graecized Court and hierarchy, a restive Bulgar
nobility and a discontented Slav peasantry, disguising passive
rebellion under the name of heresy. The Byzantine historians
could afford to ignore Bulgarian affairs, except to notice in passing that the Greek Tsaritsa used to pay frequent visits to her
home, though she only came once more after her father's death:[1]
that Prince John of Bulgaria tried to lead a rebellion of the
nobility against his brother the Tsar, but was captured and made
a monk; whereupon Romanus by a timely embassy managed to

[1] Theoph. Cont. p. 422.

secure his person, and, releasing him from his vows, gave him a palace in Constantinople and an Armeniac bride;[1] and that Prince Michael, Peter's elder half-brother, escaped from his monastery prison, to lead a band of malcontents in the Albanian hills, who after his death were audacious enough to invade the Empire and sack the important city of Nicopolis.[2] The peace lasted on; but there must have been occasional *refroidissements*, as when Romanus set up Prince John at his Court, showing that even against his granddaughter's husband he liked to have a pretender at hand; and in 930 or 931 he actively patronized the revolt of Serbia against the Bulgars;[3] while sometime there occurred the mysterious affair that made Romanus withhold the title of Basileus from the Tsar.[4] But Bulgaria could not afford to be unfriendly; she had troubles enough of her own. She was powerless to resist foreign raiders, while at home in reaction to the Graecized Court the Bulgar nobles sulked in their feudal castles, and the peasantry began to fall under the socialist sway of one Bogomil, the preacher of the puritan-Manichaean heresy that for centuries was to be the bane of the Balkans. So relations between Preslav and Constantinople remained officially cordial, and the Bulgars took on the air of being almost a client people, sending warnings to the Empire of movements and raids from the Steppes, and bearing the first brunt of them all. It was a sorry situation for the proud Empire of Symeon. Peter was being punished for the sins of his father. And the Byzantines barely noticed it all, having now no Bulgarian question to solve.

Of the nations beyond the Balkans, the one whose invasions most disquieted the Empire was the Hungarian or Magyar (Τούρχοι). The Hungarians had not long appeared in history, and only very recently had come to the country now called after them. They consisted of a collection of ethnologically related tribes, each under its own prince, closely organized in times of war under a head prince, from whom eventually there evolved the Hungarian monarchy. In the latter half of the ninth century they were inhabiting the country close to the Chazars, on the

1 *Ibid.* p. 419.   2 *Ibid.* p. 420.
3 *D.A.I.* pp. 158 *et seq.*   4 See above, Chapter V, p. 100.

banks of the river Don; but about 880, owing to a reshuffling of
the tribes of the Steppes, due apparently to pressure from the
Uzes on the east, they had moved a little westward, to the eastern
slopes of the Carpathians. There they came close into the range
of Byzantine politics.[1]

The Empire at this time seemed lost among the Slavs. Just
to the north lay the great kingdom of Bulgaria, by now pre-
dominantly a Slav kingdom; to the west of that were the Slav
Serbians and Croatians; further north was Sviatopulk's huge
Moravian Empire, and still further north, Poland and Bohemia;
on the east on the Dnieper was the growing power of Russia.
And in addition the Empire itself was filled with unruly Slavs.
The Hungarians came as a deliverance. About 895 the Emperor
Leo, at war with Symeon of Bulgaria, called in the Hungarians
to take Bulgaria in the rear—he found it more pious and less
expensive to use them to fight against his co-religionists. During
the Hungarians' absence in Bulgaria, the Petchenegs, with whom
Symeon managed to ally himself, raided and destroyed their
homes; and on their return the Hungarians were obliged to move
elsewhere. Accordingly, about the year 900, under their Chief
Prince Arpad they crossed the Carpathians and fell upon the
plain of the Danube and the Theiss, and the hills of Transylvania, then shared between the Moravian and the Bulgarian
monarchs. By 907 the Moravian kingdom had vanished, and
the Hungarians were firmly settled in the empty place.[2]

The Anonymous Hungarian historian declares that they met
with opposition from the Bulgarians and from a small body of
Greeks.[3] That the Bulgarians opposed them is certain; but the
Greeks can scarcely have objected to the fall of Moravia
and the loss to Bulgaria of half its territory. The Hungarians
were still close enough to raid the Empire, but now they had
the tempting riches of Western Europe nearby, to divert their
attention; and Byzantium must have relished the disappearance
of Slav Moravia and the partial isolation of the Bulgars. Once

1 *D.A.I.* pp. 164, 168 *et seq.*
2 *Ibid. loc. cit.* Anon. Hung. pp. 16 *et seq.* Joannes de Thwrocz, pp. 132 *et
seq.* The story is told with many picturesque legends. It is remarkable how
quickly the huge Moravian kingdom fell.
3 Anon. Hung. p. 42.

settled in their new home, the Hungarians raided freely and successfully. It was Germany and Italy that suffered most; but France was not unspared, and the terrible cavalry rushed down as far as Andalusia. Nor could the Empire hope to escape entirely. About the time of Arpad's death (907) a band of Hungarians under two prominent princes crossed south as far as Macedonia, to the terror of Bulgars and Macedonians, and raided Rascia and the theme of Durazzo. This band lingered so long that at last it forgot the way home, and stayed to be a new ingredient in the ethnological hotchpot of the Balkans.[1]

For about twenty-five years the Balkans seem to have rested; though during all the Bulgar war Byzantine diplomats were busy among the princes of the Magyars. Then soon after 930 the invasions of the Empire recommenced, with details hard to be deciphered. The account in all the Greek chronicles—an account that there is no reason to doubt—is that in April, 934, the Hungarians, for the first time, ravaged Thrace on the way to Constantinople. The Protovestiarius Theophanes went out to meet them and to arrange terms. This he managed with great success, satisfying both Greeks and Hungarians—though the former paid heavily, while Romanus, from the goodness of his heart, spared no money in the redemption of captives.[2] The Hungarian historians are vaguer; one version, dating the invasion in the twenty-first year (from the conquest of Moravia, i.e. about 928) says that the Hungarians captured Adrianople (Hydropolis) and besieged Constantinople, and then tells the story of a single combat and of perfidy on the Emperor's part. Eventually the Hungarians retreated, devastating all Greece.[3] The other version, dating it in the twentieth year, merely says that Constantinople was too strong to take, so the Hungarians ravaged the rest of Greece:[4] while the Anonymous Hungarian, without dating the legend, merely states that it was untrue that the Hungarians ever burnt the Golden Gate of the City.[5] Thus

1 Anon. Hung. p. 46. This raid is also recorded by Nestor (p. 19) as having reached the neighbourhood of Thessalonica.

2 Theoph. Cont. p. 422.

3 Thwrocz, p. 147. 4 Petrus Ranzanus, Index IV, p. 581.

5 Anon. Hung. p. 42: but this seems to be in connection with the story of Greek help to the Moravians.

far, the stories fit well enough; the difficulty arises with the version of the contemporary Maçoudi. According to him, on the frontiers of the Greek Empire, in a strong position between the mountains and the sea, lay the important town of 'Valander'. The 'Turks' could not penetrate through here. Owing, however, to a squabble kindled by an insulted Moslem merchant from Ardebil, the population of Valander raided into Turkish territory. The Turks therefore formally united—and the context implies that this was a union of Hungarians with Bashkirs and Petchenegs, under a Petcheneg chieftain—and set out with 60,000 horse against Valander. The Emperor 'Armenus' (Romanus) sent 50,000 Greek troops with 12,000 newly converted Christians against the Turks; but there was a terrific Greek defeat, and the Turks were so sated with captives that a woman could be bought for a silk dress. Then after lingering a little outside the walls of Valander, the Turks moved off to Western Europe. All this Maçoudi dates in the year 932.[1]

The obvious, and usually admitted, theory is that these stories refer to the same raid. Marquart[2], who went fully into the question, accepts, though with surprise, the union of Magyars with Petchenegs, and identifies Valander with Develtus, on the Gulf of Burgas. But he does not overcome certain difficulties. Develtus, it is true, was in a key position on one of the main routes to Constantinople, the route that the Petchenegs, though not the Magyars, would certainly use; it was also situated close to the Greek frontier, and was, I believe, a Greek city.[3] But if its citizens wished to raid 'Turkish' territory—even Petcheneg territory—they would have to journey at least a hundred and fifty miles through Bulgaria and then cross the Danube. There was no place where the imperial frontier impinged on the 'Turkish', whether Magyar or Petcheneg. Indeed, how the Empire could play the rôle ascribed to it is very hard to see. Neither in 932 nor 934 could Romanus, busily engaged in both years in conducting grand campaigns in the East, have managed

1 Maçoudi (Barbier de Meynard), 11, p. 58.
2 Marquart, *Streifzüge*, pp. 60 *et seq.*
3 See Chapter v, p. 98. If Develtus was in Bulgarian hands, the question is still more obscure.

to produce an army of such size so quickly in Thrace. Moreover, it is inconceivable that the Greek chroniclers should have omitted so sensational an event when giving their quite coherent version of the invasion. And finally, though it is possible to envisage a union between the Magyars and the Petchenegs, such a union is inherently highly improbable.

One can only guess at the truth. Maçoudi almost certainly derived his information from Moslem merchants resident at 'Valander', and almost certainly the story grew more and more sensational on its journey to Maçoudi. The episode of the citizens of Valander raiding into Turkish territory must surely be dropped; but it is quite possible that the Magyars were raiding in Bulgaria close to the border, and the inhabitants of one of the frontier towns were rash enough to attack their camp. The Magyars then invaded Thrace and beat the militia of the theme, and after this victory, till Theophanes's embassy reached them, ravaged the theme so successfully that as a result of it and of their previous ravaging in Bulgaria, the price of captive slaves among them became very low. We know that when Theophanes treated with them Romanus generously bought back all his captive subjects; probably he paid for them by presenting silk robes, a favourite Byzantine export, to the Magyar leaders; and thus Maçoudi's story arose. If this is the correct version, Develtus is much the best identification for Valander. If the Magyars were raiding in Bulgaria they would probably have made towards Preslav, where the wealth of the country was chiefly concentrated; and to advance from the neighbourhood of Preslav into Thrace, it would be natural to use the route through Develtus. It is, however, possible (though, I think, improbable) that Maçoudi's story refers to some raid that actually took place in 932, further west, and that Valander should be identified with Avlona or some such town on the west coast of the Balkans.

The only other recorded Magyar raid during the reign of Romanus presents no such difficulties. In April, 943, the Magyars appeared in full force in Thrace; but at once Romanus sent Theophanes out to negotiate. He was successful enough to conclude a five years' peace and, in return no doubt for handsome sums of money and gifts, to take back to Constantinople several illustrious hostages.¹ This peace was renewed after Romanus's fall, in 948, and lasted throughout the reign of the Porphyrogennetus.

It is interesting to note that while Western Europe trembled so frantically before the Hungarians, and made them for all time the villains of their fairy stories,² the Eastern Empire, better used to invasions, treated them quite calmly. Besides, the West had no sense of proportion; it did not know the Petchenegs.

All the world that knew them feared the Petchenegs. Even the Hungarians, when begged by the Greeks to ally against them, recoiled in terror from the prospect.³ And the one advice that Constantine Porphyrogennetus urged with reiterated firmness on his son was the absolute necessity of keeping peace with them. Their territory stretched without definite boundaries along the north of the Black Sea from the Danube to the Don. They had only recently settled in it finally, about the year 900, when they drove the Hungarians over the Carpathians; formerly they had lived further east, by the Volga, where some were still left behind. Ethnologically they seem to have been of Turkish origin and had the usual Turkish organization, being divided into eight tribes with their various areas—Constantine calls them 'themes'—each under its prince; and no doubt in times of war, one prince took the lead, as among the Hungarians.⁴ Even more than the Hungarians, they were incorrigible barbarians, nomads living in tents and disgusting their neighbours by the savagery of their practices.

Constantine's advice shows the anxiety with which the Petchenegs were regarded at Constantinople, where they were con-

1 Theoph. Cont. p. 430.
2 The derivation of 'ogre' from 'Ougre' is now challenged in etymological dictionaries (see *N.E.D.*) on the grounds that 'ogre' does not appear in literature before the seventeenth century. But surely what would necessarily be a purely popular word need not appear in literature for centuries; and certainly no other satisfactory derivation is provided.
3 Probably in 948, when the five years' treaty was renewed. Bury however dates it in Leo's reign, soon after the Magyars' arrival in Hungary. But it seems to me unlikely that the Emperor should wish to fight the Petchenegs, when a strong Bulgaria lay between; and though peace with the Petchenegs was a state policy by the time that the *D.A.I.* was written, there is no reason to suppose that Constantine obeyed that policy in the first years of his reign.
4 *D.A.I.* pp. 164 *et seq.*

sidered almost invincible; and he emphasizes the need for yearly
embassies to their princes and gives instructions for their behaviour. The embassies went either from Cherson, or directly
from Constantinople by sea to the mouths of the Dneiper or the
Dniester.[1] But probably these direct missions were only on
special occasions, and ordinarily Petcheneg affairs belonged to
the department of the Stratege of Cherson; certainly under Zoe
it had been Bogas, Stratege of Cherson, who reported to the
capital Bulgar intrigues among the Petchenegs, and undertook
negotiations with them himself.[2] Cherson's existence as a Byzantine colony almost entirely depended on peace being preserved.

During Romanus's reign the peace policy was apparently
maintained; and the rich presents provided and the hostages
demanded by the yearly ambassadors thus achieved their result.
In Zoe's time the alliance had been close enough to bring the
Petchenegs to attack Bulgaria in the rear; and, though that campaign had come to no result, the excellent terms existing between
the Petchenegs and the Empire would serve successfully to awe
the Bulgars, the Hungarians, the Russians or the Chazars. There
were very few lapses. Possibly in 934 the Petchenegs joined the
raiding Hungarians; in 941 they allowed the Russians, no doubt
in return for richer gifts than were provided that year by the
imperial ambassador, to pass through their territory on their way
to raid; and in 944 came an agonized warning from Bulgaria:
"The Russians are coming, and they have the Petchenegs in
their service". Well might the Bulgars cry; for it was they that
suffered. Romanus was astute enough to pay for an agreeable
peace.[3]

Behind the Petchenegs were the Russians, a vast confederacy
of Slav tribes stretching from the Gulf of Finland to the Lower
Dnieper, under the leadership of the house of the Scandinavian
Rurik. Here was a different type of organization. Many of the
outlying tribes, such as the Drevlians or the Severians, were
sunk in an uncouth barbarism that horrified Nestor, but the bulk
of the nation was—for the Steppes—comparatively civilized,

1 *D.A.I.*, pp. 68 *et seq.*   2 See Chapter III, p. 53.
3 Nestor, p. 35.

living in rough cities, some of which, as Novgorod or Kiev, were places of considerable importance, and now organized in a decidedly feudal arrangement under the Varangian (Swedish) aristocracy. The Greeks had already been in relations, good and bad, with Russia; treaties of a sort seem to have been made between them as early as 839, and under Theodora and Michael there had been a Russian raid on Hierum.[1] Under Rurik (about 880) and his successors Russia developed greatly, and by the early tenth century was conducting considerable trade not only with Constantinople but also with the Chazars and, it seems, the tribes of the distant Baltic; the route from Novgorod to the Dnieper was proving, as so often throughout history, one of the great trade routes of Europe.[2]

Under the Grand Prince Oleg, according to Nestor, the Russians had undertaken an enormous land and sea expedition against Constantinople in 907; and as a result of Oleg's successes, the Greeks made a treaty, which he quotes in full.[3] The expedition, unmentioned elsewhere, is probably legendary—a case of imaginative wish-fulfilment—or perhaps it was Bulgaria that suffered from it. But the treaty may well be authentic, concluded by the Greeks at the news of a projected expedition. By this 907 treaty, *bona fide* Russian merchants were to be admitted under a guard into Constantinople and were to reside outside the walls at Saint Mamas, and they were to be given an allowance for their board during their visit. Later, in 912, more clauses were added, regulating the punishments when a Russian murdered or stole from a Greek and *vice versa* (no doubt the new colonists of Saint Mamas did not bring highly refined manners with them) and the laws about slaves, and—probably a necessary precaution for the Greeks—ensuring that Greek boats wrecked or stormbound where Russians were, should not be raided, but the sailors should be helped to a Christian country, and compensation should be given for any cargo taken. At the same time

1 Theoph. Cont. p. 196.

2 Nestor, *passim; D.A.I.* pp. 74 *et seq.* For details of the Russian trade, which consisted chiefly of skins and slaves, see Kluchevsky, I, chap. vi, who describes its annual gathering.

3 Nestor, pp. 22 *et seq.* The whole of the early part of Nestor's story has been called mythical, including the lives both of Oleg and Igor.

it seems that the Empire agreed to pay the Russians an annual subsidy, no doubt similar to that paid to the Petchenegs.[1] Zoe's and Romanus's contemporary as Grand Prince of Russia was Rurik's son Igor, who escaped from the tutelage of Oleg in 913 and did not die till 945. The subsidy was probably paid to the Russians punctiliously all through the Bulgar war, to prevent a Russo-Bulgar alliance; or else the imperial diplomacy was enabled to entangle the Russians in wars against the Petchenegs —a feature of the early years of Igor's reign. Igor was also busy for several years fighting against the Drevlians, the savage Slavs that ultimately proved his death.[2] Anyhow in 941 the subsidy was no longer paid, and Igor was strong enough to plan a vast attack on Constantinople.

Igor's preparations were made in the utmost secrecy; it was only just before the Russian fleet appeared that warning came through from Bulgaria. It was an attack only by sea; but the size of the armada was considerable. The Greek historians, some of them quite angrily, insist that there were no fewer than 10,000 or even 15,000 boats[3]—dromites, swift light vessels like the Franks'—and Nestor copies them; but the Italian ambassador, who had no patriotism involved, informed his stepson Liudprand that the number was a little over a thousand:[4] that is to say, about 40,000 men—the Russian adventurers, as opposed to a *levée en masse* of the Slavs.[5] The Greek navy was away in the islands or fighting against the Saracens; and Romanus passed sleepless nights in his despair. Fifteen old chelandia were discovered in the harbour, and these the shipbuilders received orders to patch up as best they could; and the Protovestiarius Theophanes, armed with fasts and lamentations and (perhaps still more useful) Greek fire, set out in them to guard the northern entrance of the Bosphorus. On June 11th the Russian

1 Nestor, *loc. cit.*

2 *Ibid.* pp. 32, 33. Some time fairly soon after 912 there was also a Russian expedition against the Chazars which penetrated as far as Aderbaijan (Maçoudi, II, p. 21): see d'Ohsson, p. 105.

3 10,000 in Theoph. Cont. p. 423; Zonaras (III, p. 476): "not 10,000 as has been said, but 15,000"; Nestor, p. 33.

4 Liudprand, *Antapodosis*, pp. 137 *et seq.*, who gives very vivid details.

5 Soloveiv, I, pp. 111–112.

armada came in sight; and Theophanes sent his fireships out to attack. The awe-inspiring novelty of the attack achieved its primary object; the Russians, after losing several ships, turned to the east and sailed along the Bithynian coast to Sgora. There they landed and split into large bands that ravaged the countryside from Heraclea to Nicomedia, inflicting terrible deaths on all their captives and torturing with especial venom the clergy. But meanwhile the Greek armies were summoned from Armenia and the navy from the Saracen seas. The ex-Stratege Bardas Phocas with a band of cavalry and infantry (presumably the militia of the theme) destroyed a large party of the foragers; and soon with remarkable speed the great Domestic John Curcuas appeared in full force; and the raiding companies began to suffer. As autumn came on, in fear the Russians began to long for the safety of their homes. But escape was difficult, for Theophanes was watching with a strong and well-armed fleet. In September they surreptitiously tried to cross by night to Thrace; but Theophanes was prepared and attacked them on their way. The Greek fire fell like the fire of heaven, and the Russians in terror leapt into the sea. Many were drowned, and some even burnt among the waves. Only a few of that great expedition returned home to Russia, to tell of the terrors of Greek sea warfare, and to plot a vast revenge. In Constantinople Theophanes was received in triumph and raised to be Paracoemomene; all of the Russian captives (a very large number) were beheaded in the presence of the ambassadors.[1]

The expedition of 941 was really a Viking raid in the grand manner, out for booty and destruction. Had it been successful Constantinople would have been sacked, but left again for the Greeks.[2] Three years later Igor planned his revenge on a much more solid scale. Nestor gives an impressive list of the Slavonic tribes whom Igor collected (in a truly feudal manner) from all parts of his dominions; and Igor managed to pay the Petchenegs

1 Liudprand, pp. 137 et seq.; Theoph. Cont. pp. 423 et seq.; Cedrenus, II, p. 316; Zonaras, III, p. 476.
2 It is this fact, that only the Russian adventurers took part, that makes me disinclined to believe Rambaud when he suggests that it was a trade war. It seems to me far more likely that the raid was merely to remind the Greeks to pay up their subsidy.

to accompany him—perhaps the Greek embassy that year was late or inadequate, or the Stratege of Cherson tactless. This time, no doubt because it was apparently to be a land expedition, Romanus received timely warnings from Bulgaria and from Cherson; and, not wishing to risk his capital again, he hastily sent out ambassadors with a most conciliatory air. The ambassadors met Igor on the Danube, and with costly gifts patched up a truce, and bribed off the Petchenegs. The Russians returned home, while the Petchenegs stayed to ravage Bulgaria, whose Tsar had been less alert. Igor was determined, however, not to waste his great armament, and took his troops off to the southeast, over the Caspian, where they perished victorious, of dysentery, far from home, on the borders of Armenia.[1] Early next year (945) ambassadors arrived in Russia to settle permanent peace terms; they had left Constantinople before the fall of Romanus, in whose name, with Stephen's and the Constantines', the treaty was made out. The treaty, quoted in full by Nestor, was a résumé of former treaties, regulating prices and punishments, the procedure of Russians at Constantinople and Greeks in Russia, and providing for the Greek integrity of Cherson. It shows Russia as a well-organized state with large commercial interests, divided feudally between a number of cities under princes and princesses of the ruling and noble houses, all under the Grand Prince of Kiev. It also shows the exact control that the Byzantine government kept over the policing of the city (aliens only admitted under a guard and fifty at a time; and no Russian to winter on the Bosphorus) and over the trade of the Empire.[2] This treaty proved satisfactory to both parties; and peace was kept for twenty-five years.

To the east of the Petchenegs and the Russians, occupying the land from the sea of Azov and the Crimea to the Volga and the northern shores of the Caspian was the kingdom of the Chazars.[3] The Chazars, once long ago a nomad Turkish tribe,[4] had been

[1] Nestor, p. 35; Maçoudi, II, p. 21.　　　　　　[2] Nestor, loc. cit.
[3] For the Chazars, see Ibn Foszlan (trans. Frähn) who gives the fullest account.
[4] Vivien de Saint-Martin decides on a Finnish origin for the Chazars but gives them a Turkish ruling family.

already for over two centuries settled in more or less their present homes and were by now infinitely the most civilized nation of the Steppes. The Chazar kingdom was unlike any of its contemporaries. The state religion was Judaism, which the Chazar monarch, when searching for a respectable religion (probably about the year 800 or slightly earlier) had decided was more reasonable than either Christianity or Islam; and Chazaria was the centre of considerable Jewish missionary movements among the neighbouring tribes. Nevertheless, in normal times, religious toleration was complete, and the bulk of the population was allowed to be Christian or Mahometan as it pleased. The constitution was equally unexpected for the Steppes. Chazaria was an absolute monarchy. There was a *fainéant* supreme Khagan (the Ilek) who lived with his twenty-five royal-born wives and sixty concubines in his brick palace at Itil; his life was shrouded in mystery; he only emerged thrice a year and then with no one within a mile's distance of him, and he was only visited by the three highest dignitaries of the State. In former years he had been obliged after a reign of a fixed number of years to die; but by now so barbarous a custom had been discarded. The country was ruled by a hereditary mayor of the palace, the Khagan Bey, commander-in-chief and prime minister, who even appointed the Khagan. Both he and the Khagan were obliged to be Jews. Justice was administered by seven judges, two Jews who judged according to Hebrew law, two Christians who judged according to Gospel law, two Mahometans who judged according to Koran law, and one heathen who judged according to reason. The Chazars were sufficiently civilized not only to live in cities— their capital, Itil, in the Volga delta, was, it is true, except for its palace, a city of tents; but there was also the Greek-built Sarkel on the Azov, and Balanjar on the west coast of the Caspian, both considerable centres of commerce—but also they kept up and recorded diplomatic correspondence with countries even as distant as Spain. Their trade connections must have been great, though, curiously enough, Ibn Foszlan states that there was practically no export trade from Chazaria.[1]

1 Ibn Foszlan, p. 18.

Long ago the Chazars had been a formidable military nation, but their growing civilization had brought them to a peace-loving condition that contrasted sharply with their neighbours. By now they were dependent on mercenaries, chiefly Moslem, such as the Khagan's guard of 7000, who insisted on choosing their own vizier and on having to fight no wars against their co-religionists. Thus to some extent Chazaria had diplomatically to rank as a Moslem power; but its relations seem to have been if anything more intimate with Constantinople than with Bag-dad; the persecution of Jews in Albania (Albaboundje) in 922, probably by the fanatical Emir Nasr, produced reprisals in Chazaria against the Moslems; whereas Romanus's persecution, which caused many Jews from the Empire to take refuge in Chazaria, seems to have led to no hostile result. It had long been Byzantine policy to keep on the friendliest terms with the Chazars, even to the extent of intermarriage; this policy had once been very necessary, for the preservation of Cherson and even of the Balkans. But now owing to the decline of their strength and the power of the intervening Petchenegs, Byzan-tium found that it could treat the Chazars with a cynical con-tempt; they were still the chief power in the Crimea and a danger to Cherson, it was true, but they could so easily be kept in order by paying the Alans, the Bulgars of the Volga or the Uzes to attack them, though to employ the Petchenegs would be rather too severe; one does not want to destroy the Chazars utterly. They had their uses; the Khagan boasted that he held the mouths of the Russian rivers, and could prevent the Russians flooding the world; and though this was no longer true with regard to the most important Russian river, the Dnieper, he still com-manded the Don and the Volga and thus controlled their move-ments further east. The Chazars were still an important factor in the subtle interwoven diplomacy necessary to preserve the balance of power on the Steppes; the Emperor took care to main-tain constant intercourse between his Court and that of Itil; and he resented the attempts of foreign potentates to get into touch with the Khagan. The Spanish rabbi Hasdaï's ambassador (in about 950) was met at Constantinople with refusals on the Emperor's part to forward a letter from Hasdaï to the Khagan;

and the letter had eventually to journey by a dangerous route through Germany, Hungary and Bulgaria.[1]

During Romanus's reign the Empire seems to have remained on friendly terms with the Chazars, unbroken even by the Emperor's pious persecution of the Jews. No details of any actual negotiations between the two Courts have come down to us; but, to judge from results throughout the period Byzantine diplomacy in Chazaria maintained its effective level.

Beyond the Chazars, to the north, were their subject tribes, the Burdas, who despite the fact that they were all either Christian or Moslem in religion (their king was Moslem) were still predatory and primitive.[2] Beyond them lay Black (White or Silver, Volga or Kama) Bulgaria, inhabited by the Bulgar tribes left behind by their better known relatives who had migrated to the Balkans. The Volga Bulgars were a moderately civilized race, tilling their lands and taking a considerable part in the commerce between the Russians and the Chazars. For themselves they used fox skins as currency, but were beginning to recognize the value of specie for foreign trade. Their chief town, Bulgar, close to the Volga, was of such a size as to astound the Moslem geographers.[3] But the Volga Bulgars were still unsophisticated enough to enjoy raiding their neighbours, and even could undertake the two months' journey to the lands of the Greek Empire.[4] In 921, at the request of their monarch, who realized that a civilized potentate should have a higher class religion than Altaic naturalism, Ibn Foszlan was sent from Bagdad to instruct him and his people in Islam. He arrived next year in Black Bulgaria, where he found the converts ready, and built them not only a mosque but also a strongly fortified castle on the Arab model.[5] It was no doubt as a result of his missionary and political zeal that in 923 the Volga Bulgars raided into the Empire as far as 'Phenedia' on the Greek Sea, where they met the ships of the Emir

1 Harkavy, pp. 338, 366–7.
2 d'Ohsson, pp. 72–75.
3 d'Ohsson, pp. 77 et seq., quoting Ibn Foszlan; *Camb. Med. Hist.* IV, pp. 192 et seq.
4 Maçoudi, II, p. 16.
5 Ibn Foszlan, *De Bulgaris, passim.*

of Tarsus—and some of them accompanied him back to the lands of the Califate.[1] It was careless of the Byzantine diplomats to let Black Bulgaria thus enter into the Moslem system of alliances; but it took place at a time when the Empire was too anxiously involved with the Balkan Bulgarians to be able to take action further afield. Besides, to a nation so primitively oriental in its tastes, Islam with its bellicosity and polygamy was bound to be more seductive than Christianity. However, though the Black Bulgars had now a religious inducement for raids into the Empire, their raids must have been very rare—the raid of 923, which does not seem to have been very serious, is the only one recorded in all this period—and they retained a certain value in Byzantine eyes as being able and willing to attack the Chazars, should they threaten Cherson.[2]

To the east of the Chazars were the Uzes (the Ghuzz of the Moslem geographers) whose recent advent on the outskirts of the European world had caused the tribal commotions of the early years of the century. They were in a state of barbarism similar to that of the Petchenegs; and their importance to the Byzantine Court was simply as a possible corrective to the Chazars; moreover, they were the one people of whom the Petchenegs stood slightly in awe.[3] The Cumans, later to feature in Russian history as the Polovitzes, were still in the Urals, similarly barbaric. The southern neighbours of the Chazars, the Alans, who were also diplomatically valuable for the Steppes, were essentially a Caucasian tribe and will be treated in connection with the politics of the Caucasus. The Vissou and the Youra, who lived to the north of Black Bulgaria, in a land where night lasted only for one hour and in such a state that should one of them chance to enter Bulgaria the temperature of the whole country immediately dropped, fortunately did not extend their frigid influence any further afield.[4]

The Empire's dealings with regard to the Steppes were fundamentally purely defensive. The Emperor had no ambition to add

1 Maçoudi, *loc. cit.* This is the raid that Vasiliev (see above, p. 90) attributes to Symeon. Phenedia has never been satisfactorily identified.

2 *D.A.I.* p. 81.   3 *Ibid.* p. 80.   4 d'Ohsson, pp. 80–82.

the plains of Hungary or Russia to his dominions; his one aim was to maintain an equilibrium so delicate that no tribe could venture to raid into the imperial territory owing to the risk of itself being raided by its neighbours. It was impossible entirely to prevent every raid, but one of the tests of a good Emperor was that he kept the Empire as undisturbed as possible from the Steppes. The Emperor Romanus had a particularly difficult task in dealing with the northern tribes. In the early years of the tenth century the movements of the Hungarians and the Petchenegs had completely altered the situation, and a new factor had been introduced by the growth of Russia under the house of Rurik; and the collapse of Bulgaria suddenly brought the Empire into more intimate relations with the Steppes than it had known for over a century. Yet by about 950 the new situation was sufficiently settled for Constantine Porphyrogennetus to be able to record as of more than ephemeral value the diplomatic dealings that Byzantium found most useful at the time. These rules for foreign policy must therefore largely have been the work of Romanus himself or of his Foreign Minister Theophanes, evolved since the close of the Bulgarian war in 927.

Romanus was very successful in carrying out these rules. The hardest nation to restrain was the Hungarian, situated farthest to the west. The armies of the west were not yet able to put up an effective resistance against them—and indeed the Empire cannot have desired action that, limiting them on the west, might make them pay more attention to the east; and the Petchenegs, who most easily could be brought in against them from the east, had to cross the arduous Carpathians to reach them, and might well prefer to raid with less trouble on the Steppes. Yet even from the Hungarians the Empire under Romanus underwent only two raids, and before he had fallen Romanus had arranged a five years' truce, easily renewed by his successor. The Russians only once actually penetrated into imperial territory; and with them he arranged a peace that outlasted the reign of the Porphyrogennetus and was indirectly a step in the Christianizing of Russia under the aegis of Constantine's visitor, Igor's widow, the Grand Princess Olga. And, apart from Hungarians and Russians, no other foreign tribe raided the Balkan provinces from Symeon's death to Romanus's fall.[1] The story proves what historians have been slow to recognize—the brilliance with which, in spite of the apparent dogmatism of their treatises, the Byzantines adapted their diplomacy to the new and changing circumstances that they so often met.

Two things stand out in the narrative. One is the easy readiness with which the Byzantines paid subsidies to foreign tribes, thus proving that not only were they rich enough to afford them, but also that they knew, what few nations have properly realized, how utterly expensive is war. The other is the care with which the Byzantine government looked after Cherson, the solitary possession left to the Greeks on the north of the Black Sea.

Cherson enjoyed a unique position. While officially forming a theme of the Empire, it was only treated as a vassal state and sent a κέλευσις. Till the reign of Theophilus it had had its own self-elected magistrates (πρωτεύοντες), but now it was under the straiter control of a stratege, who probably also was the official chiefly employed in dealings with the Steppe tribes. Cherson, enjoying as it did the traditions of an old Greek municipality unspoiled by Rome, was restive under imperial control, and was fitfully rebellious. But on those occasions the Empire could employ an easy remedy—a trade blockade; for without their trade, as Constantine tells in the last lines of the *De Administrando*, the Chersonites cannot live.[2] The importance of Cherson to the Empire was twofold, first as a trade emporium—it was the port of embarkation of most of the trade of the Steppes, a trade that with peace and civilization was rapidly on the increase—and second, as an outpost on the Steppes, a watch-tower from which any strange or suspicious movement among the nations could be hastily told to Constantinople. It was therefore essential that Cherson's integrity should be preserved, and that she should be kept well under control by the Emperor, not only as a means but also as an end in the preservation of peace on the Steppes.

1 Or indeed for several years after. The Black Bulgars' raid of 923 was during the Bulgarian War. Possibly they called themselves allies of their relations.
2 *D.A.I.* pp. 244 *et seq.*, a long history of Cherson.

CHAPTER VII

The Eastern Frontier

O N the Steppes and in the Balkans nations might wax and wane; on the eastern frontier the Empire had a constant, implacable enemy. In the eyes of the statesmen of Constantinople the themes of Europe, overrun and impoverished by numberless invaders, were of no very great importance; it was in Asia Minor, on whose frontiers Byzantium for three centuries had been the bulwark of Christendom against the Moslems, that the most vital provinces lay, provinces with still rich and fertile plains and valleys, the home of the sturdiest of the Empire's peoples, and its great recruiting ground. On the integrity of these provinces the strength of the Empire depended. But their defence meant incessant war; for over the frontier lay another great empire challenging with Byzantium the supremacy of the world—the Empire of the Calif, by faith and tradition inevitably hostile.

The history of the eastern frontier was always one of remarkable intricacy, particularly during the period of the Macedonian dynasty. Not only were there raids almost every year by the Arabs into Byzantine territory, but simultaneously the Byzantines would frequently carry on organized campaigns into Arab territory; and the whole warfare was further complicated by the incalculable politics of Armenia and the principalities of the Caucasus, nominally the vassals of either Constantinople or Bagdad or of both, and usually at war with their suzerains and themselves. Nor is much light thrown by contemporary writers. Of these the Greeks though intermittent are the most reliable historians, the Arabs the most regular chroniclers, and the Armenians more prejudiced than the Arabs and worse at dates than the Greeks. And prejudice has descended; the conventional view in Western Europe, introduced by jealous Crusaders and firmly rooted in their descendants, is to regard every Arab as a hero and every Byzantine as a corrupt and incompetent coward, and to interpret their history accordingly. To sort, in such a miasma of preconceptions and boastful patriotism, the muddled snippets of fact from those of fiction is a task that no historian has yet dared completely to undertake.

In 912, when Alexander ascended the throne, there had been little change on the frontier for the last two centuries. The frontier line left the Black Sea about a hundred miles east of Trebizond, at the mouth of the river Tsorokh, and ran roughly to the south-east up that river, keeping the towns on the river such as Kalmakh outside the Empire, but turning sharply south to include the fortress of Paiperte, and to cross the northern branch of the Upper Euphrates some way to the west of Erzerum.[1] How much of the land between the two branches of the Euphrates belonged to the Basileus it is impossible to say. Leo VI had added to the Empire by annexing the territory of Prince Manuel of 'Teces', territory large enough, when the towns and turmae of Camakha and Celtzene were transferred to it, to be raised to the dignity of a theme called Mesopotamia[2]—the two rivers of the name being presumably the two branches of the Euphrates. Somewhere about the confluence of two branches the frontier left the Euphrates and ran due west to the neighbourhood of the towns of Abara and Lycandus, of which the latter had only been occupied and fortified during Leo's reign. From Lycandus it turned again more to the south and ran, as it had for centuries, along the top of the Anti-Taurus and Taurus ranges, the passes of which seem mostly to have been in Moslem hands, though Basil I had won permanently for the Empire Lulum, the northern key of the most important of all, the Cilician Gates.[3] On the Mediterranean coast the Empire included the country past Cilician Seleucia to the river Lamus;[4] but the hinterland was in a highly disturbed state and overrun by the Moslems, who probably commanded the two passes from Barata to Seleucia.[5]

1 D.A.I. p. 182; Vivien de Saint-Martin, p. 235   2 D.A.I. pp. 226–7.
3 Theoph. Cont. p. 277. At the Cilician Gates Podandus seems to have been the frontier town. An exchange of prisoners took place there in 938.
4 Ibn-al-Fakih, quoted in 'Arabic Lists of the Byzantine Themes' (Brooke, J.H.S. XI, p. 75).
5 D.T. p. 36.

The frontier subdivided itself into three sections, the northern frontier, from the Black Sea to the Upper Euphrates, the Euphrates frontier, and the Anti-Taurus and Taurus frontier. Of these the northern frontier was the least important; beyond it lay only the Kingdom of Abasgia, traditionally a loyal vassal of the Emperor, and various of the small principalities of Iberia and Armenia, which if left to themselves were too busy in internecine quarrels much to trouble the Empire. There was, however, one permanent irritation for the Stratege of Chaldia, the official in charge of this section—the fortress-city of Erzerum, near the sources of the Euphrates, commanding the route down the Araxes into Armenia, one of the furthermost outposts of Islam in Asia Minor. The wars on the northern, 'Chaldian', frontier consisted almost entirely of campaigns against Erzerum. The southern, Taurus and Anti-Taurus, frontier provided more danger; it was usually from Tarsus in Cilicia that the yearly Moslem raiders set out to ravage Asia Minor; and the Moslem command of the passes was apparently sufficiently strong to hinder the Greeks from counter-raiding in Cilicia. But the mountains prevented the warfare on that section from being more than raids and forays; it was too difficult a country for a grand campaign. It was on the central section, the Mesopotamian frontier, that the most important fighting took place. Here the country was less abruptly mountainous, and was interspersed with flourishing cities, through which ran the great high road from Asia Minor to Southern Armenia and Persia. For some time past it had been the Emperors' policy to concentrate on this section, particularly since Basil I's recapture of Lulum had re-established the Byzantines in some control of the passes of the Cilician Gates; and it was on this section that the Byzantine possessions had recently been markedly increased. Basil's great contribution on this frontier had been to destroy the community of the Paulicians, Armenian heretics whose creed made them inevitably hostile to the Orthodox Empire, centred round Tephrice, and to annex their territory to the Empire. Leo VI, though militarily he had enjoyed no successes, had pushed the frontier further east by his annexation of Teces and his establishment of the theme of Mesopotamia, beyond the northern branch of the Euphrates. Thus to the north of this section the Empire was rapidly growing; but it was further south that the richer cities lay and the main road ran. And it was there that Romanus made his greatest contribution to his country. Naval affairs were connected almost exclusively with the Taurus frontier. The Arabs and Greeks alike used naval action to supplement or hinder raids by land from Cilicia, the Arabs operating from Tarsus and the Greeks from the ports of the Cibyrrhaeot and Samian themes. The expeditions from the Moslem pirate-base of Crete were for the most part unconnected with affairs on the eastern frontier.

In 912 the immediate situation along the frontier was not particularly cheerful for Byzantium. Despite Leo's annexations, during his reign the imperial troops had been uniformly unfortunate and compelled for the most part to remain on the defensive: while the raids from Tarsus had been especially severe. To a large extent this was due to the political affairs over the frontier. The great enemy in Asia was the Califate, whose domains still stretched with unbroken allegiance from Persia to Egypt and away down into Arabia. In Basil's time the Califate had been undergoing a period of decline, and the Calif himself had been the prisoner of his Turks at Samarrah; but under the Califs Motadid and Moktafi there had been a slight renascence, and the government had returned to Bagdad. However, in 908 the boy Moktadir ascended the throne, and the troubles of a minority were to be followed by a weak man's rule. But as yet this was not visible. Of the provinces of the Greek frontier, Cilicia was more or less directly under Bagdad, and its Emir, 'Emir of Tarsus and the frontier province', seems to have been in close touch with the capital. It was moreover usually governed by competent officers; the Emir Damian who died in 913 and his successor the eunuch Bishra were alike loyal to the Calif and the terror of the Greeks. Further to the north-east, the cities of the Euphrates, such as Samosata, Melitene or Hisi Mansur, were self-governing under their emirs, but acknowledged themselves to be vassals of the Calif, and relied on his help in the event of a Christian attack. To the north-east of them lay the principalities of Armenia interspersed with several small Moslem

States, which while often, such as Erzerum, too isolated to keep in constant touch with Bagdad, called themselves its vassals and under normal circumstances would oppose any Greek aggression as endangering their faith. The Armenian principalities, which considered themselves in times of prosperity under no allegiance, were counted as vassals by Bagdad as by Constantinople. And at the moment the Arab influence predominated in Armenia, to a degree seriously alarming to the Byzantine Court.

At first sight the wars on the eastern frontier seem to be incessant and muddled; but a closer survey will divide them up into separate wars brought about by separate situations and terminated by separate truces, though there was usually a running accompaniment of raids on the mountain frontiers, that only ceased for a short period immediately following each peace. In 912 the Byzantines were engaged in no definite war on the frontier; it was not till 915 that the first war of the period, the 'Armenian' war, began. But already for some time past there had been on the Taurus frontier a sequence of almost yearly raids, accompanied for the most part by sea raids, that continued up to the peace of 917. With these raids I shall deal first, before entering on the causes and campaigns of the Armenian war. They were aimed solely at obtaining as much booty, in goods or prisoners, as possible, and were for the most part unconnected with any desire either to annex territory or to achieve some diplomatic object. Consequently, though they were irritating to the Empire and a continual expense, they were nothing more than painful pinpricks; they would never destroy the Empire or tear her limbs from her. The Byzantine policy with regard to them was, whenever practicable, to organize a counter-raid, particularly by sea; if that was impossible, an attempt was made to capture and hold the passes through which the raiders had to return: while if nothing expensive or on a large scale could be organized, the Stratege of each affected theme had to undertake the best defensive measures that he could manage with his local militia.[1]

It was usually from Tarsus that the raiders set out, though

1 Leo, *Tactica*, Const. XVII, pp. 913 *et seq.*; Nicephorus Phocas, *De Velit.* pp. 936–7.

sometimes they would come from Mesopotamia through the passes of the Anti-Taurus. In 913 the terrible Emir Damian set out from Tarsus by sea; but during the course of his expedition he died at Strobyle, and his fleet returned unsuccessful.[1] Meanwhile, by land, Hussin-ib-Hamdan raided from Mesopotamia, it was said with success.[2] In 914 there was no sea raid; and the land expedition of Damian's successor, the eunuch Bishra, was unsuccessful and necessitated help from the Arabs.[3] This no doubt was due to the greater activity that characterized the Empire in that year, for which the credit should be given to the Empress Zoe. In the early spring of 915 Bishra again raided by land, with greater success; indeed, he claimed to have captured one hundred and fifty Patricians[4]. Later in the year fighting broke out along the Euphrates frontier owing to the Greek campaigns in Armenia, and the situation changed. Consequently, in the summer of 916 there was a double raid. Munis, the Calif's chief general, and later general of the bodyguard, set out from Melitene; and at the same time Abu-l-Kasma was ordered to attack from Tarsus. Munis met with great success and returned triumphant to Bagdad; but Abu-l-Kasma's fortune is not recorded by the Arabs, so one may guess that it was less happy.[5] In 917 Zoe decided to enter into negotiations with the Arabs; but before the negotiations were concluded, the eunuch As-Suml had raided by sea from Tarsus and Bishra by land, both raids being considered highly successful.[6] After the peace of 917 was actually made, the raids ceased till 922.

These raids were little more than an accompaniment to the main theme. From 915 the centre of the warfare and its cause were to be found in Armenia. The history of Armenia was one of incredible complexity; I shall attempt to deal with it later on; here I shall only give the bare outline. Armenia in the early Middle Ages consisted of an agglomeration of variously sized

1 Ibn-al-Asir, *V.P.* p. 104; Theoph. Cont. p. 388.
2 Tabari, *V.P.* p. 19.
3 *Ibid. loc. cit.* (copied by Ibn-al-Asir, *ibid.* p. 104).
4 Tabari, *V.P.* p. 19.
5 Ibn-al-Asir, *V.P.* pp. 104, 105; Sibt-ibn-al-Djauzi, *V.P.* p. 125.
6 Vasiliev, p. 312; he does not give his authorities.

principalities, the ruler of one of which would periodically emerge supreme over the others and be crowned, as a rule by some foreign potentate, King of Kings. It was a Christian country, but followed the monophysite heresy; its Church was therefore independent of Constantinople, under its own Catholicus. Its geographical position made it an inevitable battleground of Arab and Byzantine influence. Though the routes through Armenia ran for the most part east and west, it could be extremely unpleasant for Arabs living in Mosul or Mesopotamia to have a strong aggressive power among the mountains close to the north: while Persia and the Byzantine Empire in Asia Minor, standing at either end of the great Armenian roads, wished necessarily for their self-preservation each to control as much of the country as was possible. Though there were many Armenians within the bounds and in the service of the Empire, in Armenia itself the Arab influence on the whole predominated, and on the whole was preferred by the Armenians, who with the dogmatism then fashionable would welcome a complete infidel much more gladly than a fellow-Christian separated by the chasm of Chalcedon. The Emperor had never ceased to regard the Armenian princes as his vassals; but the Arabs had for over a century been in the habit of appointing an Armenian prince their chief client and almost viceroy, as well as usually keeping in the country an Arab governor or ostigan. In 885, in pursuit of this policy, the Calif Motamid had sent a royal crown and the title of King of Kings to the Bagratid prince Ashot, the most powerful of the potentates of Armenia—a title which Ashot thought it wisest to have confirmed by the Basileus also.[1]

The Bagratids enjoyed the leading position amongst the princes of Armenia. Their territory lay in the very centre of the country, on the northern slopes of Ararat and on the Araxes, and included the great metropoles of Armenia, Dovin where the Catholicus, the head of the Church, had long resided, Bagaran and Ani. Of the other Armenian princely houses by far the greatest was the house of Ardzrouni, ruling over Vaspourakan

---

[1] John Catholicus, p. 125 and notes p. 414. Since 859 he had been recognized as prince of princes or leading client by the Arabs, but in 885 they revived for him a title that had been in disuse since the Arsacids.

and the neighbouring cantons—roughly all the country between the Araxes, Lake Van and Lake Ourmiah. The Ardzrouni were profoundly jealous of the Bagratids—a fact that greatly facilitated the Arab control of the country. The rest need not concern us here. All, except for the house of Siounia which on the whole remained close allies of the Bagratids, spent their days in a mass of intricate and changeful intrigues, alliances and wars directed solely by envy and the desire of self-aggrandizement. The State of Taron, on the west, deserves a slight mention. Geography had forced it into closer contact with Byzantium; and as it lay surrounded by the Moslem cities of the Upper Tigris and Lake Van it could not afford to declare its independence of the Empire; but, as the Empire was not always in a very strong position on the frontier, it wisely also became a paid spy for the Moslems.[1]

Ashot I had taken care to remain on good terms with both Bagdad and Constantinople; but his son, Sembat, who succeeded him in 890, adopted a pro-Byzantine policy and eventually definitely split with his Arab overlords. From early in the reign his deference to the Emperor made him suspect to his neighbours and involved him in several petty wars with them; and by the year 908 he was in a state of war with the Arabs. The Arabs were competent to deal with the situation. It was from Persia that Armenia was most easily entered and most vulnerable; accordingly the Emir Youssouff of Persia, who had been appointed Ostigan of Armenia, took the matter in hand, determining to reduce Armenia into a state of real vassaldom that would be too strict to permit of Byzantine influence. Youssouff's first move was to declare Sembat deposed and to crown, in 909, as King of Kings, Gagic, head of the Ardzrouni of Vaspourakan, a prince whose power made him a useful ally, while its position on the left flank of any invader from Persia, and on the shortest route to the Tigris made his territory of great strategic importance. Gagic fell to the bait of a crown, and thus promptly provoked a civil war, which removed any difficulties from the path of the Arab conquerors.[2] And so, from 909 onwards, the conquest of the

1 See next page.
2 John Cath. pp. 199 et seq., notes p. 417; Hist. des Ardzrouni, p. 229 and notes; Chamich, II, pp. 33 et seq.

country by the Emir Youssouff proceeded steadily, on a kaleidoscopic background of changing alliances and treacheries among
the Armenian princes.

The Bagratids bore the brunt of the attack, and gradually lost
everything: though in recompense they gained a sentiment of
patriotic admiration for their dynasty as being the one steadfast
opponent of the infidel invader. The Arabs, dispossessing the
Siounian princes on the way, penetrated victoriously up the
Araxes and captured the old capital of Dovin. The King of Kings,
Sembat, appealed first to the Calif to restrain his terrible lieutenant; but Moktadir was occupied with troubles nearer his
home. Then Sembat turned to Constantinople; but in 912, when
he was almost at his last gasp, news came through of the death
of the Emperor Leo VI and of the utter incompetence of his
successor Alexander. There was no help to come from there.
The Arab conquest grew more and more complete, accompanied
by ghastly atrocities and tales of martyrdom—indeed, to be used
as a shield was about the best fate that could befall a Christian
prisoner. Finally, early in 913, Sembat, closely besieged in the
fortress of Kabouda, gave himself up to Youssouff, to save
Christian lives, and was horribly done to death. His martyr's
end sent a thrill through all the Christian world; and all men's
eyes turned to Armenia. Meanwhile, his two sons fled into exile;
and Youssouff ruled the country from Dovin.[1]

This was the pitiable state of Armenia in the year 913. Gagic
of Vaspourakan, the anti-King was enjoying the insecure position
of a traitor and was tormented by his Christian conscience. The
princes of the eastern districts, Siounia and Sisagan, were fugitives in exile; the other princes spent their time in elaborate
quarrels, making and unmaking ephemeral alliances and providing more help than resistance to the Emir Youssouff. The
Arab penetration was complete. Only Gregory of Taron lay outside; and he, though carefully scrupulous in swearing allegiance
and sending tribute to Constantinople, ingratiated himself with
the Moslems by handing on all the information that he could
glean thence to Bagdad. Nor could the Christian princes of the
Caucasus provide much help. Georgia was a broken reed; of

1 John Cath. p. 233.

very recent years the King of Abasgia had filched Karthli, the central province, as far as the Alan Gates, from his wife's relatives the Iberian branch of the Bagratids, whose head, Adarnase, despite the title of King that he claimed in the east and the title of Curopalates allowed to him at Constantinople, held now only the country close to the Tsorokh, bordering on the Chaldian theme and Erzerum. The Iberians, therefore, were not in a position to come to the rescue of Armenia; and even the King of Abasgia, though more powerful, was not prepared to venture into dangerous commitments so far from his home. The countries of the east of the Caucasus were already completely in the Moslem sphere. Unless the Empire would help, Armenian independence was doomed.

For about a year there was chaos. Ashot, Sembat's elder son and heir, wandered round the edges of the country, and eventually induced the King of Abasgia to crown him King of Kings.[1] To keep them out of mischief, the anti-King Gagic and his brother were sent by their Arab ally, to fight for him in Aderbaijan, where they met with little success.[2] The other princes were already in exile or in hourly fear of it, while their princesses languished in Moslem captivity. The neighbouring nations put their fingers in the pie to pull out what plums they could, and raided at their will. Martyrs were innumerable; and famine was rife.[3] "It was thus that the children of our race were punished because of our corruptions and our apostasies", sighed the Catholicus John, head of the Armenian Church.[4] He indeed was the only person capable of action left in Armenia. He had an appallingly difficult part to play, as spiritual adviser-in-chief to a number of eternally quarrelling princes, especially now when his country was overrun by the infidel Arabs and the only help could come from the heretic Greeks. Nevertheless he did his best, journeying to and fro making peace wherever he could, and retiring now and then to acquire more strength in spiritual meditation—and describing all these movements and all the intrigues and tragedies in their bewildering details in a history of Armenia that, prompted no doubt by the desire for self-

1 John Cath. p. 239. 2 *Ibid*. p. 240.
3 *Ibid*. pp. 253, 258. 4 *Ibid*. p. 260.

justification, he wrote in his later years. Unfortunately, he had a poor head for dates. Of the only two that he mentions during this period, one is certainly some forty years out.[1]

At last news came from Constantinople. The Byzantine Empire had passed from the hands of the incompetent Alexander and the insecure regency council into those of the Empress Zoe; and the government could turn its attention to the eastern frontier. Certainly it was time. For the integrity of the eastern frontier, it was absolutely essential to the Greeks that either they should control Armenia themselves or that Armenia should at least be well out of Arab control. So long as that was the case, the Arabs could never make any serious attack except on the southernmost portions of the frontier: while an Armenian alliance could be very helpful for Byzantine offensives further north. But an Armenia in Arab hands was a danger that no Byzantine statesman could afford to permit.

The Empress decided upon action; but she knew the folly of being rushed. Accordingly, the Patriarch Nicholas, as diplomatic spokesman of the Empire, wrote an official letter to the Catholicus John, urging, besides prayer, a settlement of the Armenian private quarrels and an alliance with the neighbouring Christian princes. He himself, he says, has written to the Curopalates and the King of Abasgia recommending this alliance. If all this is arranged, then the Emperor, generously forgiving his former enemies, will send out help.[2] John hastened to make these arrangements; after securing promises from the Abasgians he went to visit the Taronites, and from Taron wrote to the Emperor (Kosdantianos) urging him on—a long diffuse letter full of flattery and not very apt scriptural allusions.[3] Meanwhile, Ashot won a few skirmishes against the Arabs; and King Gagic, weary of being used as a tool of Youssouff, openly broke with him, and with the help of Sembat of Siounia successfully withstood his attacks.[4]

---

1 John Cath. p. 362, gives date 332 Armenian era (A.D. 883) for the siege of Piourakan, which must have occurred in approximately 922.
2 *Ibid.* p. 265. Nicholas's letter does not occur anywhere else, but there is no reason to doubt its authenticity.
3 *Ibid.* pp. 267 *et seq.*   4 *Ibid.* p. 268.

On receipt of John's letter, the Byzantine Court sent an envoy Theodore, a well-known Armenian interpreter, to Armenia to summon Ashot to the capital.[1] Ashot promptly obeyed and, in the summer of 914,[2] arrived in Constantinople. He was received by the Empress with honours highly gratifying to Armenian pride, while the Greeks marvelled at his physical strength.[3] At Constantinople plans were made for a joint campaign. It was probably too late in the year to start fighting at once among the Armenian mountains; but in 915 Ashot returned to Armenia, accompanied by a considerable Greek force under the Domestic (probably Leo Phocas).[4] It seems that this army marched roughly by the main road along the southern branch of the Upper Euphrates, to enter Armenia through Taron; meanwhile, a second Greek army under the 'Logothete', to guard the exposed right flank, crossed the Anti-Taurus, defeated a large army from Tarsus, and then proceeded to ravage the Mesopotamian province by Marash and Samosata, capturing the town of Hisi Mansur and as many as 15,000 Moslem prisoners, and only retiring when special reinforcements were sent up from Bagdad.[5] Under cover of this action Ashot and his imperial allies were able to advance unmolested.

Youssouff, who could not have failed to hear of these new developments, had taken precautionary measures. He began by a fresh attack on the treacherous Gagic; but Gagic successfully

1 John Cath. p. 282. Theodore also conducted many of the negotiations between the capital and Taron.

2 I give my reasons for this date, as opposed to that given by Saint-Martin (921) and followed by subsequent sheep-like historians, in Appendix II.

3 Theoph. Cont. *loc. cit.*; John Cath. p. 283.

4 John Cath. p. 292.

5 Arib, *V.P.* p. 56; Ibn-al-Asir, *V.P.* p. 104; Ibn Haldin, *V.P.* p. 171. Arib dates this campaign Nov.–Dec. 915, but does not mention the capture of Hisi Mansur. Ibn-al-Asir implies three campaigns, indicating that the first was the Greek capture of Hisi Mansur, the second the defeat of the Tarsus troops and the third a raid of 'Melikh-al-Armeni' against Marash. Ibn Haldin also alludes to Melikh-al-Armeni's raid. I think that probably there were two raids, the first, in the summer, resulting in the capture of Hisi Mansur, after which the Greeks retired with their booty, and the second in the late autumn when the Tarsus troops were defeated and the Mesopotamian province ravaged again, and when the Greeks were accompanied by Armenian troops under an Armenian prince, or (more probably) by the troops of the Armenian-born Melias.

resisted with the help of the princes of Mokh and Andsevatsi.[1] Youssouff next tried to complicate Ashot's position by receiving another pretender to the throne, Ashot's cousin the Sbarabied (Commander-in-Chief) Ashot, who, after wandering round the country, uncertain how to act, came to Dovin where Youssouff crowned him King—ensuring his loyalty better by sending his mother and sisters as hostages into Persia.[2] This new anti-King, though less powerful than Gagic, could not fail to embarrass Ashot and lead to more civil wars.

Ashot and the Greek Domestic, having passed through Taron, were held up by the resistance of the town of Goghp (Gop, near Manzikert). Eventually the Greeks captured it, and, to the annoyance of the Armenians, kept it;[3] and the army passed on, travelling, it seems, through Manzikert and the passes to the north-west of Ararat, and joined on the way by Sembat of Siounia and a Taronite prince. The Sbarabied Ashot and the Arabs opposed them; but the Domestic managed to penetrate as far as the outskirts of the enemy capital at Dovin,[4] before retiring, no doubt when the Armenian snows began to fall. As a result of this action Ashot was well enough restored in the western portion of his ancestral territory (though he never recovered Dovin) to attend to the recapture of outlying possessions which neighbours and lieutenants had taken the opportunity to steal, and to advance as far as Vaspourakan:[5] while very soon the Siounian princes were able to return to their own lands to the east of Dovin.[6] The Greeks could go home with the comfortable feeling of victory. Armenian independence had been saved.

The Armenians however, despite the defeat of the Arabs, did not end their troubles so lightly. All John's boasted tact could not induce the princes to give up their quarrels; and the civil wars dragged on, with their eternally shifting alliances and

1 John Cath. p. 290.
2 Ibid. p. 293.
3 Ibid. p. 293.
4 I take it that Asoghic's campaign of 921–2 (Asoghic, p. 23) belongs to this year. See Appendix II.
5 John Cath. pp. 295 et seq.
6 Ibid. p. 299.

pathetically small results. Even when in the course of them, the Emir Youssouff revolted from Bagdad and was defeated, recalled and imprisoned,[1] the Armenians let the opportunity slip past unheeded. It was only in about the year 919 that the Armenians closed their disagreements and both Gagic and the Sbarabied Ashot recognized the supremacy of King Ashot; and some sort of peace fell upon the country.[1]

Though it was only for a tiny respite, it was well that Armenia so composed herself; for she could no longer look for help from Byzantium. In 916 the Byzantines rested on their laurels, and attempted no more offensives. Now that the most pressing danger on the east had been removed, the Empress Zoe was turning her attention to Europe; and by 917 she had decided that she must concentrate with all her forces against Bulgaria. Accordingly two envoys, John Rhodinus (Rhadinus) and Michael Toxaras, were sent to Bagdad to treat for peace. The Calif was as eager as the Empress; but it was several months before the ambassadors were allowed to enter the city; a reception had to be staged that would be truly impressive even to eyes accustomed to the luxury of Constantinople. Finally, in the summer, the ambassadors were received amid scenes of the most gorgeous ostentation that the Arab imagination could devise.[2] A peace was concluded and an exchange of prisoners arranged to take place on the frontier in October. When in due course the exchange took place, the Greek victory was made manifest; the Calif had to pay 120,000 dinars to buy back the surplus Moslem prisoners.[3] It seems also that the Empress acquired some territory round Lycandus, as she raised its district from a clisura to a theme.[4] The peace thus inaugurated lasted for five years— a period almost unequalled in the history of the eastern frontier. At the same time the Patriarch Nicholas, on the behest of the Empress, wrote to the Emir of Crete suggesting

1 John Cath. p. 329. I shall deal in more detail with Armenia later.
2 Theoph. Cont. p. 388, and other Greek chronicles; Arib, *V.P.* p. 56; Maçoudi, *V.P.* p. 40; reception described fully in Arib and in Sibt-ibn-al-Djauzi, *V.P.* p. 126.
3 Ibn-al-Asir, *V.P.* p. 105.
4 *D.A.I.* p. 228. *D.T.* pp. 32–3 says that Leo created the theme, but the *D.A.I.* shows that it was only a clisura that he created.

a truce; but whether the pirate Emir accepted the suggestion is unknown.[1]

These five years of peace were the salvation of Byzantium; for during them the Empire was undergoing the worst disasters of the Bulgar war and the paralysing effect of a long-drawn-out palace revolution. When in 922 war broke out again in the east, the clouds were lifting in Europe, and Romanus Lecapenus was firmly seated on the imperial throne. The cause of the war was once more Armenia: King Ashot's independence had been challenged again by the Arabs. Youssouff's successor, Nasr, was a man of considerable energy; though at first King Gagic alone had felt its effects. But in about 920 troubles in Bagdad[2] induced the Calif to release Youssouff, who returned to Armenia eager to be avenged, particularly on the traitorous Gagic.[3] Gagic, realizing with what John calls 'extreme sagacity' that he was not popular with Youssouff, fled into the mountains of Kokovit, where Adom of Andsevatsi, another fugitive, joined him.[4] Youssouff marched through the country demanding and receiving tribute; but within a short time he moved into Persia, leaving Nasr behind as ostigan.[5] Nasr set promptly about the reconquest of the country, stirring up civil wars and adopting violent anti-Christian measures so successfully that soon he was able to overrun the whole land, plundering and martyring as far as Erzerum.[6]

The situation recalled that of 914, though it was not quite so serious. Ashot, behind the walls of Bagaran, was in a stronger position than Ashot the homeless exile. Nevertheless, things were serious enough to attract the attention of the Emperor. Romanus decided that he must break Zoe's peace; but, occupied as he was by the Bulgar war in Europe, his powers of action in the east were restricted. It is possible that Asoghic was right in

1 Nich. Myst. Ep. ii, p. 36. I am inclined to place this letter here, though it is couched in terms vague enough to suit any date. But it seems unlikely that Zoe, when making peace with the Arabs of both the east and the west, should omit those of Crete, the nearest and most troublesome of all the Moslem bases.
2 Probably the riots of 919–920. John (p. 331) calls them the sack of the Calif's residence at Babylon by the Turks of Egypt and Arabia.
3 John Cath. p. 335.   4 Ibid. p. 337.
5 Ibid. p. 338.   6 Ibid. pp. 342 et seq.

dating the Domestic's Armenian campaign to Dovin in 922; but it is most unlikely, as the Domestic (Pothus Argyrus) was defeated in Thrace at Pegae in April, 922.[1] All that we can be certain happened was that the Greeks invaded the district of Melitene, possibly on their way to march to Armenia or at any rate to secure one end of the main road thither, but an army from Tarsus came upon them and defeated them, so that they retired.[2] It was not Greek arms that this time rescued Armenia; but fortunately in 923 Nasr was removed to Aderbaijan, and his successor as ostigan, Bishr (possibly the former governor of Tarsus), seems to have been less formidable.[3] However, the Greeks, despite a brightening on the Bulgarian front, were incapacitated that summer owing to a serious revolt in the Chaldian theme by the Stratege Bardas Boelas, who with some rich Armenian friends, encouraged no doubt by the presence of Moslem armies as close as Erzerum, captured and held the town of Paiperte against the Emperor's troops. A new Domestic of the Schools had just been appointed—Romanus's Armenian friend, John Curcuas; and he was soon able to put down the rebellion.[4] But meanwhile the Arabs had been able to raid with great success from Tarsus—Munis by land and the eunuch Suml by sea.[5]

To subsequent historians the most important event of the year must be the appointment of John Curcuas as Domestic; for John Curcuas inaugurated the sequence of triumphs in the east that characterized Byzantine history till the fall of the Macedonian house. With Curcuas there seemed to come a new spirit into the imperial eastern policy, a spirit of confident aggression. He was well able to lead his armies to victory, and was admirably seconded by his brother Theophilus, the rebel Boelas's successor as Stratege of the Chaldian theme, and therefore general in charge of the northern section of the front.

Towards the close of the year the Greeks enjoyed a sensational

1 See Chapter v, p. 88.
2 Ibn-al-Asir, *V.P.* p. 106.
3 John Cath. p. 365. His campaigns against the Armenian princes (which included a sea battle on Lake Sevan) seem to have been failures.
4 Theoph. Cont. p. 404.
5 Ibn-al-Asir, *V.P.* p. 106.

victory. The renegade pirate Leo of Tripoli, the terrible con-
queror of Thessalonica, was met, when raiding, by John Rhodinus at Lemnos, and was overwhelmingly defeated. His fleet
was destroyed, and he himself barely escaped.[1]

In 924 Symeon of Bulgaria was known to be planning a grand
attack on Constantinople; and Romanus, like Zoe in 917, decided
that he must make peace with the Moslems both in the east and
in the west. Accordingly, he sent ambassadors to Bagdad, and
a truce and an exchange were arranged. But this time the
Moslems were the victors; they refused to make peace until the
summer raids were over.[2] The extent and success of these raids
are unknown. It was perhaps now that Suml's fleet met the
Black Bulgars at 'Phenedia' on the Greek Sea.[3] Finally, the
exchange was concluded in October, 924, taking place on the
river Lamus. (Maçoudi says in 925, but it seems unlikely that
a year should elapse between the embassy and the exchange.)[4]

This peace lasted only two years. In 926 war broke out again,
but war with a difference. It was not a question now of fighting
for a defensive object, for the preservation of Armenia from the
Arabs. Armenia was sufficiently free of Moslem influence to
provide no more danger. The ostigan still ruled at Dovin, but
the Bagratid King of Kars or Ani was strong enough to deal by
himself with the infidel. There may, however, have been events
in Armenia that contributed to the fresh outbreak of war; but
we have already lost our only detailed informant on Armenian
history; John the Catholicus in the retirement of his palace at
Dsoroï-Vankh laid down his writing and died in 925.[5] This new
war was essentially a war of aggression for the Greeks. Everything was ready for an offensive. In Europe the Bulgar peril had
practically disappeared—indeed next year it entirely ceased to
exist—and so the bulk of the Greek armies could be moved to
the east. In John Curcuas the Greeks had a general whose ability,
popularity and spirit all combined to make for a successful con-
queror. Moreover, the Califate under the feeble Moktadir was
obviously in a decline, involved in riots and intrigues in the

---

1 Theoph. Cont. p. 405.   2 Ibn-al-Asir, *V.P.* p. 106.
3 See Chapter VI, p. 117.   4 Maçoudi, *V.P.* p. 41.
5 Preface to John Catholicus, p. xliv.

capital and devolution in the provinces, and the savage and triumphant attacks of the Carmathians of Bahrein.

In 925 Romanus already felt himself strong enough to demand tribute from the Moslem frontier towns of the Euphrates, and to threaten to attack them if they refused, saying that he "had exact knowledge of the weakness of their governments".[1] The towns refused; so next year Curcuas began his offensive. In June, 926, accompanied by the Armenian Melias with his contingent of compatriots,[2] he set out against Melitene and ravaged the countryside. The Melitenians, seriously alarmed, sent for help from Bagdad; but none arrived. Curcuas took the town, though the citadel held out, and after ten days retired with hostages and a promise of peace and tribute. So long as their old Emir lived, the Melitenians kept the peace; but after his death in about 928 they threw aside their promises.[3] This campaign was probably slightly hampered by an Arab raid from Tarsus, which occurred in the summer:[4] while Bagdad was cheered by a rumour of the death of the Domestic, whose fame was already considerable. In this same year, according to the thirteenth-century Arab Al-Makin, a huge Greek armada set out against Egypt. A ship was captured when spying and gave the news; and another was later blown ashore. The Egyptians took steps to fortify their coast; but the fleet was scattered by a terrific storm, and a large number of ships foundered.[5] It is difficult to estimate the truth of this story. Historical fiction usually has some basis in fact; but it seems most improbable that such an obviously hopeless expedition should have taken place. Probably it was just an imposing raid, ruined by the weather.

In 927 the final peace with Bulgaria enabled the Empire to turn all its energies to the east. It is probable that Armenia had

1 Ibn-al-Asir, *V.P.* p. 106.

2 It is I think almost certain that the Melikh-al-Armeni of whom the Arab chroniclers often speak about now is Melias, the famous Armenian who commanded an Armenian contingent for the Empire (*D.T.* p. 33; *D.A.I.* p. 227) and who certainly accompanied Curcuas against Melitene.

3 Ibn-al-Asir, *V.P.* p. 107; Sibt-ibn-al-Djauzi, *V.P.* p. 128; Kitabu'l, *V.P.* p. 152; Theoph. Cont. p. 415, whose story, undated by him, must belong to this year when we know that Curcuas temporarily occupied Melitene.

4 Ibn-al-Asir, *V.P.* p. 107.

5 Al-Makin, *V.P.* p. 142.

been alarmed by a fresh Moslem attack. About now, according to Chamich, King Gagic wrote to the Byzantine Court suggesting the union of the Churches. But it was not so easy to forget Chalcedon; and nothing came of it.[1] However, it showed that Gagic was anxious at the time to secure imperial sympathy and support. He seems to have secured it; for Curcuas's campaign in 927 was partially directed against the Ostigan Nasr. Curcuas began in the spring by an attack on Samosata; the Greeks succeeded in occupying the town for a few days, and scandalized pious Moslems by beating the gong in the mosque at the prayer hour. However, the approach of Moslem troops forced the Greeks to retire; and as a counterstroke the Moslem General Munis was ordered by Moktadir to raid, from Mesopotamia, and invaded Asia Minor in June or July. The fate of this raid is unknown, but a simultaneous raid from Tarsus was defeated by the Greeks.[2] Later in the year Curcuas entered Armenia, and penetrated to Debil (Dovin) where Nasr was living, and where his machines for shooting Greek fire terrified the inhabitants. Here again the Greeks temporarily occupied the town, but had soon to retire, with, so the Moslems declared, very considerable losses.[3] In the winter (December, 927–January, 928) Suml raided from Tarsus with great success, defeating and killing a Kurdish renegade called Ibn-al-Dahhak, and returning with 300,000 head of sheep.[4]

In 928 Curcuas was engaged on reducing to submission the Moslem towns in the south of Armenia. He took Khelat, on Lake Van, and concluded a peace with the population, ordering them to put a cross over their mosque and to destroy the minarets. The news terrified the neighbouring towns; Bitlis and Arzen sent to Bagdad asking insistently for help; and when none came,

---

1 Chamich, II. p. 73, says that in 926–7 Gagic wrote to Romanus and Tryphon the then Patriarch (actually Tryphon became patriarch in 928) about Church unity, but received no answer. I do not know his authorities for this episode, but clearly he had access to more material than has reached Europe or a European language. See later, p. 156, about Nicholas's letter on Church unity.

2 Ibn-al-Asir, V.P. pp. 107–8. Munis usually raided from Mesopotamia and Suml from Tarsus, so I incline to think that there were two raids.

3 Ibid. p. 108. Debil must be Dovin, as it was the seat of the Ostigan.

4 Ibid. p. 108. Kitabu'l (V.P. p. 152), when talking of the Greek occupation of Samosata, says that the Greeks wanted a truce this year.

many of the inhabitants deserted the province.¹ According to Ibn-al-Asir a stratagem was tried this year by the Greeks and their Armenian allies to capture Melitene by disguising soldiers as artisans out of work. It failed; but as he says that it was also proposed to hand the city over to the Armenians, the story is open to suspicion.² The only other event of the year was the death of the Bagratid King Ashot, who was succeeded by his brother, Abas.³

There may have been other unrecorded Greek victories; certainly the balance of the war was sufficiently in the Greeks' favour; for the Arab towns of the frontier, Melitene, Mayyafaraquin, Arzen and Amida, in 929 made a last desperate appeal to the Calif for help. It was in vain, for in 929 Bagdad was undergoing a series of revolutions in which Moktadir lost and recovered his throne and his greatest general Munis was involved. When no help came, the towns consulted together and decided to submit to the Greeks. But they were given a respite. Muflikh-as-Sadji, one of the reigning family of Aderbaijan (a relative of Youssouff), forced the Domestic to retire before him, and penetrated into the Empire.⁴

In 930 the only warfare reported on the frontier was a raid by 'Melikh-al-Armeni' (presumably Melias) near Samosata, which was badly defeated by the Arab Nedjm; one of 'Melikh's' sons was captured along with other distinguished persons and sent ignominiously to Bagdad.⁵ It was probably in this year that the Domestic and his brother Theophilus were engaged on the siege of Theodosiopolis (Erzerum).⁶ Erzerum was now an isolated Moslem fortress in Greek and Armenian country; but its inhabitants seem to have owned considerable territory round about, and to have been by no means feeble. Commanding as it did the

---

1 Ibn-al-Asir, *V.P.* p. 109.   2 *Ibid.* p. 109.
3 Samuel of Ani, p. 435; Chamich, II, p. 74.
4 Ibn-al-Asir, *loc. cit.*   5 Arib, *V.P.* p. 57.
6 The episode of the siege of Erzerum in the *De Administrando* (pp. 200 *et seq.*) is left undated; but as Erzerum was of such prime strategic importance I am inclined to think that Curcuas would deal with it as soon as possible; and 930 is the first year in which Curcuas was not obviously occupied on other things. Rambaud (p. 422), in his garbled account of the event, dates it 928. But clearly the devastation of the country when Curcuas passed through to Dovin (927) was on a separate occasion to the siege.

northern route to Armenia[1] Erzerum was much coveted by the Greeks. In 927 when Curcuas was marching to Dovin he had apparently passed by Erzerum and with Theophilus had devastated the countryside. Now he decided to capture the town. The siege involved difficulties with the Iberian Bagratids, who, while nominally allies against the infidel, had no desire to see the Empire firmly entrenched on their borders. Accordingly, they took care that Erzerum was well supplied with provisions from their neighbouring town of Cetzeum. Curcuas and Theophilus then asked to be allowed to occupy Cetzeum for the duration of the siege. This the Curopalates refused, on the grounds that the other Armenian and Caucasian princes would be angry with him; all that he could permit was that a Greek superintendent should reside there, whose superintendence it was easy to evade. At the same time the Iberians clamoured vociferously to be given cities captured during the campaign, supporting their demands by the wholesale misquotation of Romanus's Golden Bulls; and when at last Curcuas handed over to them the captured town of Mastatum, promptly they broke their solemn pledges and gave it back to the enemy. Such behaviour made Curcuas's task very difficult; but as it was essential for him to protect his flank and to appear generous and unruffled in the eyes of the Armenians, he acted with admirable patience. When finally after a seven months' siege Theophilus took Erzerum, the Iberians were given, by Curcuas's orders, all conquered territory to the north of the Araxes—a handsome allowance that Constantine Porphyrogennetus rather regretted. Erzerum itself was probably, like Melitene after the first capture, made a vassal tributary State, and as such was restive; we find the Greeks taking action there again in 939, and it was not till 949 that it was finally captured and made part of the Empire.[2]

The year 931, opening probably for the Greeks with the siege of Erzerum still unfinished, was at first a season of Arab triumphs.

1 One road ran from Erzerum down the Araxes into Armenia, and another over the hills to Manzikert.

2 *D.A.I.* pp. 200 *et seq.* The geography is puzzling; Erzerum itself was to the north of the Araxes, but certainly the Iberians were not given it. For subsequent attacks on Erzerum see below, p. 143, and Yachya of Antioch, *V.P.* p. 65.

In March three raids organized by Munis entered Greek territory, that of Suml from Tarsus being particularly successful. In conjunction eleven ships set out from Egypt, but their fortune is unknown.[1] In August Suml, encouraged by his previous successes, took a grand expedition into the Empire, penetrating even as far as Amorium and Ancyra, returning in October with very lucrative results—prisoners worth 136,000 dinars.[2] But meanwhile the Greeks were enjoying successes further to the east. In September Muflikh of Aderbaijan began a fresh campaign against Armenia, with the usual result that the Greeks, at the request of the Prince of Taron and the neighbouring princes, hastened to the help of the Armenians and captured Percri, with a large number of prisoners, on their return sacking the country round Khelat. These victories alarmed the Melitenians, who sent again for help—this time with success. The Greeks had advanced beyond Melitene to Samosata; but there Saïd-ibn-Hamdan, one of the powerful family now engaged in establishing its independence at Mosul, came upon them and for the time being drove them out of the district.[3]

In 932 the Arab writers record no action on the frontier. Among the Moslems civil troubles in Bagdad no doubt hindered any attempt at a campaign, while the Greeks probably only engaged in desultory warfare. But in 933 John Curcuas crossed again into the province of Melitene, and the Melitenians sent eagerly to Munis for help.[4] The Greeks met with many minor successes,[5] and took a large number of captives; but Munis so directed his lieutenants as to prevent the Greeks from risking any attack on the city itself, and eventually they retired.[6]

Nevertheless, Melitene was doomed. Early in 934 Curcuas again crossed the frontier, at the head of 50,000 men, including Melias's regiment of Armenians. The fall of the Calif Quahir was occupying the Moslem world, and he met with no serious opposition. As he approached, crowds deserted the city; and he was easily able to force it to capitulate, on May 19th. Only

1 Arib, *V.P.* p. 57; Ibn-al-Asir, *V.P.* p. 109.
2 Ibn-al-Asir, *V.P.* p. 110; Zahabi, *V.P.* p. 163.
3 Ibn-al-Asir, *V.P.* pp. 110–111.   4 Arib, *V.P.* p. 58.
5 Zahabi, *V.P.* p. 163.   6 Arib. *V.P.* p. 58.

142   THE EASTERN FRONTIER

Christians were allowed to remain inside the walls—whereupon
the majority of the population hastened to be converted—the
Moslems were transported to a safe place far away. The town
and district were incorporated in the Empire and subjected to
a heavy tribute as well.[1]

The capture of Melitene was a landmark that caused a great
sensation.[2] It was the first occasion on which the Greeks had
annexed a large and important Moslem city to the Empire; it
showed that they were come not to raid but to stay. After the
triumph Curcuas seems to have relaxed his efforts. For the
remainder of the year 934 he was occupied in subjugating parts
of the district of Samosata.[3] In 935 we hear of no action in the
east; probably the incorporation of Melitene and its neighbourhood into a theme of the Empire necessitated a little local fighting, which prevented any big offensive.[4] In 936 again no
Greco-Arab fighting is recorded; there was, however, in this
year an Arab invasion of Armenia; but as the Armenians were
able to repulse it themselves, it did not affect the main course
of the war.[5] 937 was another uneventful year; and in 938 the
Greeks began to treat with the Calif about peace. There were
several reasons to induce them; they wished their conquests to
be officially recognized, particularly at a time when the Califate
was not strong enough to withhold recognition; and clearly it
would facilitate the organization of the new theme if its rebels
were not supported by Bagdad. But perhaps most important
was the common desire of Constantinople and Bagdad to have
no hindrance in dealing with the Hamdanids of Mosul—a family
who controlled now all the Moslem frontier provinces from
Mosul to Aleppo, whose independence was a *fait accompli*, and

1 Ibn-al-Asir, *V.P.* p. 111; Vartan, p. 113; Asoghic, p. 37; Theoph. Cont.
p. 416.
2 It is almost the only event in the Greco-Arab wars that the Armenian
historians notice.
3 Ibn-al-Asir, *loc. cit.*
4 Prof. Vasiliev (p. 240) places here the capture of Samosata by the Greeks.
But Samosata was certainly in Moslem hands in 938, and was not finally
captured by the Greeks till 959. It had, however, it seems, been reduced
into the condition of a vassal to the Empire (probably during Curcuas's
942-3 campaign), as the Hamdanid Arabs attacked and sacked it in 944.
5 Thomas Ardzrouni, p. 241.

whose energy and ambition were unbounded, particularly under its present young representative· Saïf-ad-Daula. Accordingly, the Emperors wrote a letter to the Calif—the Greek text in gold, the Arabic translation in silver—suggesting an exchange of prisoners. The exchange took place on the Lamus in October; but there was a surplus of 800 Moslems to be redeemed. These were only recovered six months later, at Podandus, after a considerable search had been made for as many Greeks in Moslem hands.[1] At the same time Romanus sent an embassy to Mohamed-Ibn-Tugdji, the Governor of Egypt.[2]

That the Hamdanids did not consider themselves bound by any such truce was already apparent, when after skirmishes in the neighbourhood of Samosata, lasting a month, Saïf-ad-Daula fell upon the Domestic at Hisi-Ziad and defeated him very severely, capturing, it was said, his throne and seventy Patricians.[3]

The Hamdanids kept the offensive. In 939 Saïf-ad-Daula attempted, like so many Arabs before him and with the same ephemeral success, the conquest of Armenia. Setting out from Nisibin, he marched up the Tigris past the Moslem cities of Lake Van to Manzikert and thence turned north-west to Erzerum, where he put to flight the Greeks who were building a fortress close by (called by the Arabs, Hafdjidj), to keep the population of Erzerum in order. After staying there a short time he returned south, to spend the early winter in Arzen. At the beginning of 940 he recommenced his campaign, marching through Khelat, where the King of Armenia (Abas) came to vow submission to him; Abas was well received and given presents, but made to cede several fortresses. Saïf then invaded Taron and captured its capital, Moush, destroying its very holy church, and passed on into Greek territory (probably by Romanopolis-Palu). He received an angry letter from the Emperor, no doubt justly incensed at his invasion at a time of peace between Constantinople and Bagdad. Saïf, so the story went, wrote a rude

---

1 Maçoudi, *V.P.* p. 41; Ibn-al-Asir, *V.P.* p. 113; Sibt-ibn-al-Djauzi, *V.P.* p. 129; Al-Bizari and Ibn-Kesir, *V.P.* p. 169. 6200 Moslems were bought back.

2 Kitabu'l, *V.P.* p. 153.

3 Ibn-Zafir, *V.P.* p. 82. With the Arab raid in Southern Armenia that year I shall deal later.

reply, which made the Emperor exclaim: "He writes as if he were besieging Colonea". Saïf, hearing of this, determined to besiege Colonea—"Victory or death for the Faith"—and indeed managed to penetrate there (probably by way of Erzerum) and from there to write to the Emperor. However, the Domestic came up from the south, and Saïf retreated, attacking him with some slight success on the way.[1] But the Domestic, on his return to the south, raided successfully to Kharpurt.[2]

In 941, owing to the Russian raid in June, the main Greek army under the Domestic was moved as quickly as possible up to Bithynia; and it was not until September that the raiders were finally defeated and the army able to return.[3] Thus the summer was lost for campaigning. Fortunately the Hamdanids' attention was now and for the next two years chiefly turned to Bagdad, where the Califate seemed in its death throes, and the vultures were gathering. And so no advantage was taken of the Greek army's absence.

In January, 942, John Curcuas made up for lost time by beginning a three years' offensive. First he raided down into the province of Aleppo, and succeeded in taking Hamus, close to the town of Aleppo itself, and returning with a number of prisoners that even the Arabs reckoned at 10,000 or more.[4] Suml countered by a summer raid from Tarsus, which was said to be successful,[5] but could not prevent John Curcuas from starting in the autumn on the last and greatest campaign of his career. Setting out from the easternmost province of the Empire through the allied State of Taron, he swept down triumphantly through the winter past Arzen, Mayyafaraquin and Amida, capturing as he came, and then branched into the heart of Mesopotamia, taking Nisibin, and turning to direct his main attack on the city of Edessa.[6]

1 Ibn Zafir, *V.P.* p. 83; Sibt-ibn-al-Djauzi, *V.P.* p. 130; Asoghic, p. 37.
2 Abu'l-Makhasin, *V.P.* p. 182.
3 Theoph. Cont. pp. 423–4.
4 Ibn-al-Asir, *V.P.* p. 113 (15,000 prisoners); Sibt-ibn-al-Djauzi, *V.P.* p. 130 (10,000 prisoners).
5 Ibn-al-Asir, *V.P.* p. 113.
6 Yachya of Antioch, *V.P.* p. 61; Sibt-ibn-al-Djauzi, *V.P.* p. 130; Kitabu'l, *V.P.* p. 153.

Edessa, though a devout Moslem city, was famed for possessing one of the most precious of Christian relics, το Μανδήλιον, an authentic portrait of Christ, the towel on which He had dried His face, leaving on it the impression, and which He had sent as a present to King Abgar of Edessa.[1] To secure this relic would be the height of Christian excellence; and Curcuas, as he approached, announced that he would spare the town, release captives and make peace in exchange for the surrender of the image. The Edessans, in despair to know what was their duty, sent to Bagdad for advice. There the Calif and his Cadis and lawyers sat in solemn conclave and at last decided that the deliverance of Moslems overrode all other considerations.[2] Meanwhile Curcuas spent the summer in ravaging Mesopotamia, capturing Dara in May and Ras Ain in November, where he stayed two days and took a thousand prisoners.[3]

At last, early in 944, as Curcuas lay outside the walls, the Edessans received word from Bagdad; and in exchange for two hundred prisoners and a peace treaty (kept until Saïf-ad-Daula caused it to be broken in 950) they gave up the image. It was received by the Greeks with the utmost honour, and sent by easy stages to Constantinople, where it made its solemn entry in August.[4] This holy triumph, more than all his hardly-won battles, made John Curcuas the hero of the moment and the cynosure of all pious Greeks of the future; but his popularity alarmed the government.

After the capture of the image and its honourable despatch to the capital Curcuas concluded his campaign, spending the late summer in the capture of Bagrae (Birijik), where he crossed the Euphrates, and of Marash (Germanicea), one of the great road centres of the frontier; though in both cases his hold was only

1 Const. Porph. *De Imag. Ed.* p. 429.
2 Yachya of Antioch, *V.P.* pp. 61–62; Ibn-al-Asir, *V.P.* p. 113; Theoph. Cont. p. 432; Const. Porph. *De Imag. Ed.* p. 448.
3 Yachya of Antioch, *V.P.* p. 63; Al Hamdan, *V.P.* p. 78; Ibn-al-Asir, *V.P.* p. 114, says that the Greeks left Ras Ain after a fight with nomad Arabs. The Domestic had 80,000 men with him. Al-Makin, *V.P.* p. 143, says that the Greeks stayed there two days and captured 1000 prisoners.
4 Yachya of Antioch, *V.P.* pp. 61–62; Ibn-al-Asir, *V.P.* p. 113; Theoph. Cont. p. 432; Const. Porph. *De Imag. Ed.* p. 448.

ephemeral.[1] Then at the close of the year, three sensational disasters fell upon Byzantium. The first was the dismissal of John Curcuas, due to the jealousy of the young Emperors. Some time before they had attempted to undermine his position, without success. But now his old friend Romanus was ill, and the young Lecapeni could have their way. Curcuas was summarily removed from his post, to be succeeded by an imperial relative, Pantherius.[2] The second disaster was the simultaneous return of Saïf-ad-Daula to the frontier. The result was that Pantherius, raiding in December close to Aleppo, was heavily defeated, and the Arabs invaded imperial territory and sacked several towns.[3] Then soon after came news of the fall of Romanus that month, and next month the fall of all the Lecapeni.[4] It was the end of an era; new actors were strutting on to the stage.

The era had however been of the most vital importance to Byzantium, marking the turning-point in the whole history of the eastern front. Hitherto for three centuries the Empire had been on the defensive; the Arabs, it is true, had succeeded in conquering no further territory since their first onrush;[5] nevertheless, they remained the aggressors. Even the campaigns of Theophilus, of Bardas and of Basil I had been primarily counterstrokes against Arab offensives. But of recent years the Empire showed signs of recovery and had even made annexations in the east, though the territory so acquired consisted either of the land of harmless Armenian princelets (such as Manuel of Teces) or of lawless frontier districts that had owed obedience to no one.[6] It was left to Romanus and John Curcuas to make the great innovation. Under their guidance the Empire at last assumed

---

1 Zahabi, *V.P.* p. 164.

2 Theoph. Cont. p. 429.

3 Ibn-al-Asir, *V.P.* p. 114; Kemaleddin, *V.P.* p. 136; Zahabi, *V.P.* p. 164.

4 Theoph. Cont. pp. 435 *et seq.*

5 Except for Crete and Cyprus (which Basil temporarily recovered) and a few frontier forts such as Lulum, held by the Saracens from 832 till Basil recaptured it in 877.

6 Basil annexed the territory of Tephrice from the Paulicians, who were however more in the nature of heretic rebels. Before they established themselves there Tephrice had been debatable territory. Leo annexed Teces, and Zoe acquired control over sufficient of the frontier districts to raise the clisura of Lycandus into a theme.

the offensive against the Califate and began to triumph. Under
Curcuas's leadership his troops penetrated to cities that for three
centuries had never seen Christian armies, to Ras Ain, to Dara
and to Nisibin, and even to the neighbourhood of Aleppo, and
what was more important, behind these brilliant campaigns there
was going on a firm and steady annexation of Arab territory.
The capture of Melitene and the incorporation of that large
Saracen community into the Empire, first showed the startled
world what was happening. It was followed by other annexations
of which we are less well informed—for Melitene's fate made
the rest seem no longer surprising. Some time before, about 940,
Romanus acquired sufficient control over the western Taurus
passes to raise the territory round Cilician Seleucia into a theme:
though the frontier on the coast still seems to have been the river
Lamus.¹ At some unknown date, probably soon after the capture of Melitene, to whom the territory apparently belonged, he
took in the country on the southern branch of the Upper Euphrates, including the towns of Arsamosata and Palu, where, on
the very borders of Taron, he founded a fortress called after him
Romanopolis.² Shortly afterwards he rounded off his conquests
by annexing the intervening district of Khanzit; and thus the
Empire acquired complete control of the main road to Armenia.³
In consequence we find that the Arabs never acquired influence
in Armenia again.

Besides the actual annexation, several other districts over the
frontier were put into a state of strict vassaldom. In the south
it seems that Samosata was in such a state, probably having been
alarmed into submission during Curcuas's 942–3 campaign.⁴
For this allegiance the Hamdanid Arabs punished it in 944 by
a sack; and indeed their proximity made it unreliable as a vassal;
eventually, fifteen years later, it was recaptured and incorporated in the Empire. More effectively reduced were the Moslem

1 D.T. p. 36. The Lamus was the scene of an exchange of prisoners in 946
(Maçoudi, V.P. p. 41; Theoph. Cont. p. 443).
2 D.A.I. p. 227. Constantine gives no dates.
3 Ibid. loc. cit. The capture of Kharpurt, the chief city of Khanzit, took place
in November, 940, and presumably the conquest of the neighbouring district
immediately followed it.
4 See above, p. 145.

towns of South-west Armenia, Manzikert, Percri, Khelat and Ardjich. These towns were rightly considered at Constantinople to be of great strategic importance, commanding as they did roads down the Euphrates into the Empire, down the Tigris into Mesopotamia, and over hills to Erzerum and the Black Sea on one side and to the Araxes valley in the heart of Armenia on the other. After about the year 932 they were effectively under imperial control.[1] Their neighbour, the Prince of Taron, was obliged to give up his espionage for the Moslems, and henceforward lived up to his professions of loyalty.[2] Further north, Erzerum admitted imperial suzerainty, though it chafed all the while; and later, as with Samosata, it was found necessary to take from it its last vestiges of independence.[3] Thus at the time of Romanus's fall, all the country to the north of a line drawn from the Taurus to Lake Van, as far to the west as the country of the Armenian and Iberian Bagratids, was under the unchallenged control of the Basileus. The Greek chroniclers lauded John Curcuas as the man that brought the frontier to the Euphrates.[4] For once they were guilty of under-praising.

At the same time it must be admitted that the Emperor's control over many of his own acknowledged districts was not always very strong. A different picture is given by the great epic of Digenis Akritas,[5] where we see the great border barons, fighting for their faith indeed and proud to be citizens of the Roman Empire, but acting always on their own initiative without any regard to what the imperial government might arrange. Digenis himself, though he receives the Emperor in his magnificent palace by the Euphrates with every honour, treats him on terms far too like equality for the Emperor to have been altogether pleased. It is probable however that the authority of these arro-

1 *D.A.I.* pp. 191 *et seq.* Their reduction to vassaldom probably took place after Curcuas's 931 campaign. In the account of Saïf's campaign of 939–40, Ibn Zafir gives the impression that Khelat lay in Greek territory, and Saïf retreated as far south as Arzen to winter.

2 *Ibid.*

3 *Ibid.* pp. 200 *et seq.* See above, p. 140.

4 Theoph. Cont. p. 427. The chronicler adds more truly that he brought it to the Tigris too.

5 *Les Exploits de Digénis Akritas* (see bibliography). Digenis is supposed to have flourished in the second half of the tenth century.

gant warriors was legalized by the Emperor appointing them to the command of the clisura in which their castle might be placed; for certainly he had every intention of using their talents and their zeal.[1] Nevertheless, though the border barons might still show an inconvenient independence, the Empire had reached and turned a new corner in the east, and was marching to triumph. The frontier was a very different thing now from what it had been at the time of Romanus's accession. Not only had its position changed, but also the border provinces, which for centuries had almost annually to expect the horrors of an Arab foray, had been released from the nightmare. During the last twelve years of Romanus's reign Moslem raiders only twice crossed the frontier —once when Saïf led his brilliant expedition to Colonea, and once (in 942) when Suml raided for the last time from Tarsus. Truly times had changed.

To assign the credit for this change is not easy. Partly it was due to the marked decline of the Califate. Byzantium, though for centuries it had been an island in the midst of enemies, had, by the grace of its admirable organization and confident traditions, emerged with unimpaired, rather, with increased vitality. The Califate, vaster in area and richer in revenue, after far briefer glory collapsed beneath the strain of it all. But the collapse was not entirely evident. The Calif himself might be a pitiable figure despised by all the world; but the Moslem world was still formidable. Right along the Christian frontier was the powerful emirate of the Hamdanids of Mosul and Aleppo, led by one of the most splendid of all the generals of Islam, Saïf-ad-Daula. There might be chaos beyond; but that would not necessarily help the Empire, unless Saïf sank himself also into it. Fortunately he could not always refrain from so doing. Thus the weakness of the Califate provided the Empire with an opportunity, an opportunity which it was able to employ. The Balkan war

1 The renegade Kurd As-Sahhak, to whom the Emperor gave a castle, was probably another of these semi-independent barons (Digenis himself was the son of a renegade Arab); and so, I am inclined to think, was the Armenian Melias, who frequently appears as bringing his regiment to the aid of John Curcuas. Chroniclers, Greek and Arab alike (I identify him with Melikh-al-Armeni of the Arabs), treat him as though he were on an equality with Curcuas; yet Curcuas was complete commander of the imperial armies.

had been triumphantly finished; its victor, the Emperor Romanus, was firmly established on the imperial throne. Romanus, an Armenian by birth, took a close interest in the affairs of the East; and his interest took a practical form in his appointment as commander-in-chief of John Curcuas, the most brilliant soldier that the Empire had produced for generations. A lesser general might, by obeying the rules of Byzantine warfare, have cleared the Empire of the Saracens and successfully defended its borders; but Curcuas did more. He infused a new spirit into the imperial armies, and led them victorious deep into the country of the infidels. The actual area of his conquests was not so very large; but they sufficed to reverse the age-long rôles of Byzantium and the Arabs. Byzantium was now the aggressor, knocking at the gate of the trembling, tired empire of Islam. John Curcuas was the first of a line of great conquerors, and as the first is worthy of high praise. And in the praise, a part should be given to Romanus Lecapenus to whose judgment the Empire owed his services and under whose rule were passed those twenty glorious years.

CHAPTER VIII

Armenia and the Caucasus

IN the story of the eastern frontier, one fundamental point of
Byzantine diplomacy emerges very clearly: that on no account
could Armenia be allowed to fall into Moslem hands. It is
therefore worth while to see in detail what was this Armenia
whose independence it was so essential to preserve, and to dis-
cover what the difficulties in dealing with it were. The principalities that formed tenth-century Armenia were grouped in a
rough circle with a radius of about a hundred and fifty miles
round Mount Ararat as centre, bounded on the west by the
Empire and a few Moslem cities, on the south by Mesopotamia
and Kurdistan, on the east by Persia and Aderbaijan and on the
north by the kingdoms that clustered on the southern slopes of
the Caucasus. This territory was united solely by race and by
religion; politically it was divided up into the domains of various
princely families, and further subdivided among the various
members of these families, in a complexity somewhat resembling
seventeenth-century Germany and utterly baffling to a modern
historian.

In the tenth century by far the most important family among
the Armenian princes was the Bagratids. The Bagratids claimed
a distant Jewish origin and were divided by now into several
branches, of which the one (probably eldest) that showed most
pride of race was the Iberian, but the most powerful had long
been settled in the Araxes valley just north of Ararat, and had
been steadily increasing its dominions for centuries.[1] Ever since
the disappearance of the Mamiconian princes, the Armenian
Bagratids had taken the lead in Armenia. By the middle of the
ninth century, owing chiefly to their remarkably constant support of their Arab overlords, they had accumulated immense
territory and wealth in the most prosperous districts of the

1 These branches broke off in the eighth century, both descending from the
Prince Ashot who died 771, Ashot I's great-great-grandfather.

country; and in 862 Ashot, the head of the family, was recognized by his compatriots and by the Arabs as ischkan of ischkans, or prince of princes of Armenia. The growth of the Bagratid power had coincided with (and in some way had been due to) the feeble Samarrah period of the Califate; and, despite their subsequent renascence under Motamid, the Arabs never revived their old strict hold over Armenia; but Motamid, relying on the traditional loyalty of the Bagratids, while still keeping an Arab ostigan or governor in the country, was prepared in 886 to give to Ashot a royal crown and the title of King of Kings, that had been in abeyance some four centuries, since the fall of the Arsacid kings. At Ashot's accession the Bagratid territory stretched right across Armenia from Lake Van to the river Kur. On the south he held the towns of Khelat, Ardjich and Percri, which he gave to his dutiful tributary the Moslem prince of Manzikert, whose allegiance lasted till the débacle following on Sembat the Martyr's death; on the north he possessed the province of Gougark up to the city of Tiflis; and in the centre was his capital of Kars, and the metropolis of Dovin, the former residence of the Arab governors and the home of the Catholicus, and the Araxes plain, the richest plain of the country. As lord of so much power, his title of King of Kings expressed a reality. His most dangerous rival, the head of the house of Ardzrouni of Vaspourakan, a family whose possessions and influence were also on the increase, was pacified by the gift of Ashot's daughter as his wife. Another daughter married and pacified one of the powerful Orbelian princes of Siounia, a third the King of Abasgia.[1] None of the other Armenian ischkans was important or strong enough to play the part of rival: while the Bagratids of Iberia (Karthli), crushed between the Abasgians and their Armenian cousins, were in too much danger from the former to oppose the growth of the latter. Moreover Ashot had the support of the Church under the Catholicus at Dovin; and the goodwill of the Catholicus must have had an immense effect on the Armenian populace.

---

1 *Histoire des Ardzrouni*, p. 166; *Histoire de la Siounie*, p. 170; John Cath. *passim*; Brosset, *Hist. de la Géorgie*, p. 174. The Queen of Abasgia, Constantine's first wife, was a relative of Sembat the Martyr, probably a sister.

Ashot's reign had been mainly one of peace. Peace was a state alien to the Armenian ischkans, but he seems to have been strong enough to enforce it for the most part. In foreign politics he was continuously conciliatory to Bagdad, to which he paid regular tribute through the ostigan of Aderbaijan, the Arab official now in charge of Armenian affairs.[1] This slightly pro-Arab policy was the usual and most popular policy of the Armenians, to whom the Moslems, except when they were visited by a wave of bloodthirsty religious intolerance, were always preferable to the Greeks, who could never stop remembering that the Armenians were monophysite heretics and must be cured of their reprehensible errors. But while Ashot was reigning the situation in the East had changed. The Greeks, so long as the Arabs ruled in Armenia, had had to be content with stirring up what disorders they could in the country, and would never dare to make a grand offensive on the eastern frontier. But the growth of the Bagratids had relieved Byzantium from the fear of an Arab Armenia, and in consequence the Emperor Basil I had pushed the frontier eastward by the capture of the land of the Armenian Paulician heretics, and his son Leo, by annexations of semi-Armenian territory across the Upper Euphrates, had carried his work further. King Ashot was alarmed, and decided that Constantinople too must be humoured, in the interests of peace. In his old age he journeyed to the imperial city, where the Emperor, delighted to see his long-claimed overlordship at last recognized, received him gladly in great honour. On his way back he died and was buried in the Bagratid royal sepulchre at Bagaran.[2]

He was succeeded by his son, Sembat. Sembat lacked his father's prestige and was soon involved in difficulties. First he had to face revolts in his family. It seems that by the Armenian constitution, though the king was absolute, the post of Sbarabied, or Commander-in-Chief, was always held by a cadet of the royal house. This custom usually led to trouble, for the Sbarabied almost always had designs on the throne and the power to make his designs highly dangerous to its occupant. So Sembat found with his uncle the Sbarabied Abas. This caused preliminary

1 John Cath. *passim*. *Camb. Med. Hist.* IV, p. 158.
2 John Cath. p. 129.

warfare and unrest; and though Abas was defeated and succeeded as Sbarabied by a more dutiful and satisfactory member
of the family, Sembat's brother Schapouh, Sembat roused a far
greater storm by an unpopular and risky piece of foreign policy,
a renewal and tightening of his father's alliance with Byzantium.[1]
The reason for this policy is unknown. Probably it was about
now that Leo annexed the country of Teces beyond the Euphrates; and Sembat calculated that he would probably advance
further. It was a miscalculation; for Byzantium was soon distracted by fear of Bulgaria and by Leo's unfortunate marital
experiences, and half forgot the East: while in Aderbaijan there
were consecutively two ambitious and energetic ostigans, the
brothers Afschin and Youssouff, who had no intention of per-
mitting a Graecized Armenia; and Sembat's policy was too unpopular among the Armenians for him to receive general support.
At once he lost the reality of being King of Kings. The country
was plunged into innumerable civil wars in which the ischkans
of Vaspourakan and Siounia usually opposed the Bagratids and
during which the Arabs pushed steadily on, capturing Tiflis and
even re-entering Dovin.[2] There was a short period of peace about
the year 900, up to Afschin's death, and another, slightly longer,
about the year 905.[3] This was finally ended because Sembat
would not provide Youssouff with the necessary support to
enable him to revolt from Bagdad; and accordingly Youssouff
changed round his policy, denounced him to the Calif and,
backed with official approval, invaded Armenia. Sembat at this
juncture unwisely involved himself in a quarrel between the
Ardzrouni and the Siounians, taking the latter's side; and consequently Gagic Ardzrouni, lord of the huge domains of Vaspourakan, went over to Youssouff, who, declaring Sembat deposed,
gave to Gagic the crown and title of the King of Kings.[4] The
Siounians remained Sembat's only faithful allies; all the other
ischkans considered power and aggrandizement at the expense
of the Bagratids more desirable. Even Sembat's nephew the
Sbarabied Ashot (who had recently succeeded his father Schapouh) played traitor to his family. No help came from Byzan-

1 John Cath. p. 144.   2 *Ibid.* pp. 173, 184.
3 *Ibid.* pp. 175, 185.   4 *Ibid.* pp. 199–200.

tium. Finally, in 913, deserted by everyone except the already dispossessed Siounians, with all his territory conquered, Sembat gave himself up at his last stronghold of Kabouda, and met a martyr's death; and his corpse, denied burial, was exposed at Dovin, now once again the seat of an Arab ostigan.[1] After several years of chaos, civil wars and famine, Sembat's eldest son Ashot, who had already been crowned king by his neighbour the King of Abasgia, and who had carried on occasional guerilla wars with varying success, was in 915 replaced in his ancestral domains by the expeditionary force despatched by the Empress Zoe.[2] After defeating his cousin the Sbarabied, whom the resourceful Youssouff, mistrusting the frequent changes in Gagic's policy, had crowned as an additional anti-king, Ashot re-established himself and his family firmly in the district of Shirag (round Kars, Ani and Bagaran). But his attempts to recapture the possessions of his grandfather and father were not all successful. Dovin remained in the hands of the Arabs and the Sbarabied; and Ashot only extended his power eastward as far as Vagharschapat.[3] On the north, though Ashot succeeded in recovering his hold over the rebellious fortress of Scham-schoulde,[4] he never advanced as far as Tiflis: while, further to the north-east, the officially Bagratid districts of Oudi were per-petually in revolt under consecutive governors, Moses and Tslik.[5] On the south the tributary towns of Manzikert and Lake Van passed permanently from the Bagratid sphere of influence and were entering the Greek.[6] Ashot's title of King of Kings remained permanently meaningless.

About 919, owing to the persistent mediation of the Catho-licus, there was a general pacification of Armenia; the two Ashots became reconciled, and shortly afterwards even Gagic acknow-ledged King Ashot's supremacy.[7] This assured the Bagratids' position in central Armenia, though Ashot suffered from remark-ably continuous plots directed against him by his father-in-law, the grand ischkan of Gardman, and by his brother Abas. But

1 John Cath. pp. 226–233.   2 See above, pp. 131 et seq.
3 John Cath. p. 303.   4 Ibid. pp. 295, 320.
5 Ibid. pp. 304, 328.   6 D.A.I. p. 194.
7 John Cath. pp. 303, 329.

his power was well enough established for it to survive the new attacks of Youssouff on his return to Persia about 920, and those of his fierce successor Nasr.

Henceforward the history of the Bagratids seems to have been calmer, though about 924 we lose the guidance of the historian John the Catholicus, to whom we owe all the details of the civil wars of his time. Ashot reigned till his death in 928, recognized at Byzantium as King of Kings (though the Byzantines would only render it as Ἄρχων τῶν ἀρχόντων) and probably nominally also in Armenia; the territory over which he actually ruled was the country of Shirag, bounded on the south by Ararat and extending on the north to Schamschoulde, on the east to Oudi and the neighbourhood of Dovin, and on the west to the watershed over which lay the valley of the Tsorokh. The Bagratids probably lost in prestige by the settling in Vaspourakan of the Catholicus, who formerly had resided at Dovin under Bagratid protection, but now moved south to Dsoroi-Vankh, and later to the Ardzrouni city of Agthamar.[1] As regards the general trend of his policy Ashot rather favoured the Greeks than the Moslems. He was seldom to be found on good terms with the ostigans or the Calif; but on the contrary not only did Armenian contingents help the Greeks in their wars, but also Ashot apparently negotiated with Constantinople about the union of the Churches: though, as always, Chalcedon was too wide a chasm to bridge and nothing came of it.[2]

Ashot's successor, his undutiful brother Abas, adopted a slightly more anti-Byzantine policy. Abas occasionally was in conflict with the Arabs; in 931 Muflikh of Aderbaijan devastated Armenia[3]—though the Bagratid possessions may have escaped—

1 John Cath. p. 369; Preface to John Cath. p. xliv; Chamich, II, p. 73.
2 Nich. Myst. Ep. cxxxix, p. 361. This letter, written by Nicholas (therefore before May 925) after the death of a Catholicus, presumably John who died in 924, tells the King of Kings to send a man whom he (Nicholas) will ordain. Possibly it was written to Gagic Ardzrouni, and is the source of Chamich's story of Church union in 926 (II, p. 73). But in Chamich's version, the Patriarch is Tryphon and no answer is received from Constantinople; also I am inclined to believe that the title of Ἄρχων τῶν ἀρχόντων had not yet been given by Constantinople to Gagic. On the other hand it is quite probable that Ashot, who was always vaguely pro-Greek in policy, should wish to ingratiate himself further with the winning side and hold out hopes of a union.
3 Ibn-al-Asir, V.P. p. 110.

and in 936 Abas certainly had to deal with an Arab raid close to Dovin, and was defeated at Vagharschapat.[1] But on the whole he seems to have kept peace with them, and in 940 quite willingly made a temporary submission to Saïf-ad-Daula.[2] The Moslem world was being distracted by the Greek offensive and the Hamdanid independence; and so Abas was able to live as a nationalist king, without any serious fear of interference, except possibly from Byzantium. Though he had spent many years in his youth at the orthodox court of Abasgia and had married an Abasgian princess, he was a staunch supporter of the Armenian Church, and built several churches, whose dedication by Armenian rites he would defend by war;[3] and he welcomed gladly those pious Armenians whom Romanus, orthodox and repentant, banished from the Empire. Probably he did not attempt much to assert his authority over the other ischkans; and consequently his reign was one of the rare Golden Ages of Armenia, a period of comparative peace, in which the arts and commerce flourished. Abas lived on to an extreme old age, dying several years after Romanus's fall, in 951.[4]

The position of the King of Kings was very much that of the Emperor in mediaeval Germany. If circumstances were favourable and his own character strong, his title represented a reality; but otherwise the vassal princes acted very much as they pleased. As with the Emperor in Germany, the King of Kings frequently had an anti-king set up against him. Of the anti-kings of this period, the Sbarabied Ashot is a fugitive insignificant figure, a creature of the ostigans and powerless without their support. Far more important and effective was Gagic, ischkan of Vaspourakan, head of the family of the Ardzrouni, that ranked

1 *Hist. des Ardzrouni*, p. 241.
2 Ibn Zafir, *V.P.* p. 83.
3 Vartan, p. 112; Samuel of Ani, p. 437; Asoghic, p. 26. Ber, 'King of Aphgaz' (Asoghic) or 'prince of Sarmatians from Mount Caucasus' (Vartan) came to demand the consecration of Kars Cathedral by orthodox rites, but was defeated and blinded by Abas. Brosset (*Hist. de la Géorgie*, pp. 171–2) says, ignoring Asoghic, that only Chamich calls him King of Abasgia, and that the victim must either have been a Sarmatian (Caucasian) prince, or probably a Georgian general, as the Georgian word 'Ber' simply means 'old man'. It is hard to believe that the blinding of the King of Abasgia and Georgia would not have caused more repercussion in Georgian history.
4 Samuel of Ani, p. 483.

second only to the Bagratids in Armenia. The family of the
Ardzrouni, to the headship of which Gagic had succeeded in
908, owned the whole canton of Vaspourakan, stretching from
the south and east of Lake Van to the Araxes; and Gagic's father
had added to these possessions the districts of Her and Zaravand,
bringing his power to the shores of Lake Ourmiah;[1] later we
find even Marand in Ardzrouni hands.[2] Gagic's mother, Sophie,
was a Bagratid princess; but the marriage had not brought peace
between the two jealous houses, and Sembat had finally offended
his sister's family by assigning their ancestral town of Nakhidchevan on the Araxes to the Siounians. Consequently, while
already during Afschin's attacks the Ardzrouni had tended to
support the Arabs, now during Youssouff's attacks, Gagic committed himself absolutely against his uncle, and received from
Youssouff's hands the crown of the King of Kings.[3]

He did not find it an easy crown to wear. Youssouff's conquests grew too formidable; and alarm added to the qualms
caused by Gagic's Christian conscience. He drew back periodically, playing a game of remarkably volatile treachery: though it
seems that he always declared himself a loyal vassal of the Calif,
of Youssouff's loyalty to whom there was always some doubt;
and when Youssouff, dissatisfied with Gagic's conduct, crowned
the Sbarabied as another King of Kings, Gagic shortly afterwards
had his title confirmed from Bagdad.[4] The result of all this was
that Youssouff pursued Gagic with a deadly hatred; and while
Ashot II, when once established in his home by Greek help, was
able to come to some terms with the Arabs and avoid further
molestation, Gagic, whose territory was more surrounded by
Moslem land, suffered from continual attacks from Youssouff
and his successor Nasr, particularly from the time of Youssouff's
return to favour after his captivity as a rebel at Bagdad.[5] It was
not till about 924 that Gagic was left in peace.

Henceforward he was able to rule his dominions in prosperity.
He had occasional brushes with the Arabs, as in 936, the year of

1 John Cath. p. 126; *Hist. des Ardzrouni*, p. 263.   2 John Cath. p. 287.
3 *Ibid.* pp. 199 *et seq.* Sophie had died some time previously, before Gagic's
accession (*Hist. des Ardzrouni*, p. 217).
4 John Cath. p. 309.   5 *Ibid.* pp. 333, 334.

ARMENIA 159

his death, when he allied himself with Abas against some Arabs
who had captured Nakhidchevan; they defeated Abas, who would
not wait for Gagic's arrival, but were defeated themselves later
by Gagic before the walls of Dovin.[1] But otherwise there was
unusual quiet; and Gagic was able to indulge his taste for building. The great memorial of his reign was the island-city of Aga-
thamar in Lake Van, where the Catholicus was soon induced to
live, becoming there little more than a servant of the Ardzrouni
Court.[2] Gagic did not often come into contact with the Greeks.
Lake Van and the mountains of Kokovit separated him from the
Empire, and during the Armenian civil wars he was beyond their
sphere of influence. Curcuas's campaigns on the north and west
of Lake Van brought him nearer, and some friendly passages
seem to have occurred. There was an attempt on the part of
Gagic to negotiate with Constantinople about Church union in
926 or 927; and at some time Gagic was recognized by the
Byzantine Court as Ἄρχων τῶν ἀρχόντων, probably after Ashot's
death in 928. This brings us to one of the most obscure questions
in the history of Greek relations with Armenia. There exists a
letter written by Romanus and addressed to the Emir of Egypt,
concerning Armenian affairs and the transference of the title of
King of Kings from Gagic to the recipient.[3] The address to the
Emir of Egypt must be a mistake; in 938, two years after Gagic's
death, Romanus sent a letter to Egypt, and some muddled
subsequent scribe must have affixed the wrong address to the
Armenian letter. The recipient must have been some Armenian
prince, who, we cannot tell. Gagic was still alive, for the prince
is told that if he behaves well and keeps peace the Emperor will
recommend Gagic and the 'Magister Apaseius' to come to an
entente with him. It seems therefore that Abas had only received
so far the title of Magister from Constantinople and ranked in

1 *Hist. des Ardzrouni*, p. 241. The date is fixed by Gagic's death in 936 and
the fact that before the battle he was blessed by the Catholicus Eghiche, who
only became Catholicus in 936.
2 *Ibid.* p. 235; Chamich, II, p. 73.
3 Ep. Rom. (Sakkelion), II, p. 406 (see also Ep. p. 407); Vasiliev, II, pp.
264–5; Dölger, Cap. 630, 635, p. 78. Marc points out that the address is
wrong and an Armenian prince must be meant. I translate the Greek title
of Ἄρχων τῶν ἀρχόντων as King of Kings for convenience's sake: though it
would have sounded too royal an equivalent for Byzantine ears.

Byzantine eyes below Gagic: also that the title of King of Kings
was only allowed from Byzantium to one Armenian prince at
a time. The identity of the petitioner must remain unknown,
as there is no reason for selecting any one of the Armenian
princes rather than another. At the time of Romanus's dealings
with Tornices (Derenic) of Taron, Ashot, who was still alive,
is called King of Kings and Gagic is merely Archon of Vaspourakan (Basparacaca).[1] Nevertheless, soon—presumably after
Ashot's death, as the Greeks would hardly like to offend a good
friend, whereas Abas's conduct was less satisfactory—the title
of King of Kings was given to Gagic. At some time later,
presumably on Gagic's death, the title was given back to the
Bagratids; but it lingered in the Ardzrouni house; and when
Constantine Porphyrogennetus wrote the *De Ceremoniis*, while the
Bagratid prince was the Ἄρχων τῶν ἀρχόντων, the Ardzrouni
was Ἄρχων τῶν ἀρχόντων Βασπαρακᾶν.[2]

Gagic died in 936. His son and successor Derenic lacked his
personality; and Vaspourakan fell into the background, and does
not re-enter Armenian history till long after the close of
Romanus's reign.[3]

The third great family of Armenia was the Orbelians of Siounia.
Siounia was the large canton to the east of the country, which
stretched from Lake Sevan to the southernmost bend of the
Araxes. Siounia was subdivided amongst various members of the
princely house, and possessions seem to have changed hands
among them fairly frequently. There were two main branches
of the family; of the elder the head at the time of Sembat's
martyrdom was the Grand Ischkan Sembat whose possessions
lay on the west of Siounia, including Vaiotzor and Sisagan[4] (which
he apparently acquired from his cousins of the younger branch)
and extending down to Nakhidchevan. He had married an
Ardzrouni princess, Sophie, Gagic's sister, and was one of the
most prominent figures in Armenia. His brother Sahac owned
the districts of Siounia on the east, with his capital probably at

1 *D.A.I.* p. 187.   2 *D.C.* p. 687.
3 Thomas Ardzrouni's history closes after Gagic's death, and Derenic is
barely mentioned by any Armenian historian.
4 Rambaud, p. 510, identifies Vaiotzor (Baitzor) with Sisagan, but the
Histoire de la Siounie mentions that Sembat was lord of both districts.

Erendchac;[1] a third brother Papgen, the villain of the family, owned a town or two on the east and was jealous of his richer brothers; a fourth, Vasac, had already been killed in the interminable civil wars. The possessions of the younger branch clustered round Lake Sevan. It was represented also by four brothers, of whom one died young, fighting; the survivors were Grigor Souphan, the eldest, another Sahac and another Vasac. They were the sons of Vasac Gabourh, who had ruled in Sisagan, and the Bagratid princess Mariam.[2] Situated on the borders of Aderbaijan, the Siounians were usually the first to suffer in the advent of an Arab invasion; consequently, though the princes of the east of Siounia were apt to come to terms as quickly as they could with the Arabs (like Sahac and the renegade Papgen who "made their pact with Hell"[3] during Nasr's invasion of 922), the western princes, to secure their rear, kept in close alliance with the Bagratids. During the wars of Ashot II's early reign, the Grand Ischkan Sembat appears as a fairly steady ally of Ashot, and a victim of Youssouff's ravages—the family lost their ancestral town of Erendchac—while the sons of Mariam, who were dispossessed early in the war, appear as their cousin Ashot's most constant helpers, recovering their lands when the Greek armies brought him to Dovin.[4] Siounian history after the pacification of Armenia and the close of John Catholicus's history is dim. The History of Siounia tells of little save ecclesiastical and dynastic arrangements, which are without great historical importance. As yet the country was too war-weary and divided to play a grand rôle; the great days of the Orbelians were to come.

Of the other princes of Armenia John Catholicus allows the title of grand ischkan only to the prince of Gardman, on the north of Lake Sevan, Ashot's unsatisfactory father-in-law, who does not seem to have been a figure of any great importance,[5] and to the Bagratid prince of Taron, with whom I will deal later. The ischkans of the south, of Mokh and Andsevatsi, appear to

---

1 Which his wife and mother defended against Youssouff (John Cath. p. 235). *Hist. de la Siounie*, p. 116, says that it was Sophie (Sembat's wife) that defended Erendchac; but as she appears later as building churches in Armenia (*ibid.* p. 148) she can hardly have been taken to a life captivity in Persia.

2 *Hist. de la Siounie*, p. 170.   3 John Cath. p. 340.

4 *Ibid.* pp. 279 *et passim*.   5 *Ibid.* p. 301.

have followed the lead and been almost vassals of the Ardzrouni princes:[1] though the latter, Adom, son of an adventurous cadet of the Ardzrouni, Gourgen, who had married the Dowager Princess of Andsevatsi,[2] was rich enough to impress and attract Arab raiders, and to defeat them; in 938 he repulsed the razzia of Lachkari, a lieutenant of the governor of Iraq.[3] Kokovit, to the north of Vaspourakan, was another possession of the Ardzrouni, apparently belonging always to a cadet of the family— during these years to Gagic's brother Gourgen.[4] To the north of the Bagratid lands and Gardman lay the large canton of Oudi, part of which was a province of the Bagratids,[5] ruled by governors whom they appointed; part was owned by the Sevortians, an alien race that most probably were Slav in origin,[6] and the rest was probably in the hands of the Aghovans, whose country (Albania) lay just to the east.[7] The Aghovans were not, strictly speaking, members of the Armenian empire. Their ruler bore the title of king,[8] and their Church was under its own Catholicus. But they shared the Armenian heresy, and their Catholicus was consecrated by and subordinate to the Armenian Catholicus:[9] so that for practical purposes they counted as members of the Armenian confederacy. The Aghovans appear occasionally in the narrative of John Catholicus, always as being well disposed to the Armenians; apart from that their history is obscure.

I have left to the last the canton of Taron, which, situated to the west of Lake Van, came early into the Greek sphere of influence and thus had a slightly different history from the other cantons: though the dealings of the Taronites with the Empire are typical of the attitude with which Byzantium was regarded by the Armenian east. The Taronite territory stretched roughly from Lake Van to the imperial frontier, with its capital at

1 John Cath. p. 291. The ischkan of Mokh was certainly a tributary of Gagic's.
2 Laurent in *Rev. des Etudes Arméniennes*, II, p. 183.
3 Ibn Miskawiah trans. Huart in *Rev. des Etudes Arméniennes*, I, p. 419.
4 *Hist. des Ardzrouni*, p. 273; John Cath. p. 181.
5 John Cath. pp. 304 *et passim*.
6 *Ibid.* pp. 175 *et passim*; Rambaud, p. 510–11.
7 *Saint-Martin*, p. 86.
8 John Cath. p. 209. He was a cadet of the Siounian house.
9 *D.C.* p. 688; John Cath. p. 209; Brosset, *Hist. de la Géorgie*, p. 488.

Mousch,[1] on the high road from the Empire to southern Armenia. Close relations between Taron and the Empire began certainly after Leo's annexations across the Euphrates. The princely house of Taron was a branch of the Bagratids; in the early years of Sembat's reign the grand ischkan had been a certain David; but he seems to have died soon and been succeeded by his son, almost certainly the Gregory of Constantine Porphyrogennetus's narrative, and the husband or brother-in-law of a sister of the Sbarabied Ashot. The Taronites did not keep on very good terms with their more prominent cousins; and during Leo's reign King Sembat had to petition the Byzantine Court to induce the Taronites to release two of his nephews whom they had captured. Its situation saved Taron from the horrors of the Arab wars; and to John Catholicus it provided a frequent safe refuge. Early in Romanus's reign an arrangement was made by which Gregory of Taron was given a fixed income from the Byzantine treasury in return for large periodical gifts of goods: while his younger brother Apoganem was allotted a house in Constantinople and a Greek wife. The arrangement did not work well; Ashot II, Gagic and Adarnase of Iberia all jealously asked if they could not have incomes too, while Gregory found it rather too expensive satisfying the imperial greed for presents. So the agreement lapsed, and Gregory took merely to paying a small regular tribute. Meanwhile, after Apoganem's death, quarrels occurred over the house at Constantinople, which Gregory considered his and which he exchanged for a country house at Celtzene, nearer his home, to the indignant protests of Apoganem's young son Derenic (Tornices). Throughout it all the Emperor acted with great patience, gradually extending his influence where he could—marrying Gregory's son and heir Bagrat (Pancratius) to a Byzantine, probably an Armeniac relative of the Lecapeni, and later using the excuse of Bagrat's maltreatment of Derenic to annex a little territory and further to divide up and weaken the Taronite inheritance.[2] Thus Taron became practically an imperial province and as such enjoyed immunity from

1 Vartan Vartabied, p. 429.
2 *D.A.I.* pp. 182 *et seq.* The dates can only be fixed by the fact that Ashot II was one of the princes who protested against Gregory's income.

the Armenian civil wars, but instead suffered from occasional
Arab raids, as when Saïf-ad-Daula in 940, though he was willing
to be friendly to the Armenians, sacked the Taronite capital of
Mousch and destroyed its very holy church.[1]

There were probably many other minor Armenian princes
whose names history has not handed down to us, and whose
importance was slight.[2] More powerful was the Armenian
Church, a large organization that extended throughout the
country, promoting unity, and apparently very free from the
secular arm. The Catholicus was elected by the Church and himself appointed his bishops and subordinates, probably with a
certain amount of nepotism.[3] The fact that it was the one great
nationalist institution in the kingdom won for it a sentiment
among the people that must have seemed menacing to the lay
powers; and consequently the princes constantly made attempts
to unite the Armenian with the Orthodox Church—attempts
that invariably ended in failure.[4] The importance of the Catholicus's political rôle is well brought out in the narrative of John
Catholicus. Even making due allowance for John's fondness to
emphasize his value, he appears as the one ambassador that can
deal for Armenia as a whole. Moreover, the clergy had the great
advantage of being the most cultured section of society. Their
political influence was on the whole directed against the Greeks.
Their bugbear was the Orthodox Church, of whom they disapproved doctrinally and therefore with profound bitterness,
and whom they dreaded as threatening their ecclesiastical independence. It was only when the Arabs persecuted Christianity

1 Ibn Zafir, V.P. p. 83.

2 The list of Armenian vassals given by Constantine in the De Ceremoniis
(p. 687) is: Bagratids (ἄρχων τῶν ἀρχόντων), archons of Βασπαρακᾶν, ὁ νῦν
τιμηθεὶς ἄρχων τῶν ἀρχόντων, of Κοκοβὶτ (Kokovit), of Ταρὼ (Taron), of
Μῶεξ (Mokh), of Αὔζαν (Autzoun in the province of Koukarkh, according
to Rambaud, p. 509; but I am inclined to identify it with Andsevatsi, whose
prince was of considerable importance), of Συνῆς (Siounia), of Βαιτζὼρ
(Vaiotzor, which need not necessarily be identified exactly with Sisagan),
of Κατζιένης (Artsakj, Saint-Martin, I, p. 149, identified by Vartan Vartabied
p. 419; the archon of Chatzienes was probably the King of Aghovania), and
the archons of the Σερβοτιῶν τῶν λεγομένων Μαῦρα παιδία (the Sevortians
of Oudi).

3 John Catholicus appointed his nephew Ter Hacob as bishop of Siounia in
918 (Hist. de la Siounie, p. 148).

4 As both Ashot II and Gagic (see above).

so fiercely that it would be scandalous not to protest, that they would look with friendly eyes to Constantinople; otherwise they much preferred the Moslems.[1] Engrained by their religious upbringing, this distrust and dislike of the Empire characterized all the Armenians. Though Bagdad was several hundred miles nearer than Constantinople, and the Arab armies usually more menacing than the Greeks, it was the Arabs that they liked the better. The Arab civilization and religion were too different ever to threaten Armenian national individuality; but the Empire, essentially cosmopolitan, with a civilization akin to their own, only further advanced, and a religion divided only by a tiny clause, could so easily absorb them and crush their independent life for ever. The number of Armenians already taking service under the Empire, entirely submerging their nationality in its cosmopolitanism, must have appeared very ominous, particularly at a time when both the Emperor and his chief general were of pure Armenian birth.[2] Consequently, relations between Armenia and the Empire were always undermined by fear and suspicion, except at moments when Moslem persecutions reminded the Armenians of the Empire's fellow-Christianity; and the Empire had to make the most of those opportunities. The Armenians were willing occasionally to make professions of loyal vassalage to the Empire (though they more frequently did so to Bagdad); but when an Armenian like Sembat too frequently showed to the Emperor the respect due to a superior and the obedience owed to a father,[3] he quickly lost popularity. Almost the only thing on which the Armenian princes would agree was to compose a sort of Trade Union against their grasping master the Basileus. Sembat showed signs of becoming a blackleg, therefore he fell; Gregory

1 John was frequently to be found engaging in friendly intercourse with the Moslems, whereas even at the worst moment of the Arab conquest he refused to visit Constantinople for fear of attempts to convert him (John Cath. p. 204).
2 Laurent, in "Les Origines Médiévales de la Question Arménienne," *Rev. des Etudes Arméniennes*, I, pp. 35 *et seq.*, says (p. 47) that the Armenian never was able to fraternize completely with the Greeks; however high he mounts (in the Empire) he always keeps his own language, customs and religion. That statement seems to me to be fantastic nonsense.
3 John Cath. p. 189.

of Taron has to give up his income as it is against the rules of the union, and the Curopalates of Iberia (the Iberians held much the same views with regard to the Empire) refuses to hand Cetzeum over to the Greeks as that too would be a breach and bring on him the wrath of the other members.

Nevertheless, intercourse between Armenia and the Empire was practically unbroken. Armenia lay across the great trade route to Persia, and itself provided much raw material from its mines and its pastures for the workshops of Constantinople; and the continual flow into the Empire of Armenians tempted by its riches and opportunities to leave their own crowded valleys and desolate mountains, involved a constant interchange of ideas. Armenian art, with its purer Sassanian heritage, found its place in the styles that formed the imperial art of Byzantium, while the refinements of Byzantine culture and luxury were eagerly copied at the Courts of Agthamar and Kars. But the civilization of Armenia, fortified by its religion, its mountains and the mutually cancelling Greek and Arab influences, remained a thing apart, particularly now that the native Sassanid civilization that could enter so easily from Persia was dead. It was on a much lower level; the recitals of any of the historians show how childish and improvident the policies of Armenian statesmen were; an excellent realization of the two levels is to be found in the narrative of John Catholicus by comparing the letter of the Patriarch Nicholas to the Catholicus with John's reply. Nicholas's letter is terse and to the point, showing a wide comprehension of the problems of Armenia and reasonable schemes for their solution. John's, on the other hand, is extremely long and diffuse, full of crude flattery and scriptural quotations that point rather to ignorance than to knowledge of the Bible. Even in his history he thus innocently shows up the backwardness of his country.

John's letter shows one more point. Individual—aggressively individual—though its civilization was, it was to the West that Armenia turned in times when it was seriously attacked. When really alarmed it looked to the Empire and the holy person of the Emperor as the ultimate fountain-head of Christian culture. Like all their fellow-Christians, the Armenians could not but be impressed by the age-long past of Rome and New Rome. Their fear, their hostility and their final reliance is explained when we remember that though the Arabs might rule their bodies from behind the walls of Dovin, it was the Empire that dominated their minds.[1]

North of Armenia were spread the tribes of the Caucasus—tribes "of whom God alone knows the number".[2] Most of them were counted as the vassals of Constantinople; but for the most part they were considered as of little importance by the Byzantine politicians save when their periodical wars and movements produced repercussions in Armenia or near the Greek frontier, or to the north towards the Chazars. A few however were given special notice, as being potentially dangerous or of value.

Nearest to the Empire, stretching from the frontier of the Chaldian theme to the valley of the Kour, were the principalities of Iberia, divided *de jure* among the members of a branch of the Bagratids; but actually several foreign tribes had their share. With the Iberian Bagratids the Empire had frequent and complicated dealings, such as those recorded by Constantine Porphyrogennetus. In order in the least to understand the situation, it is necessary to unravel their genealogy, a genealogy all the more involved in that, for reasons of family pride, as befitted the descendants of Bathsheba and the cousins of the Virgin Mary, they preferred to marry each other. In the first half of the tenth century the Iberian Bagratids were subdivided into two main branches, of Karthli (upper Georgia) and Tao (on the Greek frontier). Being orthodox in religion[3] they had always been on close terms with the Empire; and the head of the family was given at Constantinople the special title of Curopalates. The house of Karthli, in which the title of Curopalates had descended, was now in a decline. It seems that Ashot I of Armenia had

1 See Rambaud, pp. 521 *et seq.*, for the Byzantine influence in Armenia.
2 Maçoudi (Barbier de Meynard), II, p. 3. He estimates it at 72 (*ibid.* p. 2).
3 I am inclined to question the orthodoxy of the Karthli branch; it was so intimately bound up with Armenia. That of the Tao branch was more spotless; indeed to one of its princesses (Dinar) is due the honour for converting from heresy her husband's principality of Hereth. It is possible that the conquest of Karthli by the Abasgian King was aided, or even perhaps originated, by some lapse from orthodoxy on the part of the Bagratids, which was resented by their subjects.

reduced Karthli to a state of strict vassalage, so much so that it was an honour to the Curopalates Adarnase II (881–923) when Sembat, to whom he had been extremely loyal, raised him to the rank of King of Iberia and second person in the kingdom of Armenia.[1] Later a far worse disaster had befallen Adarnase; his sister's husband, Constantine, King of Abasgia, had in about 908 attacked and annexed the bulk of the province of Karthli, leaving Adarnase with probably only a small rim of land in the hills north of Ani and Erazkavors.[2] Henceforward Adarnase was a figure of slight importance, continually intriguing against his nephew George of Abasgia, the viceroy of Karthli, and following King Ashot in many of his campaigns.[3] After his death in 922 or 923 it was even considered whether the title of Curopalates should not be transferred to the house of Tao, particularly as his four sons quarrelled so much between themselves; but eventually it was given to the eldest Ashot, who came to Constantinople to be invested.[4] The history of the Bagratids of Karthli during the next few years is very obscure.

The branch of Tao was more powerful. Its elder subdivision, that ruled in Tao itself, seems never to have troubled Byzantine politics and soon became extinct. By 912 it was reduced to two members, Gourgen, whose daughter married an Abasgian prince and who died in 941, and his sister the proselytizing princess of Hereth.[5] The younger branch was less negligible in that it owned the important town of Ardanoudj (Adranutzium), the key to Iberia and Abasgia and one of the great trade centres of Armenia and the Caucasus. On the death of Sembat of Ardanoudj (889), Ardanoudj had gone to his elder son Bagrat, and some less important territory to his younger son David. On Bagrat's death (909) the territory of Ardanoudj was further divided between his four sons,[6] who soon started quarrelling amongst themselves.

1 John Cath. p. 172.
2 He owned a little territory in Gougarkh where John Catholicus took refuge in 914 (John Cath. p. 262).
3 John Cath. pp. 312 et seq. et passim.
4 D.A.I. pp. 211 et seq. Theoph. Cont. p. 402, dates it 922. Brosset, from Georgian sources, dates it 923 (Hist. de la Géorgie, p. 273).
5 Brosset, op. cit. p. 155.
6 Const. Porph. gives only three sons, but one of them (David) may have pre-deceased his father, though he left a posthumous son (Brosset, loc. cit.).

Constantine's narrative is very complicated. One of Bagrat's sons, Gourgen, he says, died without issue, but he talks soon of a Gourgen the son-in-law of another of Bagrat's sons, Ashot Ciscases, who inherited Ardanoudj from his brother Gourgen. This second Gourgen must, I think, be the son of the former Gourgen, a person whose existence is reported in the annals of Georgia. This second Gourgen was determined to capture Ardanoudj from his father-in-law Ashot Ciscases. Romanus, wishing to be on good terms with the strongest of these princes, sent an envoy, the Patrician Constans, to create Gourgen Magister; but before he arrived, Ashot, who was holding Ardanoudj precariously against Gourgen's attacks, offered to hand the town over to the Greeks in return for help, rather than let Gourgen have it. Constans, not knowing what to do, created Gourgen Magister, after a stormy interview with the sons of the recently dead Adarnase of Karthli, who feared that the dignity of Curopalates was going to be taken away from their family, and then went to take Ardanoudj over from Ashot Ciscases. This annexation outraged the trade union feeling of the princes of Iberia; and both Gourgen and a prince of Karthli threatened to go over to the Saracens unless it was restored. To pacify them Romanus disowned Constans's action, and the unhappy patrician was blamed all round. Ashot Ciscases was given back Ardanoudj; and Ashot of Karthli journeyed to Constantinople to be created Curopalates. But Ciscases did not enjoy Ardanoudj for long. Gourgen soon captured the city, and gave him some land in compensation, which also he later annexed. On Gourgen's death, his widow, Ashot's daughter, claimed Ardanoudj as her inheritance; but her neighbours decided that a woman could not inherit a town; so all took snippets of her territory, and the town itself went to her father's first cousin of the younger branch, Sembat son of David, who generously gave her a small country estate, and in whose family the town remained.[1]

1 *D.A.I.* pp. 206 *et seq.* The narrative is unintelligible unless we remember that (i) the events recorded at the bottom of p. 206 and on p. 207 are subsequent in date to Constans's mission on pp. 208 *et seq.*; (ii) that both the Tao and the Karthli branches are mentioned indiscriminately in the narrative (see Appendix IV) and Constantine himself does not seem to have his mind absolutely clear about them.

The difficult behaviour of the Iberian Bagratids at the siege of Erzerum has already been noticed. The villains in this story were, according to Constantine, the dispossessed family of Karthli, whose remaining lands may have stretched down to the neighbourhood of Erzerum, particularly the Magister Bagrat, son of the Curopalates Adarnase: though one is tempted to suspect that the Porphyrogennetus confused the Tao branch, geographically closer, with the more distant branch of Karthli.[1]

The Iberian Church was orthodox, and as such probably under the ecclesiastical jurisdiction of Constantinople. Nevertheless, there was an Iberian Catholicus, who almost certainly was the head of the Armenian Church in the country, and under the jurisdiction of the Armenian Catholicus.[2]

The kingdom of Abasgia was an infinitely more satisfactory vassal-State. It was scrupulously orthodox; indeed, the king, who at Constantinople was given the title of ἐξουσιάστης, slightly higher than ἄρχων, prided himself on being the champion of the True Church, of which his country was an eparchate. Abasgia stretched along the Black Sea coast three hundred Greek miles, from the frontier of the Chaldian theme to the mouth of the river Nicopsis,[3] with the Caucasus behind it. In the early years of the tenth century it was one of the most powerful States of the Armeno-Caucasian world. In about 908 its King Constantine (906–921) had annexed from the Bagratids of Karthli the bulk of their territory, bringing his empire up the valley of the Phasis and across to the Upper Kour valley, the neighbourhood of Tiflis and the Alan Gates.[4] This province of Karthli was, it seems, governed by the heir to the Abasgian throne as viceroy.[5] Constantine figured as the representative of Byzantine influence in the Caucasus and Armenia; he was the ally of Sembat in his

---

1　D.A.I. pp. 200 et seq. I have not been able to identify Cetzeum, the position of which would enable one better to judge which branch was really involved.

2　D.C. p. 688, where he is mentioned in conjunction with the Catholici of Armenia and Albania, both certainly heretics. John Cath. p. 265, shows that there were Iberians under the Catholicus's jurisdiction.

3　D.C. p. 182; Vivien de Saint-Martin, ii, pp. 234–5.

4　John Cath. p. 189.

5　In John Catholicus George (Gourgen) always appears as ruler of Karthli during his father's lifetime (e.g. pp. 325, 326, 327) and his son Constantine ruled there during his own (see below).

pro-Greek wars, and was suspect amongst his neighbours for his friendship with Constantinople.[1] During the *débacle* of the Armenian Bagratids, he had befriended Sembat's sons, providing Abas, who married his granddaughter, with a refuge for several years, and crowning Ashot King of Armenia.[2] His son George (Gourgen), who succeeded in 921, continued this friendship with Byzantium, and even won the thanks of the Patriarch Nicholas for his good work among the recently converted Alans.[3] George reigned till his death in 955 in prosperity, marred only by trouble with his son Constantine, viceroy of Karthli, whom eventually he made a eunuch and who died in his father's lifetime.[4]

Of the other Caucasian tribes whose rulers Constantine Porphyrogennetus counted among his vassals, none were of any importance. He mentions the Archon and the Catholicus of Albania (Aghovania) with whom I have dealt among the potentates of Armenia. He also mentions eight further archons:[5] of Crebatan (a Slav name, possibly referring to the kingdom of Kabalah, with Moslem towns and a Christian countryside, situated somewhere at the east end of the Caucasus[6]); of Cedonia (Khaïdac, or Djidan, north of Derbend, a country dominated by the Chazars, with a Moslem royal family and a Christian populace[7]); of Tzanaria (Sanaria, a Christian nation claiming a Semitic origin, situated to the south-east of the Alan Gates—the pass of Dariel—and ruled by a chorepiscopus[8]); of Sarban, between Tzanaria and the Alans (another Slav name, the Christian kingdom of Serir, to the north of Sanaria[9]); of Azia by the

1 John Cath. pp. 197–8.
2 *Ibid.* p. 209. I presume that Constantine is the King of Georgia mentioned, not the Curopalates Adarnase, who is always called King of Iberia.
3 Nich. Myst. Ep. LI, p. 241. Nicholas also wrote to George condoling on his father's death (*ibid.* Ep. XLVI, p. 236), and recommending him to follow his father's admirable conduct *vis-à-vis* the Empire.
4 Brosset, *Hist. de la Géorgie*, p. 175.
5 *D.C.* p. 688.
6 d'Ohsson, p. 19; Vivien de Saint-Martin, II, p. 244.
7 d'Ohsson, pp. 19–20; Vivien de Saint-Martin, II, p. 246, who calls the name of Khaïdac an invention of d'Ohsson's.
8 d'Ohsson, p. 18; Vivien de Saint-Martin, p. 246.
9 d'Ohsson, p. 21; Vivien de Saint-Martin, p. 245.

Caspian Gates (possibly Ossethi round the Alan Gates, or possibly
some unidentified country by the Caspian Gates; Ossethi should
probably be identified with the country of the Christian Gou-
mikes, placed by the Arab geographers at the Alan Gates[1]); of
Chrysa (either the valley of Kasara, south-west of Ossethi, or
more probably Circassia, the land of the handsome Caschakes
of the Arab geographers, to the north of Abasgia[2]); of Breza
(probably Ertso, between the rivers Aldran and Agri[3]); and of
Mocas by the Maeotid Lake (undoubtedly Mugan, where the
Kour comes out into the Caspian[4]). This list probably included
all the Christian States of any importance in the Caucasus[5]; there
were, however, several Moslem States. Tiflis had been a Moslem
city since about 900;[6] further east there was on the Caspian
coast of Albania the strong kingdom of Chirvan, which commanded the Caspian Gates,[7] and to the north of it the country
of the Gourdjes where a Christian people was dominated by
Moslem rulers.[8] The Moslem power in the Caucasus was however
declining;[9] and the Arab ostigans of Albania and Iberia were
probably meeting with increasing disobedience and revolt that
they were powerless to crush.

Just beyond the Caucasus, to the north of the Alan Gates,
was the country of the Alans, who were treated by the Emperor on
a slightly different footing. The exusiastes of Alania, though he
was the Emperor's 'spiritual son', did not receive a κέλευσις,
and so was not, strictly speaking, a vassal.[10] The Alans had

1 Vivien de Saint-Martin, II, p. 247, identifies Azia explicitly with Ossethi, but
it seems unlikely that Constantine would have muddled the Alan Gates with
the Caspian Gates. d'Ohsson, p. 22.

2 d'Ohsson, p. 25; Vivien de Saint-Martin, II, p. 247, identifies it explicitly as
the valley of Kasara.

3 Vivien de Saint-Martin, loc. cit.

4 Vivien de Saint-Martin, loc. cit., firmly denies that Mocas can be Mugan,
despite the fact that Constantine places it by the Maeotid Lake, which must
be the Caspian, but identifies it instead with the inland district of Morakani,
by the junction of the Kour and the Ardzan.

5 The Arab geographers mention a few more Christian nations, such as the
Schekis and the Somekhis (d'Ohsson, pp. 18–19) but they were probably of
no significance.

6 John Cath. p. 173; d'Ohsson, p. 13.

7 Vivien de Saint-Martin, II, pp. 268–9.

8 d'Ohsson, p. 12.   9 Ibid. p. 17.

10 D.C. loc. cit.

become Christian early in the century, and no doubt the Emperor had hopes of his spiritual .fatherhood bringing material power. But things did not go smoothly; Peter, the Archbishop sent out from Constantinople, had considerable difficulty with them, particularly as regards their views on marriage. Nicholas the Patriarch sent him consoling messages and advised him to be tactful, and George of Abasgia offered help.[1] In vain, for later, in about 932, so Maçoudi informs us,[2] the Alans turned out all their bishops and priests and reverted to the more comfortable state of heathendom. Nevertheless, the Alans seem to have remained on good terms with Constantinople; and Byzantine diplomacy found them useful, not so much as a Caucasian power but as a power for controlling the great tribes of the Steppes, particularly the Chazars, whose territory probably abutted on their own and who if they were hostile would never venture out against the tempting province of Cherson.[3]

In conclusion, whereas in the wars on the Greco-Arab frontier the personality of the head of the government at Constantinople had a great effect on the course of events, the diplomatic dealings of Byzantium with the nations of the Armeno-Caucasian world ran always along more or less fixed lines. In that world circumstances were constantly changing; but the changes were never important enough to distract the attention of the Emperor. His only fear was that it should fall into Moslem hands; this he would take violent action to prevent. Otherwise the government at Constantinople was content to let the Caucasus look after itself, merely employing (probably with a handsome salary) some client-prince, during this period the kings of Abasgia, to spread his influence as far as was possible, particularly through

1 Nich. Myst. Ep. LII, p. 243.
2 Maçoudi, V.P. p. 24.
3 Const. Porph. D.A.I. p. 80. The exact position of Alania is impossible to place. It was vaguely to the north of the Alan Gates—probably not a very large country, but very thickly populated. Maçoudi lays great stress on its population, saying that one cock crowing will eventually wake all the cocks in the country (Maçoudi, p. 45).
I have not dealt here with the ethnology of the various Caucasian tribes; it was extremely complicated and has never been adequately elucidated. Practically every known Indo-Aryan race was said to be represented in the Caucasus.

religion, among the Caucasian tribes. They were too far off for more positive action to be worth while, except just in the Armenian and Iberian districts abutting on the frontiers. It was not till a century later, in the reign of the Porphyrogenneta Zoe, that the annexation of Armenia brought the Empire for a short while into a direct connection with the Caucasus.[1]

[1] In connection with the eastern frontier it should be noticed that apparently the Empire sometimes had diplomatic intercourse with countries so far off as India and Arabia Felix (*D.C.* p. 688). Such dealings must, however, have been rare.

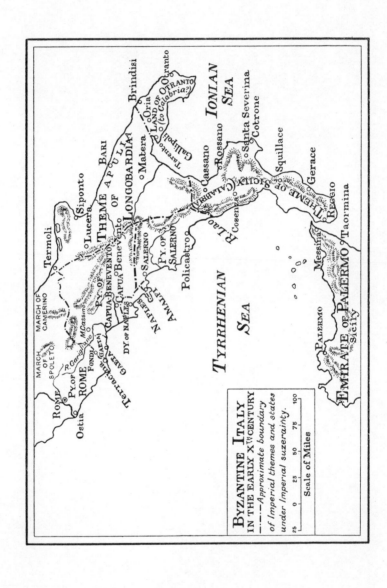

BYZANTINE ITALY
IN THE EARLY XTH CENTURY
— — — Approximate boundary
of Imperial themes and states
under Imperial suzerainty.

Scale of Miles
25   0   25   50   75   100

ROME
Ostia
Py. of ROME
March of Spoleto
March of Camerino
Termoli
Siponto
Lucera
Fondi
R. Garigliano
GAETA
Py. of (GAETA)
Terracina
Py. of CAPUA
Capua
M. Cassano
Benevento
Py. of BENEVENTO
Dy. of Naples
Napoli
Amalfi
Py. of SALERNO
Salerno
BARI
THEME OF APULIA
LONGOBARDIA
Matera
Brindisi
Oria
LAND OF OTRANTO
(to Calabria?)
Otranto
Taranto
Gallipoli
Policastro
Cassano
Rossano
Santa Severina
Cotrone
R. Lao
Cosenza
THEME OF SICILY (CALABRIA)
Squillace
Gerace
Reggio
Messina
EMIRATE OF PALERMO
PALERMO
Sicily
Taormina

IONIAN SEA

TYRRHENIAN SEA

CHAPTER IX

Byzantine Italy

IT was not only in Asia that Byzantium had to face the implacable hostility of the Saracens. At the other end of the Empire, in the provinces of Southern Italy, there was a second battlefield. Here the surroundings were very different. The eastern frontier was inevitably the most important to the Empire, opening as it did straight on to its very heart, the themes of Asia Minor. Italy on the other hand lay across the Adriatic Sea; between it and the capital there were many lines of defence. Nevertheless, though at times of crisis the west would be sacrificed to the east, the Emperor could never afford to ignore Italy, despite the difficulties with which his interest there provided him. Geographically, far though it was from the heart of the Empire, Apulia in the hands of an energetic enemy could be a base for very unpleasant attacks on the coasts of Albania and Greece: whereas a foothold across the Straits of Otranto was valuable for the control of the Adriatic and its growing commerce. Diplomatically, the Emperor's interest was more urgent. Italy contained the city of Rome, the centre of Western civilization, the city with the greatest spiritual prestige in Europe. A close connection with Rome was vastly useful for the Emperor in his dealings, not only with the Western powers but also with the inhabitants of his own dominions.

Byzantium therefore took care to play a leading part in the politics of Italy. But it found the part both difficult and costly. On the east there was only one enemy, the Califate, now in its decline; the Armenian vassals, though they were guilty of incorrigible double-dealing, never dared, with the Moslems so close, openly to declare themselves against the Empire. On the west things were not nearly so simple. The Saracen power—the African Califate—showed no such hopeful signs of decadence despite an occasional Sicilian revolt. The imperial vassals, the Lombard princes, lay protected on the side of the imperial provinces away from the Saracens; they had therefore no qualms in taking up arms against their suzerain. Moreover, across the frontier, in Central and Northern Italy, things were changing with kaleidoscopic rapidity. In the hurried procession of emperors, kings, popes and senatrices that passed to and fro, there always might arise some forceful potentate who from Rome or Spoleto would cast greedy eyes on the districts of the south. And finally, the spiritual and cultural capital of the western world was Rome, not Constantinople; and Rome was inevitably the rival of Constantinople.

Leo the Wise's reign had been inglorious in the west. By 912, the year of his death, Sicily was utterly lost to the Empire; the Saracens had completed their conquest by the capture of Taormina in 902. A few Christian villages up in the mountains still held out, notably the fort called New Taormina, which the ambitious Ibn-Kurhub could not capture even in 912;[1] and a few more revolts were still to occur. But the reconquest of the island was, now at any rate, quite impracticable. This gloomy situation was slightly modified by internal troubles among the Saracens; not only Sicily but also Africa was disturbed by civil wars. It was during these years that the Shiites were occupied in chasing the Aghlabite Emir out of Kairouan, and the Fatimites were in their stead establishing their dominion over the country from Mehdia. In Sicily the Emir Ibn-Kurhub, lord of Palermo from 913 onward, was taking advantage of the troubles of his African suzerains to declare Sicily under the Calif of Bagdad and no one else—the Calif's suzerainty being of necessity only nominal.[2] Ibn-Kurhub and his son Ali had their time well filled in trying to consolidate their independent position, all the more energetically in that Ibn Kurhub knew that "the people of Sicily did not love him".[3] Consequently, though Sicily was firmly in the hands of the Moslems, they were not in a position at the moment to use it as a base for dangerous aggression.

The state of affairs in Italy was infinitely more complicated. In Basil I's time, the Byzantine government had considered the reconquest of Southern Italy of more importance than the reten-

1 Ibn-al-Asir, V.P. p. 103.   2 Gay, L'Italie Mér. p. 158.
3 Ibn-al-Asir, loc. cit.

tion of Sicily; and Nicephorus Phocas, the first great member of that great family, had admirably performed the reconquest. Now the whole country south of a line drawn roughly from Termoli on the Adriatic to Terracina on the Tyrrhenian sea was officially under the Basileus. North of that was the city of Rome, and the March of Spoleto, the frontier provinces of the Frankish kingdom of Italy; to them the Basileus laid no claim. He had enough to do with the territory nominally his own. Only a part of Byzantine Italy was directly under the Empire—Calabria, Lucania (Basilicata) and Apulia—the country to the east of a line drawn roughly from Termoli to the river Lao.[1] Calabria was considered to be a remnant of the theme of Sicily, and in Constantine's list of themes it only appears as a subdivision of that theme.[2] And this was absurd only geographically, for Calabria was now largely populated by Greek refugees from Sicily, and the Greek stratege, residing at Reggio, had still great influence over the Christians of the island. Affiliated to this theme was the other entirely Hellenized portion of Italy, the land of Otranto in the extreme south-east.[3] The boundary of the theme is hard to place; the population was probably more or less Hellenized all over Lucania (certainly round Monte Pellino[4]), and round the shores of the Gulf of Taranto and across to Brindisi; but the political frontier can hardly have been ethnologically exact. Nevertheless, whereas Calabria was Greek, the other Byzantine theme, the theme called Longobardia, was preponderantly Latin. It consisted roughly of the provinces now called Apulia, from Termoli to Brindisi, with its capital at Bari. This theme was really the creation of Nicephorus Phocas, before whose time Longobardia, only nominally under the Basileus and possessed by Saracens and Lombards, counted merely as a subdivision of the theme of Cephallenia. Now Longobardia, won back to the Empire, officially even included the vassal states of

1 See maps in Gay.
2 *D.T.* p. 60.
3 Gay (pp. 128–9) does not decide whether the land of Otranto was part of the theme of Longobardia or of Calabria. Ecclesiastically Gallipoli at any rate depended on the Calabrian metropolis of Santa Severina, though Otranto seems to have formed an archbishopric apart (George of Cyprus, p. 57).
4 This was the heart of the district inhabited by Greek monks and hermits.

Capua-Benevento and Salerno.[1] It was a theme unique[2] in the Empire; alone it did not naturally look to Constantinople as the centre of the universe, but instead it was Latin-speaking and looked to Rome. Consequently the Basileus found it difficult to govern, and it was a triumph to Byzantine tact and statesmanship that he was able to govern it for so long. Chiefly he adopted the usual Byzantine policy of respecting local institutions; but probably he also tried to cure the Latinity by Greek colonization, for which the recent devastations of the Saracens provided an opportunity—though we only know of one case, when the slaves of Danielis, god-mother to the Macedonian dynasty, were liberated in their thousands and sent across to Longobardia.[3] But such methods can never have made more than a slight effect; the post of stratege of Longobardia (later he was always known as the Catapan) was always one that required an occupant of unusual capacity.

Within the bounds of the official imperial territory there were five self-governing principalities, the Lombard duchies of Capua-Benevento and Salerno and the seaport states of Naples, Amalfi and Gaeta. The Lombard duchies had been formed over three centuries before, at the time of the early Lombard invasions. Their fortunes had varied according to the history of Italy; when there was no strong power in Italy they were recklessly independent and behaved as they pleased, otherwise, they tended to submit, nominally at least, to the dominant potentate. Nicephorus Phocas had reminded them of the existence of the Basileus, and the Saracen menace still kept them in a sufficient alarm to ensure their loyalty. The more important of these states was that of Capua-Benevento. In 899 Atenolf I of Capua had profited by the discord that was rending the family of his cousins, the Dukes of Benevento, and had succeeded in ousting them and occupying their whole duchy. By his death (in 909) he controlled the whole centre of Southern Italy, from the Garigliano into Basilicata. The present rulers were his two sons (who governed jointly), Landolf I and Atenolf II, they were still punctiliously

1 *D.T.* p. 10.
2 Except for Dalmatia, which more properly ranks as a collection of vassal states.
3 Theoph. Cont. p. 321.

respectful to Constantinople; in 909 Landolf had even been sent on a visit there, and had returned with the title of imperial patrician.[1] The other Lombard principality was that of Salerno, a thin strip stretching down the Tyrrhenian coast from Salerno to the Calabrian border. It had been ruled since 901 by Guaimar II, a prince without much vigour, a brother-in-law (through his wife Gaitelgrima) of the Capuan princes,[2] whose lead he tended to follow. He, too, was still a dutiful vassal of the Emperor, and had visited Constantinople, returning with the same title of patrician.[3]

The maritime states were of purer Italian origin, and consisted each of a seaport and its suburbs and a little territory around. Naples was the largest and most prominent. Rich and commercial it was settling down into a state of comfortable independence under its dukes of the house of Sergius. The present duke (Consul et Dux) was Gregory, a grandson of the founder of the dynasty.[4] Naples had just avoided becoming a Church-State ruled by its bishops, but by now the lay hereditary power was firmly established. The civilization was still a blend between the Greek and the Latin, with the latter predominating. Greek monks and Greek churches were still to be found in the city, and everyone of any education spoke Greek; but the literary renaissance at the close of the last century had been purely Latin, and that also was the language of the populace. Nevertheless, Naples kept an intellectual interest in the affairs of the east, and Byzantine arts and luxuries were highly fashionable among the upper classes.[5] Besides their growing industrial town and suburbs, the Neapolitans owned a small strip of fertile territory

1 Gay, p. 231.

2 *Chronicum Salernitanum*, p. 551. Gay (p. 209) says that Gaitelgrima was the daughter of Atenolf II. It seems to me, however, to be clear that she was Atenolf I's daughter, especially as we are told in the same context that Atenolf II married Guaimar's daughter, Rothilda. He might have married his niece, but surely not his granddaughter.

3 *Anom. Salern. Chron.* (in Muratori, II, pt II), p. 272 *et passim*; Gay, p. 152 *et passim*.

4 Gregory (898–915) succeeded by John II (915–919); Marinus I (919–928) and John III (928–963).

5 Gay, pp. 240 *et seq.* Byzantine robes were used to buy back captives from the Hungarians in 922. (*Chron. S. Monasterii Casinensis*, p. 328.)

behind, round the foot of Vesuvius. Their foreign policy tended
to be renegade; though the dukes were connected by marriage
with the Capuans,[1] they found it more profitable to ally themselves with the Saracens, and ignore the attendant Papal
anathemas.

South of Naples was the tiny state of Amalfi,[2] that had successfully resisted all the Neapolitan and Salernitan attempts at
conquest. It had long been more republican than its neighbours,
but recently the system of two annual prefects had broken down,
and the prefecture had become hereditary. The present holder
was either Manson, who held the Byzantine title of Spathatius
Candidatus, or his son Mastalus I, who was certainly ruling in
915. Amalfi's great strength lay in its mercantile marine; it was
already the chief trading state in Italy, and there is reason to
suppose that it had counters established as far away as Antioch,
while certainly it held nearly all the carrying trade of the Tyrrhenian coast. In all this it was immensely helped by keeping,
with profitable impiety, on excellent terms with the Saracens.

The last of the vassal-states was Gaeta,[3] a small state stretching along the Tyrrhenian coast from the Garigliano to Terracina,
only some fifty miles south-east of Rome. Like Naples and
Amalfi (whom it also resembled in its Saracen alliance) Gaeta
kept considerable traces of Greek culture, its educated classes
often spoke Greek and used Greek script, and its chief magistrates, hereditary since 867 or thereabouts, were usually called
by the Greek name of Hypati ($\H{\upsilon}\pi\alpha\tau\iota$). The founder of the
present dynasty, Docibilis I, had died quite recently (between
909 and 913), and the Hypatus in 912 was probably his son,
John I. It is interesting to note that while the rulers of Capua
and Salerno and Naples were called at Constantinople by the
transliteration of their Latin titles ($\pi\rho\acute{\iota}\gamma\kappa\iota\psi$ for Capua and Salerno, $\delta o\acute{\upsilon}\xi$ for Naples), those of Amalfi and Gaeta were known
only as $\H{\alpha}\rho\chi o\nu\tau\epsilon\varsigma$. It is tempting to see in this an indication that the
last two states still were more Hellenized than their neighbours.[4]

---

1 Landolf of Capua had married Gregory's sister Gemma (*Chron. Salernitanum*, p. 547).
2 Gay, pp. 247 *et seq.*   3 *Ibid.* pp. 251 *et seq.*
4 *D.C.* p. 690: certainly Amalfi's princes when once they received the title
of imperial patrician, kept it in use longer than their neighbours (Gay, p. 250).

The rest of Italy, outside the Byzantine sphere, was in a state of peculiar disorder. Rome itself·was in the power of its nobles, or rather of the lurid ladies of the house of Theophylact, the Senatrices Theodora and Marozia.¹ The Pope, at the moment an obscurity called Anastasius III, was entirely in their hands, and consequently his prestige in Christendom was low. The Duchy of Spoleto, in the centre of the Peninsula and recently, under its duke, the Emperor Lambert, the main Italian power, had since his death in 898 lost its importance, and now was an appanage of Marozia's adventurer-husband, the Margrave Alberic. The only power in Northern Italy was Berengar of Friuli, King of Italy since 905, who ruled somewhat precariously over the Lombard plain, and, nominally, over all Italy to the Byzantine frontier, and who had ambitions to wear the imperial crown.²

The one great problem facing all Italy at this time was the Saracens. Since the capture of Bari in Basil I's time, the Adriatic coast was fairly free of them. But on the Tyrrhenian side of Italy they were a portentous feature. Before Leo VI's death, the long wars of the Byzantines had succeeded in driving them out of the Byzantine themes; but the Lombard princes had been less successful, chiefly owing to the renegade diplomacy of the maritime states. There was still unconquered a huge fortified Saracen colony on the banks of the Garigliano, in the lands of the Prince of Capua, from which the Saracens could raid with ease all over Central Italy, to the very gates of Rome, the city of the old fool Peter that they had vowed to destroy. So long as this colony of freebooters lasted, there could be no peace for Italy.

Besides these terrible forays from the Garigliano castle, the coasts of Italy, particularly Calabria, were raided almost yearly by the Arabs from Sicily and Africa, while Northern Italy further suffered from a second Saracen colony close by at Fréjus.

This was the Italy that the Emperor Alexander saw on his

---

1 Theodora died somewhere about 915. Marozia came into full power about 925, though from about 915 onwards, as the wife of Alberic, she was a considerable figure in Rome.

2 The history of Venice in regard to Byzantium fits more properly as an adjunct to the history of Byzantine Dalmatia.

accession in 912—Sicily entirely in the hands of the Moslems and the Italian provinces continually raided by them, his vassal-states in virtual independence, docile only from fear of the Saracens, his subjects in Calabria chiefly poor refugees, in Apulia restive Latins: outside his dominions no strong power, for good or for evil, in all the peninsula, but only the continual irritant of the Saracen nest on the Garigliano. This last was the sore that needed curing most urgently; till the Saracens were ejected from their Campanian fortress, disorder would reign in Italy. And the realization of this was inducing a tentative peace among Italy's Christian rulers.

The Emperor Alexander, as might have been expected, did nothing. During his thirteen months there is no record of any Byzantine action in Italy; the only event seems to have been an Arab raid of Calabria.[1] The Regency that followed his death was too short and too insecure to occupy itself in Italian affairs. But the Empress Zoe, who came into power in the autumn of 913, was energetic and bellicose; negotiations were busily set on foot for the formation under the Basileus of an Italian league against the infidel. In 914 Nicholas Picingli yielded to the persuasions of the Patriarch and reluctantly consented to become stratege of Longobardia,[2] and the Byzantine forces were considerably increased.

Fortunately in 914 the Papal Chair was vacant, and the Senatrix Theodora decided to fill it with one of her former lovers, the Archbishop of Ravenna. John X, who thus became Pope owing to his bodily charms, was in other ways worthy of his position. Almost his first action was to get into touch with Constantinople, which was easy, as Zoe, like her late husband, found the Papal alliance useful against the Patriarch, and it was probably at his instigation that additional forces were sent to Picingli. In 915 everything was ready. Nicholas Picingli marched up from the south, and the Duke of Naples and the Hypatus of Gaeta were induced by fear and the promise of titles to break all connections with the Saracens (though the latter insisted on a special treaty confirming him in his possession of Fondi and other Papal lands) and even to follow him. From the north came

1 Ibn-al-Asir, V.P. p. 103.   2 Nich. Myst. Ep. cxliv, p. 372.

the Pope himself, with Alberic of Spoleto, driving the Saracens from the Tiber valley, and close at hand from the east was Landolf of Capua. Against such forces the Saracens could not long hold out. They had no help from their co-religionists in Sicily, where Ibn-Kurhub was fighting against the Fatimites; and the blockade of the fortress, completed by the presence of Greek ships in the river, was close and severe. Starved out, the Saracens attempted to fly to the mountains; but, owing, it was thought, to St Peter and St Paul, who were present at the battle, not one of them escaped alive, except a few captives. And so ended the last Moslem fortress in Italy.[1]

This was the high-water mark of Byzantine power in Italy. The victory of the Garigliano had been primarily a Byzantine victory, organized and carried out with a Byzantine stratege in command. And Byzantium was rewarded. For once the ideal limits of the imperial dominion were realized. The princes of Capua and Salerno, the Duke of Naples and the Hypatus of Gaeta admitted the suzerainty of the Empire and gloried in their titles of imperial Patrician. The Greeks were the dominant factor in Italy. In December, 915, Berengar of Friuli moved south to be crowned Emperor at Rome, induced probably by jealousy of the Greeks; but that only added to the chaos of the country beyond the frontier.[2] Civil wars were occupying the Arabs of Sicily—in 914 Ibn-Kurhub had raided Calabria, but a Fatimite invasion of the island had hastily ended the raid[3]—and so there was no rival to compete with the Basileus. Unfortunately, this ideal state was ephemeral.

There were three principal causes for the decline of the Byzantine power. The year 916 passed peacefully enough, but the victory of the Garigliano had removed the terror that kept the

1 Liudprand, *Antapod.* pp. 61–2; Leo Ost. I, pp. 50 *et seq.* Gay, p. 161, establishes the date 915 as opposed to 916 which is based on the word 'triennio' as referring to John's pontificate in Leo Ost.: though Lupus (Lupus Protospath. ann. 916; *M.P.L.* CLV, p. 126), whom Gay does not mention, agrees with the later date. But ind. III (915) is found in the *Cod. Casin.* and the *Annales Beneventani*, and fits better into the narrative, as Gay has shown.
2 Gregorovius, III, pp. 265 *et seq.*, placing Garigliano in 916, makes Berengar partly responsible for the victory. That I think is impossible.
3 *Cambridge Chronicle*, Amari, p. 281.

Lombards docile, and in 917 circumstances were altered by the overthrow of the independent emirate of Palermo; the Fatimites now, as unchallenged masters of Sicily, could turn their attention to profitable raids on Italy. Still more important as regards Italy was the decision of the Empress Zoe to concentrate all her force against Symeon of Bulgaria. Probably late in 916 or early in 917 the additional troops that had been sent to Nicholas Picingli before Garigliano, were recalled to Thrace; and at the same time Picingli returned, no doubt willingly, home, to be succeeded in Longobardia by a far less capable official Ursileon.[1]

The Empress's decision had probably been timed largely by the success of her Italian policy, and she attempted to safeguard its results by making peace with the Fatimites. Eustathius, the stratege of Calabria, agreed to pay the Saracens 22,000 gold pieces yearly.[2] The date of this treaty is uncertain; Amari places it in the time of Ibn-Kurhub, that is to say, 916 at the latest;[3] Gay, on the other hand, places it in 918 or 919, after the African capture of Reggio, and he uses Cedrenus's words about war having just broken out with the Bulgars to confirm his date.[4] But Cedrenus's words, especially in their context, would apply much better to 917, when the Empress had decided to concentrate against Bulgaria; and it seems absurd not to correlate the Eustathian treaty with her treaty with the Eastern Saracens. Moreover, in 917, the recent Fatimite recovery of Sicily would make peace all the more desirable. The capture of Reggio as the one isolated Arab aggression between 914 and 922 is easy to explain. Eustathius was recalled soon after making his treaty, and John Muzalon (or Bizalon) was appointed in his place. In the business of the change of stratege, the tribute might well be late, or Muzalon might not consider himself bound by his predecessor's promises. Consequently, the Arabs took this drastic but natural step of reminding the Calabrians of their undertakings. In 918 under Selim, emir of Sicily, the Africans sailed to Reggio, and captured and sacked the town, though they made

1 Stratege in 921, and, as far as we know, Picingli's immediate successor.
2 Cedrenus, II, p. 355.
3 Amari, *Mussul. in Sicilia*, II, p. 153.
4 Gay, p. 202.

no attempt to stay. As a result, from that year Muzalon sent the money regularly—to the distress of the Calabrians, from whom it was rapaciously taken.[1]

North of Calabria, memories of the Garigliano still lingered. The vassal princes were quiet, airing obediently their imperial titles. But the imperial prestige was sinking. Almost certainly the imperial troops were reduced[2]—and troops were the most potent argument for obedience among the Italians. News of the disastrous Bulgar wars must have filtered through to Italy, while the weakness of the central government at the time of Romanus's scramble to the throne must have been to some extent reflected on the provinces, to the discredit of the emperors. Moreover, the Pope cannot have been overjoyed at the fall of Zoe and the triumph of the Patriarch—and John X had considerable influence in Italy. It is probably to these years (about 920) that the anxious letters of Nicholas to unknown Romans and to a personage called Gedo belong, letters looking for support at the Papal court; and the Pope himself was wooed in rather too grandiloquent an apologia, and next year in a complaint that no answer had been received.[3] But John remained unmoved by Nicholas's tirades against third and fourth marriages; and the coolness between Rome and Constantinople lasted several years. In Italy it was the latter that suffered by it.

Nevertheless it was in the Greek south that trouble first began. In 920 or 921 the Calabrians rose against their stratege, John Muzalon, and murdered him. The motive, according to the biographer of St Elias, was Muzalon's attempted treachery against the Empire; but that no doubt was the Calabrian excuse. The more probable cause was the tribute to the Saracens, that the stratege had to squeeze out of the Calabrians; and it is not unlikely that Muzalon, after a habit common to unscrupulous governors, squeezed out more than was necessary and kept the surplus. This was an isolated revolt, and not of an uncommon

1 *Camb. Chron.* Amari, p. 282; see below, p. 188, n. 1.

2 Liudprand in his stories of African help (*Antapod.* p. 57) says that troops were removed to put down what he calls a revolt in the East—presumably the Bulgar war.

3 Nich. Myst. Ep. XXXII, LIII, LIV, LVI, LXXV, LXXVII, LXXXVIII, pp. 196 *et seq.*, 248 *et seq.*, 252, 253, 256, 273 *et seq.*, 280, 289. Letter LVI was, we know written in 921 (nine years after Nicholas's return to the Patriarchate).

or deeply significant type. Under Zoe the Athenians had behaved just similarly with an unpopular stratege called Chases,
who was stoned to death in the Parthenon. Muzalon's successor,
wishing to live, seems to have reduced the taxes; for in 922 the
Arab raids began once more.[1]

But in Apulia there had meanwhile been a very significant
revolt. The Latin population had risen in 921 against the Stratege Ursileon, and had successfully called to their aid Landolf
and Atenolf of Capua, the 'imperial patricians'. A bloodthirsty
battle was fought at Ascoli in April between the Byzantines and
the rebels, in which the latter were victorious and the stratege
himself was slain, and Landolf became master of Apulia.[2] The
loss of Apulia was a great shock to Constantinople, proving as
it did the weakness of the imperial prestige, and presumably
what troops could be spared from the Bulgar wars were sent to
Italy. For the Apulians hastened to send an apologia to the
Basileus, blaming the iniquities of the stratege as the cause of
it all, and suggesting, as the basis of peace, that Landolf should
be made next stratege of Longobardia.[3] The Imperial Court was
naturally shocked at what was really a demand for autonomy;
to Byzantium, Landolf appeared as an audacious rebel, the villain
of the piece, and it would be insane to reward him for his villainy
—a fatal precedent and a deathblow to the imperial prestige.
The Patriarch Nicholas, through whom the negotiations were
carried, sent back a tactfully worded '*non possumus*',[4] and the
imperial troops set about the reconquest of the province. When
this was completed we do not know: certainly by 929, as in that
year Landolf made a fresh invasion. The negotiations may have
lasted two or three years; but by 925 they were finally over, for
after that year Landolf and Atenolf utterly discarded their

---

1 Cedrenus, II, p. 354; *Camb. Chron.* Costa Luzzi, pp. 42–72; *Life of Saint
Elias*, 54; Gay, p. 203. Cedrenus says that the Calabrians turned to Dandolf
(Landolf) for help, but he probably mixed up the Calabrian with the Apulian
revolt. It is surprising that no one has connected the Eustathian treaty, the
Reggio raid, the Calabrian revolt and the subsequent Arab raids in the above
sequence. Though nowhere definitely stated by the authorities, that seems
to be the obvious explanation of the course of events.

2 Lupus Protospath. ann. 921, *M.P.L.* CLV, p. 126; Gay, p. 203.

3 Nich. Myst. Ep. LXXXII, LXXXV, pp. 285, 289.

4 *Ibid. loc. cit.*

imperial titles. The whole episode had shown with bitter clarity the tenuousness of Greek rule in Latin Italy. Liudprand even declares that to recover their position, the Greeks had to ask for help from the Emir of Africa.[1]

In 922 the Arabs again made an isolated raid, as a result of the murder of Muzalon. That year an Arab emir called Mac'ud captured the fort of St Agatha, close to Reggio.[2] In this same year the troubles of Italy were increased by a Hungarian raid as far as Campania.[3] In 923 the Arab treaty was probably renewed; there were no raids, and it seems likely that it was in this year that Symeon of Bulgaria, preparing for his last great attack on Constantinople, sent an embassy to Africa to secure the help of the African fleet, to supply the sea-power that he so badly needed. His ambassadors were returning successful and bringing with them the African ambassadors, when the whole party was captured by the fleet of the Calabrian theme. Romanus, hearing of the event, kept the Bulgar ambassadors, but wisely sent the Africans home to Africa with costly presents and an offer to renew the treaty and the tribute of Eustathius. According to Cedrenus, our only authority for this episode, the African monarch was so pleased by this friendly act, that he even agreed to remit half the tribute; and the Calabrians paid 11,000 gold pieces yearly, till the reign of Nicephorus Phocas.[4] But this treaty must frequently have been broken. From 925 to 928 Arab raids were frequent, and it was never a Greek characteristic to continue paying money uselessly. Gay places this treaty after the capture of Oria, that is to say in 925;[5] but as Cedrenus gives no date, it is much more reasonable to place it before Symeon's final attempt on Constantinople in 924. After 924 he never attacked the city, and so would never need the co-operation of an Arab fleet. Also, if the negotiations took place in 923, it would explain why in 923 and 924 there were no Arab raids against Calabria.

In 925 Arab raids recommenced; perhaps the lessening of the

1 Liudprand, *Antapod.* pp. 57–8.
2 *Camb. Chron.* Costa Luzzi, p. 42; Ibn-Adari, *V.P.* p. 148.
3 Gay, p. 206.
4 Cedrenus, II, p. 356. 5 Gay, p. 207.

Bulgarian menace had made the Greeks less eager to pay their tribute. In July a large Arab expedition from Africa, after raiding the coast, landed near Taranto and marched some fifteen miles inland to the wealthy town of Oria, where the stratege seems to have been residing. The town was taken by surprise (July 9) and utterly sacked. The Arabs placed the number of the dead at 6000 and the captives (which included the famous Jewish doctor Domnolo) at 10,000; Lupus merely states that all males were killed. The stratege himself was captured and paid an immense ransom to free himself and the town.[1] This triumph satisfied the Arabs for over a year; 926 passed peacefully for Calabria. But Italy was not free from raids; in July, Michael, Prince of Zachlumia, the arch-villain of Dalmatia and steady ally of the Empire's enemies, crossed the Adriatic and sacked Siponto (July 10th).[2] In 927 the Arabs repeated their Oria coup at Taranto; a fleet under the eunuch Saïn or Sabir, after raiding along the coast and capturing a town called Heran (Gerace?), finally, in August, fell upon Taranto, where, as at Oria, men of military age were slain and the remainder led off captive. The Arabs moved on to perform a similar triumphant feat at Otranto; but here they over-reached themselves; before they succeeded in entering the city they were visited by a pestilence of such dimensions that an abject return was necessary back to Africa.[3] In 928 Sabir raided again, recapturing Heran, and capturing Cal'at-al-Hasab (possibly Policastro); but this year he sailed up the Tyrrhenian coast to Salerno and Naples, and both of these states made haste to buy him off with money and with stuffs.[4] After this last raid the Greeks hastened to re-make peace with Africa,[5] a peace which was probably finally concluded next year: as in

1 *Camb. Chron.* Costa Luzzi, p. 42, Amari, p. 283; Ibn-Adari, *V.P.* p. 148; *Ann. Bar.* and Lupus Protospath. ann. 925, *M.P.L.* CLV, pp. 125–6. See n. 3 below.

2 *Ann. Bar.* ann. 928; Lupus, ann. 926, *M.P.L.* CLV, pp. 125–6.

3 *Camb. Chron.* Costa Luzzi, p. 42, Amari, p. 282; Ibn-al-Asir, *V.P.* p. 106 (year 925); Kitabu'l, *V.P.* p. 153. It is interesting that these raids all took place in the Greek land of Otranto. Was it the Calabrian or the Longobardian stratege that was residing at Oria in 925? I believe the former, but there is no means of telling.

4 *Camb. Chron.* Amari, p. 284; Ibn-Adari, *V.P.* p. 148; Nuweïri, *V.P.* p. 159.

5 *Camb. Chron.* Amari, p. 284.

929 Sabir raided Calabria once again, winning a tiny skirmish at sea and marching inland as far as Tiriolo, which he sacked.[1] This was his last raid; henceforward Byzantine relations with Africa seem to have been friendly, even remarkably friendly, which no doubt gave rise to the stories current in Liudprand's time of how the Byzantines ruled Italy with African help:[2] while the 'Amer' of Africa was given by the Greek Court the imposing title of 'lord of the Moslems'—ἐξουσιαστὴς τῶν Μουσουλημιτῶν —a title never allowed to its more rightful claimant at Bagdad.[3] The only break in these relations was at the time of the rising of Girgenti, when the Greeks were able to take the offensive in Sicily. It is significant that this improvement in the conditions of Greek Italy occurred shortly after the end of the Bulgar war. Romanus, with the Balkan question settled, now probably reinforced the garrisons of Calabria, so that the Arabs found it wiser to content themselves peaceably with their 11,000 pieces of gold.

Henceforward, the chief foes to the Byzantines in Italy were their vassals, the Lombards. In 926 the Prince of Capua and his nephew, the hitherto loyal Prince of Salerno, finally dropped their imperial titles.[4] In 929 Landolf re-invaded Apulia, and the country remained in his possession for seven years.[5] In the only pitched battle recorded between him and the Greeks the latter were victorious; but Theobald of Spoleto crossed the frontier to help the Lombards and restored their position.[6] Meanwhile, the Prince of Salerno was invading Lucania and fighting several

1 *Camb. Chron. loc. cit.*, Ibn-Adari, *V.P.* p. 149, calls the name of the town Termoli, but it is unlikely that Sabir should have ventured so far from his base with only four ships.
2 Liudprand, *Antapod.* p. 57.
3 *D.C.* p. 689.
4 Gay, p. 209.
5 Lupus Protospath. ann. 929, *M.P.L.* CLV, p. 126; Liudprand, *Antapod.* p. 108; *Leg.* VII, p. 179; Gay, p. 209, dates this revolt 926, presumably to coincide it with the drop of titles. But that would mean that the seven years, mentioned by Liudprand, would be over before 934; and it is most unlikely that Cosmas's small expedition should have at once won back all the province; in that case Epiphanius's embassy would have been pointless. Though Lupus is careless about dates, it seems unnecessary to doubt him when no other date is given.
6 Liudprand, *Antapod. loc. cit.*

skirmishes with the Greeks, the name of one of which, at Basantello, has survived.[1] This state of affairs lasted almost unchecked till 934, though authentic records of these years are very scanty. For all practical purposes the hinterland of Apulia and large tracts of Lucania and Calabria were lost to Byzantium.

However, the situation in the rest of Italy was more favourable to the Byzantines. In 924 the Emperor Berengar had been killed at Verona. In 926 his successful rival, Hugh of Provence, was crowned King of Italy at Pavia,[2] and soon he had made his kingdom a reality down to the confines of Rome. His ambitions now were concentrated on securing Rome itself. In Rome the energetic John X had in 928 been ousted from power by the Senatrix Marozia, daughter of his former patroness, and his place was now taken by Marozia's son (it was said, by Pope Sergius III), the boy John XI.[3] In 932 this sinister lady, ruler of Rome, was conveniently widowed, and she and Hugh, who had recently become a widower, agreed to unite their dominions by marriage. There followed a dramatic scene in the Castel Sant' Angelo, when Count Alberic of Tusculum, Marozia's son by a former marriage (with the Margrave Alberic), turned against his mother, driving Hugh out on his wedding night and imprisoning Marozia for her lifetime.[4] With the help of the Roman nobility, Alberic succeeded to the rule of Rome, and henceforward, for the next fourteen years, till Hugh's defeat by Berengar of Ivrea, Italian history centres round Hugh's struggle against Alberic for Rome. The result of all this was that both Alberic and Hugh were eager to pay highly for Byzantine support. Despite the rebel Lombards, Byzantium was still the great power of Southern Italy, and the alliance would ensure victory. Romanus took full advantage of this, flirting first with one, then with the other. In 933 Alberic sent legates with the Pope's blessing (John XI, his half-brother, was his prisoner) to attend the installation of the Patriarch-prince, Theophylact.[5] Next year

1 *Chron. Salernitanum*, pp. 549–50.
2 Liudprand, *Antapod.* p. 69 n., p. 81 n.
3 *Ibid.* pp. 95, 96; Gregorovius, *Rome*, III, pp. 278 *et seq.* In between there had been Pope Leo VI (928–9) and Pope Stephen VII (929–31).
4 Liudprand, *Antapod.* pp. 96 *et seq.*; Gregorovius, *Rome*, III, pp. 286 *et seq.*
5 Liudprand, *Leg.* 62, p. 210; Theoph. Cont. p. 422.

Hugh entered into negotiations with Romanus for an alliance against the Lombards, and in 935 the alliance was definitely made.[1]

This meant the end of Landolf's seven years' rule in Apulia. Already in 934 the Thessalonican Patrician Cosmas, a previous acquaintance of Landolf's, had crossed to Italy with an imposing escort of troops from all the east. Cosmas had an interview with Landolf, and requested him to evacuate Apulia; but Landolf, though politely acquiescent, did not altogether obey.[2] But next year, when the Protospatharius Epiphanius arrived, with all his presents for King Hugh and his vassals, the Lombard game was up. With the troops of the north in their pay, the Byzantines were too formidable; the Lombards made their submission, and by 936 had evacuated Apulia.[3] But it was very different from their submission after the Garigliano; the princes did not resume their imperial titles, and they even began to leave out the year of the Emperor's reign in their charters; their vassaldom was barely even nominal. Moreover, they did not stay submissive. In 936, probably on the return of Hugh's troops to the north and the Greeks to the east, Atenolf of Benevento led a raid to Siponto.[4] And in 940 there was a pitched battle between the Lombards and the stratege, in which the latter was probably victorious.[5] The relations between the Lombard princes and the stratege were hitherto always cold. By 955 another large expedition had to set out against them from Constantinople.[6]

The maritime States remained on better terms with the Empire. By about 920 Amalfi, hitherto consistently renegade, had changed her policy sufficiently to ask for help from Constantinople for the redemption of her citizens captured by the Saracens.[7] Later,

1 Liudprand, *Leg.* 7, p. 179; *D.C.* p. 661; Gay, p. 211.

2 *D.C.* p. 660; Cedrenus, II, p. 353.

3 *D.C.* p. 661. 936 is seven years from 929 (see p. 191, n. 5).

4 Gay, p. 211, quoting *Ann. Benev.* The year 936 was further complicated by a Hungarian raid as far as Campania (Lupus Protospath. ann. 936, *M.P.L.* CLV, p. 126).

5 Lupus Protospath. ann. 940, *M.P.L.* CLV, p. 126. Lupus calls the stratege "Imogalapto", and adds the cryptic sentence "et necavit Pao in mare". The text is obviously too corrupt for its meaning to be discovered.

6 The expedition of Marianus Argyrus.

7 Nich. Myst. Ep. CXLV, p. 372.

in about 935, Naples, when making a treaty with Capua, put in a clause preserving her allegiance to the Emperor;[1] and though by 955 the Neapolitans were notorious rebels, that time had not yet come. But the history of their relations to the Empire during these years is very obscure; the growing rebelliousness of Naples may have made Gaeta and Amalfi more loyal to the Emperor; but all we know is that at the time of Romanus's fall there were Gaetan and Amalfitan embassies at Constantinople.[2] And as additional reasons for friendliness there were the rivalry of the Lombard States, and the revival of Byzantine sea power along the Tyrrhenian coast.

Thus, from 936 onwards, Byzantine Italy was enjoying as much peace as it ever had enjoyed. Since 929 the Saracens had no longer been a menace; and the Greeks had largely recovered the mastery of the seas. Indeed, in 931 a Greek fleet pursued a squadron of marauding Arabs right into their harbour Fréjus.[3] In 938 the Greeks were themselves able to take the offensive, for in that year Sicily revolted against the Saracens. The native population rose in all parts of the island, led by the inhabitants of Girgenti. In most places they were soon overcome by troops sent over from Africa; Girgenti, however, remained for some time independent. It was helped with men and particularly with provisions from Byzantine territory; its first siege, by Halil, governor of Sicily, was unsuccessful; and it was not till September, 941, after a second siege lasting eleven months, that the city was captured, and even then the citadel held out. Most of the inhabitants were allowed to cross to Calabria, but others were treacherously taken to Palermo, which frightened the citadel into surrender. Its more illustrious citizens were taken from Sicily and set on the high seas in a pierced boat, and they were drowned;[4] and thus Sicily re-entered into bondage.

Tragically though the revolt ended, it had been most con-

---

1 Gay, p. 246, quotes treaty.

2 Liudprand, *Antapod.* p. 143.

3 Flodaord, ann. 931, *M.P.L.* cxxxv, p. 441. The Saracens in 935 were able to raid Sardinia and Corsica and sack Genoa (Ibn-al-Asir, *V.P.* p. 112; Ibn-Adari, *V.P.* p. 149; Nuweïri, *V.P.* p. 159).

4 Ibn-Adari, *V.P.* p. 149 (year 937); Ibn-al-Asir, *V.P.* p. 112 (revolt, end of 938, Girgenti captured Sept. 941); *Camb. Chron.* Costa Luzzi, p. 44. Girgenti was taken November 20th.

venient for Byzantium. Not only was Calabria filled once more with loyal Greek refugees—a class of society very useful to Byzantine Italy—but also the Arab power was put out of action for three years and more. The Byzantines kept the offensive till after the fall of Romanus. In 941 ambassadors passed between Pavia and Constantinople to plan the destruction of the notorious Saracen colony of Fréjus; King Hugh was to attack by land, and the Greeks by sea. Next year the attempt was made; as at the Garigliano the Greek ships carried all before them, and the sailors, with the Italians, were able to storm the town. But Hugh, having entered Fréjus, had an attack of nerves; he sent away the Greek fleet and made an alliance with the Saracens against his rival Berengar of Ivrea. The Saracens proved unconscientious allies, and the whole work was undone.[1]

Meanwhile, Romanus was enjoying to the full the rivalry between Alberic and Hugh. The eager goodwill of each of them had solved his Lombard difficulties for him; but he was careful not to commit himself too far—at least with Alberic; Hugh was rather more powerful. Alberic sought to establish an alliance by marriage; he had dreams of a Greek princess for his bride;[2] and he offered his own sister as a bride for one of the young emperors. Romanus found this a little too definite, so he politely said that his son could not come to Rome, as was suggested; but could not the young lady be sent with her mother (her most suitable chaperone) to Constantinople?[3] Alberic was too wise to comply with this innocent request; the mother was Marozia, lingering in her prison, but still a figure of importance; it was by means like this that Byzantium acquired those most useful of diplomatic weapons—pretenders to foreign thrones. The negotiations were quietly dropped. With Hugh, Romanus felt that he could go a little further. He was looking for a wife for his eldest surviving grandson, Romanus, son of Constantine Porphyrogennetus; and at the time of the Fréjus treaty he enquired if Hugh had an eligible daughter. Hugh had to reply, rather timorously, that

1 Liudprand, *Antapod.* pp. 135, 139.
2 Gay, p. 222, quoting Benedict Soracte. Alberic actually married Hugh's only legitimate daughter.
3 Du Chesne, *L'Etat Pontifical,* p. 175 (I cannot find his original authority)

the only one left was illegitimate; she was, however, very beautiful. Romanus, on receipt of this news, reflected that, after all, his grandson was not a Lecapenus, and accepted the bastard Bertha.[1] In 944 the young girl was brought from Italy by Paschalius, Stratege of Longobardia, and, accompanied by the elderly Bishop of Parma and extremely sumptuous presents, arrived in Constantinople. There she was re-named Eudocia (a family name in the Macedonian house) and married in September to the young Romanus.[2] She died five years later, still a virgin—the first of the tragic procession of Western Empresses of the East.

This was the last passage between the Courts of Hugh and Romanus. Early in 945, when Hugh and Alberic were still quarrelling at the gates of Rome, and Berengar of Ivrea was looming in the background, news came through of the fall of Romanus and all the Lecapeni, and the triumph of the Porphyrogennetus.

Whereas the tendency on the eastern frontier under Romanus was towards the growth of the Byzantine power, on the western frontier it was slightly towards its decline. In Greek Calabria and the land of Otranto the Byzantine hold was firm, and Byzantine influence was as strong as in any province of the Empire— the Greek language was spoken for many centuries to come, and Byzantine laws merged into the laws of the land even into the days of the Normans.[3] But in Latin 'Longobardia' and among the vassal States the hold could never be anything but weak. The difficulty was not so much the racial difference—for that was a difficulty that Byzantium had often overcome elsewhere— as the religious and cultural difference. Latin Italy would not look to Constantinople and speak the Greek that served as the national language to the Empire. It was Rome that dominated the peninsula and made success impossible for Byzantium. So long as the Pope and Emperor agreed, all might be well, particularly if the imperial armies visited the country to drive off the Saracen and remind the natives that Byzantium though far

1 Liudprand, *Antapod.* p. 137.
2 Theoph. Cont. p. 431; Liudprand, *Antapod.* p. 141.
3 For the survival of Romanus's law of pre-emption, see Brandileone in *Cent. Nasc. Amari*, I, p. 38.

away was watchful and powerful: particularly when the north passed from adventurer King to adventurer Emperor and knew no government that outlasted a generation. But the seeds of decay were there, with the growing divergence of the Orthodox and Catholic Churches, seeds that would grow, watered by Popes and German Emperors, into a crop that the Normans would reap. It was a decay that Constantinople could not prevent.

It is a misfortune to Romanus's apparent record that his government began at the height of Byzantine prestige after the Garigliano, with grateful subjects and officiously dutiful vassals; for when it closed the vassals were openly disobedient and inciting the subjects to revolt. But to blame him for it would be ridiculous; the Garigliano triumph, that gave Byzantium her heightened prestige, also removed the fear that bound the vassals to their suzerain; and the chaos of the central government during the Bulgar wars was a deadly opportunity. It is to Romanus's great credit that, faced with these problems, he not only staved off the Saracens but succeeded in the end in keeping the Lombards within their own borders, thus by diplomacy and the occasional show of arms giving to Byzantine Italy a short, rare peace; and the outward effect of his policy is shown by the eagerness of his neighbours to woo him to their side. It was impossible for a Basileus to do more.

With the western powers outside of Italy neither Romanus nor the regency governments immediately preceding him seem to have had any dealings. It was no rare thing for embassies to pass between Constantinople and the Courts of France and Germany; and with the latter affairs in Central Europe, in Hungary or Croatia, would often introduce new grounds of amity or dissension.[1] But during Romanus's reign no such occasion arose; Romanus had no need to look further than Italy, and consequently entered into relations with no one more remote than Hugh of Provence, whose headquarters were fixed in Lombardy.

1 D.C. p. 689; an embassy was sent from Constantinople to congratulate Otto of Saxony after his victory over the Hungarians at the Lechfeld in 955. Previously, under the last German Carolingians, there had been coolnesses over the work of Cyril and Methodius, and the Carolingian intervention in Croatian politics.

With the Saracen Court of Cordova the Empire seems to have been on excellent terms and to have had fairly constant dealings, particularly in the years that followed Romanus's fall.[1] This intercourse, though it never led to any practical result, was probably intended to awe the Abbasids, whose hereditary enemies the Spanish Moslems were. Of the history of the western Mediterranean islands very little is known. The Balearic islands were under the Spanish Moslems; Corsica was probably in a state of complete lawlessness. Sardinia, on the other hand, was a recognized Byzantine possession. But all we know about it is that it was liable to Saracen raids,[2] that it was ruled by an ἄρχων who received the Emperor's κέλευσις,[3] and that its ἄρχων wrote in Greek, occasionally enjoyed the title of Protospatharius and was usually called Turcotorius.[4] But whether his vassalage weighed at all on his shoulders we know nothing.

The relations between Constantinople and Rome deserve further comment; for they were of a delicacy unique in history. As I have shown, Rome was to a great extent both the means and the end of Byzantine rule in Italy; but had the Romans and the Byzantines seen each other with logical eyes there could never have been peace between them. Rome and New Rome were inevitable rivals. The Byzantines were οἱ Ῥωμαῖοι, their Greek language the γλῶσσα τῶν Ῥωμαίων, their land was known throughout the world as Romania, the land of Roûm; and their Basileus was, in unbroken descent, the Roman Emperor of the world. Rome, on the other hand, though it could not compete in political continuity, was Rome, and ecclesiastically its descent was unblemished, with a long line of bishops headed by St Peter, bishops whose consequent supremacy was in some way acknowledged throughout all Christendom. The Basileus might be the

---

1 D.C. p. 664; Notice sur. Abou Iousouf Hasdai, p. 5.
2 As in 935 (Ibn-al-Asir, V.P. p. 112) when Corsica was also raided.
3 D.C. p. 690.
4 Besta, La Sardegna Medioevale, pp. 48–50, quotes three Greek inscriptions from Sardinian churches, which he dates roughly 930, 965 and 1000. In each the archon is called Turcotorius, in the second he is Protospatharius, in the third imperial aspatharius.

world's Emperor; but the Pope was lord of its Church which
he considered authority enough to raise counter-Emperors—
Charlemagne and his successors and later the Ottos. This was
an infringement of the monopoly of the Basileus; to Byzantium
none of these counter-Emperors, however wide their domains,
could be more than ῥῆξ; and for Rome to raise them to the level
of the Basileus logically implied the breaking of relations with
Constantinople. Equally fatal to good relations was the religious
question; there again the functions of Pope and Caesaropapist
Emperor must clash; and the Greek-speaking East could never
acknowledge the rule of the Latin-speaking West. In recent years
this difficulty had been heightened by the work of vehement
controversialists such as the Patriarch Photius, and by the missionary work of Cyril and Methodius, whose system was in
direct opposition to that employed by the missionaries from
Rome: while also in the creed divergencies were creeping in.

In view of all this, it is surprizing that Rome and Constantinople should ever be on terms of other than deadly enmity. Yet
during the greater part of the reign of Romanus their relations
were of an emphasized cordiality. Though fundamentally it was
impossible for the Pope and the Emperor to escape from rivalry
and antagonism with each other, superficial tendencies were
continually apt to draw them together into amity. The Emperor,
who was often involved through a determination to maintain
his Caesaropapism in quarrels with the Patriarch of Constantinople, found it of great value to play as a trump card the sanction
of St Peter's representative on earth; even in the East the prestige
of the Roman bishopric was stronger than that of the comparatively parvenu patriarchate of Constantinople; and the Pope, for
his part, was glad to accord his sanction, as the appeal enhanced
his dignity, and he knew he could never hope to govern more
intimately the Church of the East. Also, for the government of
Southern Italy, the Papal alliance was of inestimable value against
the restive Latins: while the Pope, or whoever was master of
Rome and the Papacy, often found the power of western kings
or emperors too menacingly strong, and as a counterpoise was
eager to seek the alliance of the great power of Southern Italy.
Thus it was not so very surprizing that embassies passed

frequently between the two Courts, that the Emperor was prepared to address the Pope as his spiritual father,[1] and that even the Patriarch liked to have papal approval for his more controversial actions.

The value of the Roman alliance was well realized at Constantinople; but it was not always easy to achieve. In the early years of the tenth century the schism between Leo VI and his widow and the Patriarch Nicholas caused the Imperial Court to enter into a close rapprochement with Rome: one of the direct results of which, under Zoe's rule, was the victory of the Garigliano and the docility of the Lombard vassals. Nicholas's triumph, when Romanus became Emperor, ended this alliance, and thus largely contributed to the troubles that simultaneously broke out in Southern Italy. Romanus himself was always extremely anxious to return to good relations, but Nicholas was an unsurmountable obstacle. Despite the patriarchal apologies, written no doubt at the Emperor's request (but in which the humility always sounded a little strained), Nicholas could never be an acceptable friend to a Pope so conscious of the papal dignity as John X. At last, in 923, he condescended to send legates to Constantinople, to use influence to induce the Bulgars to make peace with the Empire; but though Nicholas had made an overwhelming concession in admitting that the papal influence might be of value and even asking for it, thus showing the Byzantine anxiety to close the breach, the reconciliation was abortive; John had not really forgiven Nicholas. The Bulgars ignored the legates then; but two years later they received legates sent on a very different errand. John was unfriendly enough to the Emperor to give his sanction to the imperial title assumed by the Bulgar monarch. Meanwhile, to the detriment of Byzantium, he held two synods at Spalato[2] which captured Croatia for the Roman Church. Nicholas's death in 925 and John's fall in 928 eased the situation; the nonentities that succeeded to the papal tiara were less disposed to reject Romanus's overtures.

1 D.C. p. 686.

2 I must here insert a word of protest against the Croatian historians (such as Šišić and Manoïlovitch) who see the Council of Spalato as the result of the entente between Rome and Constantinople. The idea is manifestly absurd. See below, Chapter x.

Finally, when in 932 Rome and the Pope fell into the hands of Alberic, Romanus's patience was rewarded. Alberic, in his anxiety to maintain himself in Rome, would pay anything for Byzantine friendship; the Pope would refuse the Emperor nothing now. Romanus took the opportunity of disarming ecclesiastical criticism by securing papal support for his most cynical act of Caesaropapism—the installation of a hippomaniac child on the patriarchial throne. And the papal alliance, particularly in conjunction with its zealous rival the alliance with Northern Italy, made it a comparatively easy task for Romanus to keep his Latin subjects and vassals in control. The entente between Pope and Emperor lasted past Romanus's days, on till the coming of the Saxon kings to Rome. Fundamentally the entente was false and forced; but the diplomats of Byzantium were masters of tact—discreet silences and amiable blindness veiled the logical chasm. How necessary were the veils was shown a century later, when Michael Cerularius with dogmatic honesty tore them aside and laid bare the rift to all the world; and Byzantium lost Italy for ever.

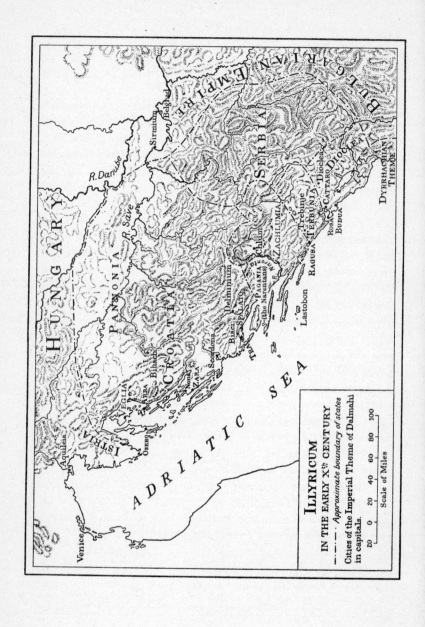

HUNGARY

R. Danube

R. Save

PANNONIA

CROATIA

ISTRIA

VEGLIA

ARBA

Aquileia

Osero

ZARA

Bihach

Nona

Scardona

Biaci

Spalato

Delminium

DIOCLETIA

PAGANIA
(the Narenians)

THE NARENTA

Chlum

ZACHLUMI

Sirmium

Belgrad

SERBIA

BULGARIAN EMPIRE

Trebunje

TERBUNI

Diocleia

Cattaro

Rosa

Ragusa

Budua

DIOCLEA

SEA

DYRRHACHIAN
THEME

Lastobon

ADRIATIC SEA

Venice

ILLYRICUM

IN THE EARLY Xᵗʰ CENTURY

— · — · — Approximate boundary of states

Cities of the Imperial Theme of Dalmatia
in capitals.

Scale of Miles

20   0   20   40   60   80   100

CHAPTER X

The Southern Slavs and Illyricum

I N the Western Balkans and up the Illyrian coast to Venice
at the head of the sea lay the Empire's third group of vassal
States, the principalities of Serbia and Croatia, and the seaports
of Dalmatia. To the statesmen of the Bosphorus their comparative isolation made these vassals of less anxious import than the
vassals of Asia and Italy; nevertheless, a recent combination of
circumstances had brought them into unusual prominence and
faced the Emperor with several irritating problems. Illyricum
was passing through a crisis that enforced the world's attention.

The vassals were of varied races and governments. The Dalmatian towns along the coast, Ragusa, Spalato, Trau, Zara, Arba,
Veglia and Osero, still officially counted as a theme of the
Empire, under a stratege resident at Zara;[1] but in practice they
were treated rather as a series of independent vassal States:
which indeed they were. Racially their inhabitants were a mixture of Latin, old Illyrian and Slav; culturally they were purely
Latin, looking like the Apulians across the sea to Rome as the
mother of their civilization and their faith. For more than two
centuries they had almost forgotten their connection with the
Emperor, whose fleet no longer sailed their waters and who lived
far away beyond the hostile heathen Slavs. It was only within
recent memory that St Cyril on the one hand and the imperial
reorganization of the navy on the other had changed all this, and
the Emperor Basil, rescuing Ragusa from the Saracens, had
reminded them of their allegiance. Meanwhile, their old-established culture and their impressive list of martyrs and churches
gave them great prestige among their neighbours.

1 *D.A.I.* pp. 128, 147. In Greek the towns were called ʽΡάουσιν, ʼΑσπάλαθον,
Τετράγγουσιν, Διαδώρα, Ἄρβη, Βέκλα and ʼΟψάρα. Constantine talks elsewhere
of Decatera (Cattaro)—*ibid.* p. 139—as though it belonged also to this group,
but as it is not mentioned among the towns (these same seven) that paid
tribute to the Slavs, it was probably under the jurisdiction of Ragusa.
Certainly the two towns were religiously connected.

The States of the hinterland around and behind them were purely Slav by race. Since the days of Heraclius these Southern Slavs had been the official vassals of Constantinople;[1] and lately St Cyril and the imperial revival had made this vassaldom less of a nullity; but actually these States fell geographically into two distinct divisions, and history followed geography. The smaller division, inland Serbia, looked towards Bulgaria and Constantinople in the distance; the larger, Croatia and the maritime Serbian principalities, sloped down to the Dalmatian coast and looked ominously across the sea to Rome. Indeed, already Croatia had had far more dealings with the Carolingian Emperor than with the Basileus.

Inland Serbia, Serbia proper, was therefore, in Byzantine eyes, the most important and the most satisfactory of these vassals. It consisted of the country round the lower valleys of the Morava, the Drina and the Bosna: though Bosnia was still a separate canton.[2] Civilization was probably on a slightly lower plane than in Bulgaria; there were towns, and a great trade route passed through the country; but the Serbs were mostly farmers. The organization was vaguely on a feudal basis. There was the chief prince with his Zupans under him; but while some were merely great lords without any territorial power, others were territorial magnates, some, such as the Prince of Terbunia, frankly independent. The princely throne was probably nominally elective by the Zupans;[3] actually the princes all belonged to one family, a large and quarrelsome family of which every male member had ambitions for the crown. In religion, as a result of St Cyril's work, they were spotlessly orthodox; and their conversion had really brought them into the sphere of Byzantine influence. This influence was further strengthened by the growth of Bulgaria. The Serbian prince had even more to dread from Bulgar aggressions than the Basileus; and the common fear made an alliance inevitable. Indeed, during the first half of the tenth century, Serbian history is entirely taken up by the wars of Symeon and their consequences.

---

1 *D.A.I.* p. 159.   2 *Ibid. loc. cit.* 'Τὸ χωρίον Βόσωνα', p. 159.
3 Symeon summoned the Zupans to receive Tzeesthlav when he appointed him prince (*Ibid.* p. 158; see below, p. 206).

At the beginning of the tenth century the Prince of Serbia was Peter, who had stolen the thròne from an elder cousin about the year 893.¹ His reign had been successful; as yet Bulgaria was at peace with the Empire, whose dutiful vassal he remained, and he consequently was able to develop his country without hindrance. About the year 915 he even extended his dominions, conquering the principality of the child Tiescimir 'King of Serbia' (almost certainly prince of Bosnia), bringing his frontier close to the coast and sharing the spoils with Michael, Prince of Zachlumia.² But meanwhile war had broken out between the Empire and Symeon of Bulgaria, and inevitably before long Peter was drawn into the net of the Empress Zoe's active diplomacy. About the time of the Achelous (August, 917) Michael of Zachlumia, who steadily opposed the Empire and had perhaps quarrelled with Peter over the division of Tiescimir's land, revealed to Symeon the extent of the Byzantine-Serbian negotiations; and Symeon, taking advantage of the Greek collapse, determined to strike first. In 918 he invaded Serbia, bringing with him as a pretender to the throne Peter's cousin Paul, whose father Peter long ago had blinded. Peter was defeated and surrendered; he was treacherously taken off to die in Bulgaria, and Paul was installed in his place.

Paul did not long live in peace on his Bulgar-built throne. In 920 the Byzantines, reviving under the new Emperor Romanus, incited and aided another princely cousin, Zacharias, an exile in Constantinople, to make an attempt on his country. With Bulgar help Paul defeated the invader, and in gratitude sent Zacharias to be a prisoner and hostage in Bulgaria. But three years later Paul himself was seduced by the Byzantine diplomats into realizing how unnatural was his Bulgar alliance, and turned against his benefactors. As usual, Bulgarian arms triumphed, and the hostage Zacharias superseded Paul as prince. But then

1 *Ibid.* p. 155–6.
2 Farlati, III, p. 87. This refers I imagine, to the episode recorded in Junius Restius's Ragusan chronicle in which Tiescimir an infant King of Bosnia was despoiled by all his neighbours except Terbunia (*Chron. Rag. Jun. Rest.* p. 26). The date given by the editor in the margin is 925 and Farlati gives the same date. As I can find no reason for choosing 925 rather than any other year, I have preferred an earlier date which seems to me to fit better. Peter, whom Farlati mentions by name, was dead in 925.

the inevitable cycle returned. Zacharias, remembering his youth at Constantinople and following the natural Serbian policy, soon broke with the Bulgars, and for a while resisted them successfully. Symeon's first punitive expedition (in 925), led by his generals Marmaëm and Theodore Sigritze (the former conquerors of Peter), ended in disaster and the generals' heads were sent as a delectable gift to Romanus. But Zacharias was only postponing his fate. Next year Symeon sent out another army, strengthened by the presence of a new pretender, the half-Bulgarian prince Tzeesthlav. It was too formidable for Zacharias, who fled into safe obscurity in Croatia. The Serbian Zupans were then summoned, under the promise of safe-conducts, to receive Tzeesthlav as their prince; but on their arrival he and they were taken off in chains into Bulgarian prisons; while the Bulgars, unchecked, set about the conquest of the country.

The Bulgar conquest was performed with a thoroughness and a ferocity remarkable even in those days. The whole land was turned into a desolate wilderness and the inhabitants fled in despair to their Greek or Croatian neighbours. Even though late in the year the Bulgar armies met with disaster in Croatia and though next May Symeon himself died and his Empire immediately crumbled, it was not till 933 that the Serbians dared to attempt to recover their independence. That year Tzeesthlav escaped from captivity and returned to Serbia. He found it a desert; in the former great city of Preslav there were only fifty men, womanless and childless. However, Romanus, eager to ingratiate himself with such useful allies, sent money and robes to Tzeesthlav to help him re-establish his principality; and gradually the exiles returned from the countries around. In gratitude Tzeesthlav undertook to be a good vassal of the Empire, and fulfilled his promise. Under these satisfactory circumstances, neither the Porphyrogennetus nor his contemporaries have any more to tell us about Serbia.[1]

Thus Serbia submitted wholeheartedly to Byzantine influence and became a Balkan State. Had the Bulgarian menace been less, Serbia might easily have reacted against Constantinople and

[1] D.A.I. pp. 153 et seq. See also above, Chapter v, pp. 86, 87, 95, where I give reasons for the dates.

joined her maritime neighbours in looking to the West; but, as
it was, geography put Serbia too close to Bulgaria, so that Bulgarian greatness was bound to threaten Serbian independence,
and the Serbians had to look to the Emperor for help. Once the
Byzantine alliance was made, it was inevitable that Serbia,
emerging during these years from heathendom and barbarism,
should fall under the spell of Byzantine civilization. These years
set the tone of her whole future history, giving her on the one
hand a dangerous yearning to found a Balkan Empire, but on
the other an orthodox Cyrillic Church whose Slavonic nationalism would carry her through all her disasters to her present-day
supremacy among the nations of the Southern Slavs. The good
vassal was rewarded in time.

But Serbia stood alone. The western group of Southern Slav
vassals was far from being so satisfactory. Of these, the most
important was Croatia. Croatia in the tenth century roughly
included the modern provinces of Croatia, Slavonia and the
western parts of Bosnia, and extended along the Adriatic coast
from about Fiume to the river Cetina.[1] The northern parts of
this territory had belonged to the separate kingdom of Pannonia,
but by Tomislav's reign were certainly Croatian.[2] This geographical position was of great importance to Croatia. She was
far removed from the dangers of Byzantine arms; though, if
necessary, it was comparatively easy to make the journey to
Constantinople by sea. On the other hand, the Latin cities of
Dalmatia, situated on her littoral, kept up a constant connection
with Italy and Rome, a connection bound to have its effect,
particularly as the Croatian monarchs were always magnetized
by the culture and the holiness of the Dalmatian cities. Even
the chief foreign danger for Croatia had come from the Latin
West, in the shape of the Carolingian Empire: which had indeed
during the ninth century established a suzerainty over the Croatians. Now, however, the Germans were weak, and the only
menace came from the central Danubian plain, where the wild
Hungarians were establishing their power.

Thanks to these foreign connections Croatian civilization was
on a far higher plane than the Serbian. There was the same

1 See map.   2 Drinov, p. 45.

semi-feudal organization—the King or Grand Zupan and under
him fourteen Zupans or (for the three northern districts) Bans
with territorial power and minor jurisdictions.[1] But the country, more compact than the straggling valleys of Serbia, was
easier to govern; the monarchs did not undergo the same catas-
trophic falls as the Serbian princes, and the throne tended to
pass peaceably from father to son: while from their palaces at
Nona or Biaci they issued and recorded decrees in a way un-
imaginable in Serbia.[2] They also kept up a formidable army;
Constantine estimates its strength as having recently been 60,000
cavalry and 100,000 infantry.[3] However, in spite of this culture
and strength, Croatian history is very obscure; and it is an
insoluble problem even to give the names of the tenth-century
monarchs in their proper sequence.

During most of the ninth century the supplementary evidence
of Carolingian and papal diplomatic papers enables us to identify
and arrange the various Croatian princes. We learn that the
throne was occupied successively by Vladislav (c. 821–835)—the
actual dates are all uncertain—Mislav (c. 835–845); then Trpimir,
the founder of a new dynasty (c. 845–865); Trpimir was succeeded by Domagoi (c. 865–876), a member of a different family,
possibly related to Mislav. It was under Domagoi that the
Frankish suzerainty was finally thrown off. Domagoi was succeeded by his son Iliko (876–8); but he was soon dethroned by
Trpimir's son Zdeslav (878–9). Zdeslav was in his turn over-
thrown by Branimir (879–892), whose family is unknown. On
Branimir's death, Trpimir's younger son, Zdeslav's brother,
Mutimir, succeeded; and here our knowledge ends.[4]

Constantine Porphyrogennetus is the only author to give us
any consecutive history of Croatia during these following years.
He mentions a monarch, Trpimir, then his son (but not necessarily his successor) Crasimir, followed by his son Miroslav, who,
after a reign of four years, was dethroned by a rebellious Ban,
Pribunia.[5] There his information, supplied without any dates,

1 D.A.I. p. 145.   2 Lucius, II, pp. 65, 67.   3 D.A.I. p. 151.
4 Šišić, Geschichte der Croaten, pp. 72–120, who gives full references to the
original authorities.
5 D.A.I. pp. 149–151. Constantine also says (loc. cit. p. 126) that the Croatian
princes all belonged to one family.

stops; nor has he anything to say about the earlier history of Croatia, beyond a legendary and muddled account of its conversion to Christianity. On the other hand, we know from Thomas Archidiaconus and from the records of the Councils of Spalato that a certain Tomislav was on the throne in 914 and again in 925 and 927.[1] The Priest of Dioclea, who professes to give a full history of the Southern Slavs, gives no help, as his list of names has no connection with any verified fact.[2] It is not till we reach a second Crasimir, the husband of a certain Helena and the father of Stephen Drzislav (c. 969–997), that we tread again on firm ground.

Farlati, the first serious historian of Illyricum, solved the difficulty by making Mutimir die about 900: whereupon his brother Crasimir succeeded. Crasimir died about 914; his son Miroslav reigned four years, and was deposed by the rebel Pribunia, who, after two years of civil war, was himself deposed by Tomislav, a prince of uncertain origin, who reigned some twenty years, till about 940. His successor was Godimir, who was followed by Crasimir II.[3] Whence Farlati drew his dates and the name Godimir, I do not know; he constantly gives information without quoting any source, and though he may have had access to oral traditions or written material now lost, the information inevitably inspires no confidence. Certainly he ignores Thomas Archidiaconus's very positive assertion: "Joannes Archiepiscopus fuit anno Domini nongentesimo quarto decimo tempore Tomislavi ducis":[4] which can only mean that Tomislav was reigning in 914. Farlati's view held the field till the days of Drinov, who declared categorically that there were no grounds for placing any reigns between those of Mutimir and Tomislav, and who placed the four monarchs of the Porphyrogennetus one after the other, after Tomislav's death.[5] The modern Croatian writers, headed by Šišić, patriotically eager to preclude the possibility of a blank in their country's history, adopt and amplify this sequence; Šišić places Mutimir's death c. 910, followed by

1 Thomas Archidiaconus, p. 321; Farlati, III, p. 92.
2 Presbyter Diocleae, p. 290. He says that Tomislav succeeded his brother Vladislav and reigned thirteen years. He gives no indication of dates.
3 Farlati, III, p. 84.
4 Thomas Archidiaconus, loc. cit. 5 Drinov, p. 44.

Tomislav (910–928), Trpimir II (928–935), Crasimir (935–945), Miroslav (945–949), the usurper Pribunia (949) and so to Crasimir II (949–969).[1] But sympathy with the Croatians for so happily rounding off Croatian history should not make us forget that after all the vital evidence is that provided by Constantine in the *De Administrando*. The *De Administrando* was written about the year 950; Bury fairly conclusively has shown that the Croatian chapters were written in 948 or 949.[2] If therefore Šišić's dates are correct, Constantine was informed about Croatian affairs with a promptitude in remarkable contrast to the dilatoriness of his information about the other Illyrian States. In the other Illyrian States Constantine has heard of no monarch later than Prince Michael of Zachlumia, and of Michael's actions the only one that he records took place in 917.[3] He seems never to have heard, for example, of Michael's nefarious raid on Byzantine Italy in 926. To argue from silence is rash, but when there is no other argument it is obligatory. Constantine makes no mention of the Councils of Spalato or even of the name of Tomislav;[4] and of the Bulgar invasion of Croatia in 926 his news clearly came only from Serbo-Bulgar sources. It is, therefore, only reasonable to conclude that Constantine did not possess any very recent information about Croatia and the other Illyrian States: that, owing to an easily explicable coldness between the Dalmatian and Croatian States and Constantinople, no diplomatic missions had lately passed to and fro; and so Constantine could only relate what was already rather old history. Indeed, Croatia's behaviour during these years was of a sort that must have prevented the Empire from entering into any friendly relations, and it must have been practically impossible for Constantine to keep up to date in Croatian history.

1 Šišić, *op. cit.* pp. 121 *et seq.*, *passim.*

2 Bury, *The Treatise De Administrando Imperio,* p. 574. He dates the Dalmatian chapter 951.

3 This was Michael's betrayal to Symeon of the Serbo-Byzantine negotiations that year (*D.A.I.* p. 156); but Constantine could have found that information from Serbian or Bulgar sources.

4 It is fashionable among certain Croat historians to identify Tomislav with Constantine's Terpemer. Drinov began the theory; and though Rački (Doc. 399) and Šišić oppose it, Manoïlovitch has reverted to it (*Sbornik Kralja Tomislava*, introduction, *passim*). There is, however, no argument to support it; and Constantine is usually rather careful about names.

In view of this it seems unreasonable not to return to Farlati's sequence, modifying the dates.. It is unnecessary to introduce a second Trpimir; the scanty evidence is best satisfied if Mutimir died about 900 and was followed by his brother Crasimir, son of Trpimir; Crasimir must have been old by now and reigned only a short while, till about 908; his son Miroslav reigned four years, *c.* 908–912, and was killed by the rebel Pribunia, during whose troubled times Croatia's strength rapidly diminished. This was the last that Constantinople heard authentically of Croatia. The Bulgar war broke out and diverted Byzantine attention; and difficulties arising out of the schism with Rome and the independent airs of the Croat rulers prevented relations from being resumed. So Constantine was unable to record Croatia's recovery under the Prince Tomislav, who acquired the throne some time in the chaos following Pribunia's revolt (*c.* 913) and reigned on till 930 or beyond.

Tomislav alone of these monarchs is more than a name to us; and of him we know very little. He was present at the Councils of Spalato;[1] he took to himself the title of king;[2] and it was almost certainly he that defeated the Bulgar invasion in 926, in a war that broke out owing probably to Symeon's jealousy of his power and fear of his designs on Serbia.[3] The vague-minded Priest of Dioclea represents him as overcoming the invasions of Attila, King of the Hungarians;[4] and it is indeed likely that he had to meet and repulsed Hungarian invaders. As his religious policy showed, he was a good friend of the Roman Pontiff, who rewarded him by recognizing his royal title and by arranging a peace between him and the Bulgars in 927. The date of Tomislav's death must remain unknown and we are equally ignorant

---

1 See below, pp. 217 *et seq.*

2 He is so addressed by the Pope in the papers relating to the Councils of Spalato. See below, *loc. cit.* Thomas Archidiaconus, however (p. 320), calls Drzislav the first king. This apparent discrepancy is explained by the fact that Thomas, a dutiful citizen of Spalato, only recognized the title when the suzerain of Spalato, the Basileus, did so: which was not till Drzislav's reign.

3 See above, Chapter v, p. 95.

4 Drinov (p. 45) makes him also conquer Southern Pannonia from the Carolingians (I do not know his evidence for this) and parts of Bosnia, so as to make Croatia abut on to Serbia in 926. But their neighbourhood might be equally explained by Serbia's conquest of Tiescimir's kingdom. We have not the evidence to be positive.

about his successor, whether it was Farlati's Godimir or no; even Crasimir II's dates can only be a matter of loose conjecture. It is disappointing to have to admit so much ignorance; but the scheme of Šišić and his followers, though beautifully finished, is dissonant with the little evidence that there is. The Croats must console themselves with the thought that after all there is no disgrace in having a decade or two without history; indeed, to accept it is less undignified than to behave like an old man who spaces out unnaturally his few remaining hairs in order to hide up his baldness.

South of Croatia, between Bosnia and Serbia and the Adriatic, were the minor Serbo-Croat principalities. The most northerly of these was the land of the Narentans, divided up between three zupans and stretching down the coast from the river Cetina (Zentina) to the river Narenta (Orontius). The Narentans were pagan and predatory and on a very low level of culture; Constantine, who calls the country Pagania, talks of its inaccessibility, which prevented either conquest or civilization. It contained a few inhabited towns; but on its subject islands, Cuzzola, Brazza and Meleda, once so prosperous, the towns were all deserted.[1] Of its history or the names of its rulers nothing has transpired. The inhabitants occupied themselves in profitable piracy—it seems unopposed except for a slight attack by Nicetas Oryphas in 870 and a disastrous Venetian attack in 888,[2] until in 948 an expedition of thirty-four ships from the Venetians (probably the greatest sufferers) caused a temporary check.[3]

Beyond the Narentans, down to the walls of Ragusa, was the principality of Zachlumia. The Zachlumians, said by Constantine to be of Serbian origin, were Christian and more civilized; they had five inhabited cities. Their prince Michael, son of Buzebutze, who was reigning certainly in 913 and still in 926, was the most considerable figure in the Southern Serbo-Croat world, and he seems to have built up a hegemony over the States around. He had at one time kept up a diplomatic correspondence with the Imperial Court where he was given the titles of anthypatus and patrician.[4] But he soon showed himself to be a very unsatis-

1 *D.A.I.* pp. 129, 146, 163.   2 *Vita Basilii*, p. 293; Lucius, II, 2, p. 64.
3 Dandolo, XIII, 6, p. 198.   4 *D.A.I.* p. 160.

factory vassal; despite the titles and his Christianity, his true profession was piracy, directed mainly against the Empire and its respectable subject-ally, Venice; and he soon allied himself with the Empire's arch-enemy, Symeon of Bulgaria. In 913 he captured the son of the Venetian doge, who was returning from paying his respects at Constantinople, and sent the captive as a present to Symeon.[1] In 917 he reported to Symeon the Byzantine intrigues in Serbia, thus enabling Symeon to strike first.[2] In 926 he went so far as to cross the Adriatic and sack the town of Siponto in Byzantine Italy.[3] He also, like Tomislav, committed himself religiously to Rome and was present at Spalato.[4] His bad behaviour towards the Empire may only have been due to rivalry with its protégé, Serbia, whose ally he had once been in despoiling the child Tiescimir of Bosnia, and with whom he had probably since quarrelled; but he seems to have adopted the definite policy of preventing wherever possible a recrudescence of imperial influence in Illyricum. The memory of Basil's squadron was not dead; but Michael was determined that such an incident should not recur. Of the date of Michael's death or of the subsequent history of Zachlumia we know nothing.[5]

The country south of Zachlumia, from Ragusa to Cattaro, was occupied by the principality of Terbunia or Canale, a Serbian State officially owing allegiance to the princes of Serbia. It contained five inhabited towns, and was ruled by Tutsemer, son of Phalimer and great-grandson of the Serbian prince Vlastimer.[6] We have no information about Tutsemer's dates or about his country's further history. From the fact that it is never mentioned in Serbian history during these years, we may presume that its allegiance did not weigh heavily on its shoulders.

1 Dandolo, x, p. 198.
2 D.A.I. p. 156.
3 Lupus Protospatharius (ann. 926) and *Annales Barenses* (ann. 928), pp. 125–6; *Ann. Beneventani* (ann. 926); Manoïlovitch, *op. cit.* p. xxi, actually calls this a move to help the Byzantines against the Lombards—the fruit of a grand Croat-Byzantine alliance that he has invented.
4 See below, p. 218.
5 Farlati, iii, p. 86, says that Michael died in 932.
6 D.A.I. p. 161. In D.C. (p. 691) Constantine mentions the archons of Canale and of the Trabuni (Terbunians) separately, but in D.A.I. he states positively that the land of the Terbunians and the Canalites is the same.

Most southerly of all these principalities was Dioclea, approximately the modern Montenegro, called after a deserted city of that name. It contained three large inhabited cities, but for the most part was rough and unconquered, and without any recorded history.[1] It was probably the country known to the Hungarians and the western nations as Rascia. Beyond its southern borders lay the imperial theme of Dyrrhachium.

Dotted down this long littoral were the Dalmatian cities, precariously placed between the Slavs and the sea. In their traditions and their culture the inhabitants were purely Latin; but their nominal allegiance to Constantinople had been unbroken for centuries. They were famed for their saints and relics, which gave them great prestige among the newly-converted Slavs; however, politically they were not accorded the same respect, but were obliged to pay yearly tributes to the princes of the hinterland—varying from the 200 nomismata paid by Spalato to the Croatians to the 72 nomismata paid by Ragusa, half to the Zachlumians and half to the Terbunians.[2] Of these towns Ragusa led the freest life; in one passage Constantine calls it the metropolis of the whole country, and certainly it was the head of a little group of towns, Budua, Rosa and Cattaro.[3] It was fortunate in having in its hinterland only the rival princes of Zachlumia and Terbunia instead of the powerful Croatian king. Thanks to this, Ragusa was already developing its independence, which was to last so many centuries; despite Constantine's words, it was rapidly becoming a thing apart from Dalmatia with a history of its own. Of that history during the early tenth century nothing is known except for an occasional visitation of the plague.[4] The true centre of the country was at Spalato. The size of its yearly tribute indicates that Spalato must have been large and prosperous. Moreover, it was the ecclesiastical metropolis; the Archbishop of Spalato was primate of Dalmatia and as such took the lead in local government. His figure occurs

1 *D.A.I.* p. 162.

2 *Ibid.* p. 147. Zara paid 110 nomismata, Arba, Osero,Veglia and Trau each 100, all to the Croatians.

3 *Vita Basilii*, p. 289. From that narrative it seems that those towns followed closely the lead of Ragusa.

4 *Chron. Rag. Jun. Rest.* p. 27.

again and again in Dalmatian history. Dalmatia had, however, a stratege appointed from Constantinople.[1] On the two occasions on which his name has survived, he was a local magnate, the Mayor of Zara.[2] Zara must, therefore, have been the seat of such Greek administration as there was in Dalmatia, and also the base from which Greek influence was disseminated. It is significant that Nona, whose bishop was the great champion of Cyrillism, is situated under twenty miles from Zara.

Of recent years Greek influence in Illyricum had undergone a revival. Byzantine suzerainty had always been recognized in Dalmatia even by the Carolingians; and among the Slavs had been admitted officially since the days of Heraclius.[3] But by the first half of the ninth century it was purely nominal. The change came in Basil I's reign. Among the Slavs it was wrought by the missionary zeal of Cyril and Methodius. The conversion of the Southern Slavs, like their political submission, stood originally to the credit of Heraclius; but their Christianity had since been very fitful and uncertain. Cyril's Moravian missions had given the Church new life, and his introduction of the Slavonic liturgy brought Christianity within the comprehension of the whole Slav peoples. In the first enthusiasm everyone looked with grateful respect to Constantinople, whence Cyril had come; and the imperial prestige rose to an unprecedented height. Meanwhile, the Dalmatian cities, cramped by the Slavs and robbed by the Narentans, had their position made still more intolerable by attacks from the Saracens who had already established a foothold in Southern Italy. Eventually a grand Saracen siege of Ragusa forced them to turn to the one quarter from which they could hope for help—to Constantinople. Basil was alive to the Saracen danger and sent out a small squadron under the admiral Nicetas Oryphas, who relieved Ragusa, and sailed ostentatiously up the whole coast, reminding the inhabitants of their obligations towards the Emperor. The demonstration was effective, and soon afterwards the Dalmatians in grateful vassaldom sent a detachment to help the imperial troops in the recovery of Italy

1 *D.C.* p. 697. He was one of the strateges who found his salary out of the local revenues.

2 Lucius, I, p. 50; II, p. 81.

3 *Vita Basilii*, p. 293; *D.A.I.* pp. 231 *et seq.*

from the Saracens. At the same time Basil further eased their position by reducing the tribute that Constantinople demanded from them (it had probably been seldom paid) and by arranging for them a regular standardization of their tribute to the Slavs. This bow to necessity, disguised as a piece of generous good government, finally confirmed Dalmatian loyalty; and even Croatia, impressed by the ships and the business-like terms, entered into a brief phase of humble obedience.[1]

Unfortunately, Oryphas's fleet, sailing back to Dyrrhachium, took away with it the main foundation of this new prestige. A decline set in. During Leo's reign the Byzantines were too busily occupied with troubles nearer home to concern themselves with the distant harmless Dalmatian theme: while the Dalmatians, freed from the Saracens and on satisfactory terms with the Slavs, could afford to forget Byzantium. Meanwhile, the Slav princes, gazing with eager admiration at the relics crowded in Dalmatia, began to be more impressed by Dalmatian Christianity, the Christianity of Rome; and like the Bulgarian princes they discovered that Rome would give what Constantinople withheld. They decided to forget Constantinople.

It is difficult to tell exactly how much influence was left to Byzantium in Illyricum at the time of Leo's death. There is no record of the Empire having affected any of the main events in Illyrian history during the following years, except as regards Michael of Zachlumia; on the contrary, the chief incident of the period, the Church settlement of Spalato, took place without the assistance of any imperial official and in defiance of the imperial policy. Even Tomislav's war with Symeon, a war that must have pleased the Byzantines, probably only arose out of rivalry between the two kings in Serbia and cannot have been in any way caused by Byzantine diplomacy. Tomislav, as his religious polity and his royal title show, could ignore the very existence of the Empire; and consequently the Emperor Constantine can give no recent information on Croatia. Zachlumia, further south, was more conscious of the imperial power, though Michael, anthypatus and patrician, was able to carry out his acts of impertinent defiance quite unpunished. The Terbunians and the

1 *Vita Basilii*, p. 293; *D.A.I.* pp. 131 *et seq.*

Diocleans tended more to follow the lead of Serbia and so probably freely acknowledged imperial suzerainty; but they were both rough barbaric states, of insignificant importance. The Narentans were distressingly independent of any control. The Dalmatian cities were probably more subservient; certainly they always stood firmly by official imperial etiquette;[1] and though, as at the Councils of Spalato, they might omit to mention the Emperor, they never actually forgot him—the Slavs might always come to threaten their liberties, and they would have to have recourse once more to Byzantium.[2] Meanwhile, the Emperor, having nothing to fear from Illyricum (so long as Serbia stayed loyal) turned his attention elsewhere, content to leave the policing of the Adriatic to the Venetians.

The great proof of the decline of Byzantine influence in Illyricum is to be found in the ecclesiastical settlement of Spalato. For some time the position of the Illyrian Churches had been extremely awkward. On the one side there was the Dalmatian clergy of the coast cities, Latin-speaking and under the jurisdiction of the Archbishops of Spalato, for centuries past loyal servants of the Papacy. On the other hand, recently introduced by St Cyril's missions, there was the Slav clergy of the interior, who used the Slavonic liturgy and were less meticulous in acknowledging the papal supremacy. Conflict was bound to rise; the Dalmatian bishops, conscious of their old-established faith, were offended and horrified by these parvenu Slavs, worshipping in a barbarous tongue and disobeying the Holy Father; the Slav bishops were proud of their popular liturgy and jealous of their freedom. Meanwhile, the secular powers waited, a little uncertain how to act.

In 914 there was appointed to the See of Spalato an active prelate, John III, who was determined at all costs to stamp out the Slavonic liturgy; and about the same time John X, the most active of the tenth-century Popes, ascended the papal throne. The Cyrillic clergy was led by the Bishop of Nona. Already

---

1 E.g. Thomas Archidiaconus's refusal to give Tomislav the title of king.

2 Constantine professes to tell of events in Dalmatia μέχρι τῆς σήμερον (*D.A.I.* p. 137). I do not think that this should be taken too literally.

there had been a certain rather unfriendly correspondence
between the Papacy and a previous Bishop of Nona, Theodosius,
and Theodosius's successor Adelfrid had taken proceedings
against the Archbishop Peter II of Spalato.[1] But John III
brought matters to a final head in his controversy with Bishop
Gregory of Nona, and the Pope determined to intervene and
settle the matter once and for all in favour of Spalato and the
Latins. In 924 papal legates passed down Croatia and Dalmatia
and summoned a Council to meet at Spalato; and the Pope wrote
two letters, one an official letter to the Archbishop, directed
against the doctrines and methods of Cyril and Methodius: the
other a declaration to King Tomislav of Croatia, Duke Michael
of Zachlumia, John the Archbishop of Spalato and all the zupans
and all the bishops and all the people of Slavonia and Dalmatia,
firmly condemning the use of the Slavonic language in churches.
The Synod met that year; owing to the greater number of their
bishops and probably also to lay support, the Latins were easily
victorious. In the decrees of the Council the Slavonic liturgy was
banned and the jurisdiction of the See of Nona was carefully
defined and limited and placed with all the province of Croatia
under the supremacy of the See of Spalato. These drastic decisions did not at once bring peace; Bishop Gregory chafed
under the restrictions and hunted for loopholes. Finally, in 926
the Pope wrote again to the Archbishop, summoning him and
Gregory to Rome for a final settlement. This proved impracticable; and so next year the papal legate Madalbert, returning from
Bulgaria where he had been giving papal sanction to Symeon's
title of Emperor, paused at Spalato and held a second Synod, less
impressively attended than the first but equally Latin in temper.
The decrees of 924 were reiterated and the rights of the See of
Spalato upheld. On Madalbert's return to Rome, the new Pope,
Leo VI, who succeeded John X in June, 928, approved his
decisions and hastened to send the pallium to John as primate of
Dalmatia and Croatia. At the same time he wrote to the bishops of
the province enjoining them to obey the metropolitan of Spalato.[2]

1 Šišić, *Priručnik*, pp. 195, 199 *et seq.*; *Geschichte der Croaten*, I, pp. 110,
115 *et seq.*
2 Farlati, III, pp. 92 *et seq.*; Šišić, *Priručnik*, pp. 211 *et seq.*—both quoting
in full the letters and decrees; also Šišić, *Geschichte*, pp. 132 *et seq.*; Šišić dates

The Latins had won, and Illyricum passed with no more resistance under the religious sway of Rome. John III lived on in the primacy for another decade. After his death in 940 there followed the thirty years' rule of the Archbishop Fruntianus, during whose primacy nothing worthy of record occurred;[1] that is to say, the Christian world of Illyricum lived on in peace. Zachlumia and its subject-parts of Bosnia followed Croatia's lead and entered the Roman fold. Terbunia swayed between the two rules; only Dioclea in the south and Serbia over the hills remained Cyrillic and Orthodox, loyal to the culture of Constantinople.[2] Isolated throughout Illyricum a few little Cyrillic strongholds lingered, keeping their Slavonic liturgy and their strange Glagolitic script even to this day. But these rare unimportant relics came to be good-humouredly tolerated by the Roman hierarchy, who managed to embrace them under the device of the Uniate Church.

The settlement was natural enough. A conflict was inevitable; and in a conflict the Latin clergy, far cleverer and more astute than the Slavs, with history on their side (for had not Illyricum been always considered a Roman province?) and a consciousness of the reverend age of their Church, would never be the ones to yield. The Slavs had no such background; they were newcomers into the fold; their original champions, the holy brothers, were dead; Constantinople, whence they might have had support, was far away and out of touch; and in any conference they were bound to be outnumbered and outwitted. Nevertheless, Croatia might have been saved for Cyrillism had it not been for the action of the princes. Tomislav and Michael came down on the side of the Latins. The reason is not, I think, far to seek. Apart

---

the Councils 925 and 928. I know of no reason for preferring these dates. As regards the second, certainly Madalbert seems to have left Bulgaria while Symeon still lived, i.e. before May, 927; and though he presumably did not reach Rome, much, if at all, before Leo VI's election (June, 928), it is probable that the Council was held before the New Year. The authenticity of the letters and decrees is now, I think, no longer challenged. See authorities quoted above.

1 Farlati, III, p. 109.

2 To-day in Bosnia and Herzegovina (Bosnia, Zachlumia and Terbunia) the Orthodox outnumber the Catholics by about two to one. But the Catholics much more than the Orthodox were affected by the Bogomil heresy and later turned Moslem under Turkish rule.

from the impression that the Christian past of the Dalmatian cities made on all the Slavs—the princes used to try to be buried within their precincts—ambitious rulers such as Tomislav and Michael inevitably longed to take complete possession of the coast; and that task would obviously be made much easier if the prince could show himself to be in complete religious sympathy with the Dalmatians—especially as their present suzerain, the Basileus, patronized an increasingly divergent Christian system. Moreover, the Pope outbid the Emperor in a flattering willingness to bestow titles. Moved by these considerations Tomislav and Michael were caught by the papal bait and brought their states into the western comity of nations.

Nevertheless, it is impossible not to question the wisdom of the move. The Bulgar monarchs, who knew how to play Rome against Constantinople without committing themselves, were finer statesmen than the Croatians. Bulgaria won an independent Church, on a national Slavonic basis; and though her independence was periodically taken from her, the nationalism remained and kept Bulgarian consciousness alive through all the darkness. Serbia, too, found her Slavonic Church an equally vigorous national strength. But Catholic Bosnia and Catholic Croatia had no such backbone. Bosnia, after suffering more painfully than any other land from the Bogomil heresy (a vain Slav attempt to found a Slav Church, which Bulgaria, its birthplace, was able to overcome) turned wearily Moslem on the coming of the Turks, and lost her national consciousness. Croatia, less afflicted by heresy, fell soon into the arms of a greater Catholic power, Hungary; and both, even to-day, though at last they are united with fellow-Slavs, are finding themselves the subordinate parts of a nation. The great countries of Western and Northern Europe were able in their rude youth to take advantage of the blessings of Catholicism and in their middle age to temper or to shake off its control, so fatal to their individualism. But in South-eastern Europe, in lands perpetually weakened by cataclysmic invasions, the great international Church had only an enervating effect. That much-abused Greek, Lucas Notaras, who preferred the turban of the Turk to the hat of a cardinal, was a profound statesman. In the long run the infidel did less harm.

While Illyricum was airing its independence and passing this ominous milestone, Constantinople remained all the time very indifferent. Tomislav's royal title and Latin sympathies might wound imperial pride and show imperial powerlessness, but they did not really matter. The coming of the Hungarians had broken the solid Slav block that had at one time threatened to dominate Eastern Europe; now Illyricum provided no menace and could be ignored. So long as Greek influence was paramount in Serbia and Venice kept down the Adriatic pirates, nothing else mattered. Even the Dalmatian cities, imperial theme though they were, brought little money to the Empire and were of little strategic importance; a Greek stratege at Zara would keep sufficient watch on the few Greek interests there. The Strateges of Cephallonia and Dyrrhachium kept open with their ships the passage to Italy; further up the sea the Emperor was content to leave things to Venice. It was enough that the forms of official etiquette were observed. And for the most part they were observed; Dalmatia remained meticulously correct in form for over a century more, till the days of Manzikert; and even Croatia, despite all Tomislav's bravado, waited for the same disaster to Byzantium before daring to throw off entirely the imperial yoke and have her King Svinimir crowned independent monarch by the Pope.

Venice, the future heir to Byzantium of the riches of the East, as yet only showed faint indications of her coming greatness. It is not the place here to give a history of Venice, but only to record her relations with regard to Byzantium and the Byzantine policy in Italy and the Adriatic. In the early years of the tenth century the city-state had been established for a century on the Rialto, and the system of government by doges was two centuries old. By now, though the basis of the State was still democratic and the people would if necessary take the law into their own hands, the government was falling more and more into the power of the great families, and the office of doge showed signs of becoming purely hereditary.[1] The Venetians were, as regards official actions, probably the most dutiful of the vassals of the Empire; till 976 the Emperors' names appeared at the

1 *Camb. Med. Hist.* IV, chap. XIII.

head of every state document, and prayers were said for the
Emperors in the churches; and the obligations of transport as
laid down in Imperial Bulls were fully recognized. It has been
often said that this dutiful vassaldom was purely nominal; but
considering that Venice already had trade interests in the East,[1]
she clearly had to appease the greatest power of the East. Certainly there is no doubt that Venice looked to the East for her
culture and all her mode of life; and the influence of Byzantium
is stamped ineradicably, almost to the exclusion of all others, on
the truest mirror of the soul of a people, her art.

But though Venice was a Byzantium *in miniature*, Byzantium
herself left her alone as regards the affairs of the Upper Adriatic
and Northern Italy, only restricting her actions as regards the
more intimate enemies of the Empire.[2] This was due to indiffer-
ence at Constantinople as to what might happen in those distant
parts. Venice had shown at the time of the Carolingian supremacy her refusal to become part of a western continental Empire;
and as her disposition was always friendly towards her eastern
suzerain, it was safe to let her control the Upper Adriatic and
even build up a little territorial state; and no interference was
made in her relations with the changing north Italian kingdoms.
Consequently, Venice made her own treaties with the Italian
monarchs; in 924 King Rudolf recognized the Venetian right to
coin money;[3] and about 930 King Hugh renewed the treaty.[4]
About 933 the Venetians, in an endeavour to put down piracy,
captured Commachio and annexed the city of Justinopolis,[5] and
defeated by means of a trade blockade the jealous Marquis of
Istria.[6] And in 948 the Venetians took it upon themselves to
send a large expedition against the Narentan corsairs.

The Venetian fleet was growing to be the most powerful in
the Adriatic. Already in 840 the Venetians had been able to fit
out sixty ships for the unlucky expedition to Taranto to aid the
Greeks against the Saracens. In 948 the squadron sent against

1 The extent of her interests at this time is impossible to define. But as early as
829 Venetian merchants had brought back the body of St Mark from Alexandria.
2 Forbidding her to trade in arms or timber with the Saracens.
3 Dandolo, x, p. 198.   4 *Ibid. loc. cit.*
5 *Ibid.* xi; Const. Porph. *D.A.I.* p.121, recognizes ' Justiniana' as a Venetian city.
6 *Camb. Med. Hist.* iv, chap. xiii, p. 401.

the Narentans consisted of thirty-four ships; and these thirty-four ships were probably chelandia or large biremes, not the smaller vessels that would have composed the expedition of Taranto. Byzantium had apparently a right to call upon the fleet whenever necessary, a right not infrequently used in the early ninth century. By the tenth century Byzantium, with her own sea power greatly revived, seems to have required the help of the Venetians no more, but to have left to them the Upper Adriatic: until, under the Emperors Basil II and Constantine VIII, the police-work was formally assigned to them, and thus their future was assured.

The doges of the period were first Ursus Particiacus II (912–932), who sent his son to Constantinople as a mark of respect; the young Ursus was received with honour, but on his return was captured by Michael of Zachlumia and sent, to annoy Byzantium, to Symeon of Bulgaria, from whom he had to be expensively ransomed. Ursus's successor was Peter Candianus II, son of the doge who had been killed by Slav pirates in 887. Peter, like Ursus, sent his son to pay his respects at Constantinople—with happier results, for the youth returned safely, bringing his father the title of protospatharius. In 939 there followed Peter Baduarius Particiacus, grandson of Ursus II; he died in 942 and was succeeded by Peter Candianus III, to whom, two years later, his envoys at the Imperial Court sent, in some detail, the story of the fall of the Lecapeni.[1]

Had the Byzantines been able to foresee the Crusades and the consequent growth of Venetian power, and the terrible mock-Crusade of 1204, they would scarcely have treated Venice with so much complaisance. But as yet that fatal story was dim in the future, and even the Seljuks were still in Turkestan; at present, it was all to the interest of Venice to keep on friendly terms with Byzantium, and it saved Byzantium much unnecessary trouble and expense to leave to Venice the affairs of the Upper Adriatic. Meanwhile, Venice profited by intercourse with the capital of civilization; and the result of the intercourse was St Mark's.

1 Dandolo, x, xi, xii, xiii, p. 198.

CHAPTER XI

The Land Laws and other Legislation

THE main interest and importance of Romanus's reign lies in his foreign and colonial achievements, in his victories and settlements on the many frontiers of the Empire. He was, however, responsible for a piece of internal legislation of the greatest significance for the Empire, a determined attempt to stay a tendency that was well on its way to ruin the whole basis of the imperial government. This was the question of land tenure, a question considered but unsolved by Romanus's predecessors but which now was demanding an answer. The Emperor was faced in the provinces with the disappearance of the small peasant-farmer, the depopulation of the countryside, and, most sinister of all, the accumulation of vast estates in the hands of single families, whose hereditary power was beginning to resemble that of the feudal barons of Western Europe. The organization of the Empire, so well centralized for centuries, was beginning to show signs of devolution.

To understand the difficulties, we must go back to the earliest years of the Empire. In those days large portions of the land were held by peasant-proprietors; they lived in village communities, and, for the obvious convenience of the imperial treasury, were taxed according to their communities—a slightly unfair arrangement but one that gave each peasant an interest in his neighbour's welfare, and thus indirectly ensured very little careless farming. The rest of the land was divided up between the estates of the rich; and under them worked peasants of two kinds: free tenant-farmers, working their farms themselves and paying a rent to the owners, and enjoying all the rights of freedom, except that after thirty years of tenure they and their families were considered bound to the soil: and labourers in the employ of the landowners, also nominally free, but in reality serfs bound to the soil, with only a few privileges to raise them above the status of slaves.

Barbarian invasions and the official transplantations of population altered the land systems—amongst other innovations,
communities holding the land in common now appeared. The
Isaurian emperors met these innovations with a very definite
policy, abolishing serfdom, and putting tenants into a new, freer
relation with the landlords. The landlords naturally objected to
this with persistent energy; and indeed it may have had the
effect of depopulating the countryside. Adventurous peasants'
sons, like Basil the Macedonian, would be induced to leave their
homes and try their fortune in the towns. Anyhow, yielding to
the landlords' pressure, and perhaps relying on his own judgment and experience (though the growth in the landlords' power,
with the rise of the great semi-feudal families, would make the
pressure decidedly formidable), Basil repealed the Isaurian
reforms, and tenants sank back into serfdom.

This was the more agreeable to the landlords, in that their
estates were increasing vastly. The only two safe investments
for capital in the Byzantine world, where the atrocious Roman
credit system[1] continually hampered trade, were land and minor
government posts, both of which could be bought and would
yield a reasonable interest; and the former was the more attrac-
tive. Consequently, the wealthy bought up land as fast as they
could, and by the end of the ninth century enormous estates had
been formed; the widow Danielis, Basil's former benefactress,
owned almost all the Peloponnese.[2] These estates, especially as
they were provided with a fixed reliable number of tenants paying regular rents or services, gave to the land-owners ominous
importance and power. And piety led to the same result; proprietors would feel a call to enter into monasteries, taking their
land with them under monastic rule, or they would bequeath
it to monasteries at their deaths. Thus the archimandrites vied
with the nobles, and both vied with the Emperor.

The Emperor began to be alarmed. The rich magnates, with
their wealth so well invested, were a menace to the imperial
authority—as the troubles of the latter half of the eleventh
century were to prove. In the tenth century this was becoming
apparent; it is now that we have the first signs of the great semi-

1 See below, Appendix III.   2 Theoph. Cont. p. 319.

feudal families of Byzantium; the Phocae, the Argyri and the Ducae are coming to the front with hereditary power. The feudalism, against which Constantinople had for centuries battled, was now creeping in. Also, the growth of great estates, besides being harmful to the agricultural profession, was inconvenient to the imperial treasury. When a magnate bought up a small proprietor's land, his irruption into the village community not only was disagreeable to the other small proprietors of the village, but also it disorganized the taxation of the community. In addition it damaged the army. The soldiers, for the most part a hereditary class, were largely paid by the gift of free and officially inalienable smallholdings; but now the magnates were absorbing by whatever means they could these hereditary holdings, and the subsequent generations of soldiers required new provision. It was therefore not surprising that the imperial policy was firmly opposed to the territorial aggrandizement of the magnates.

The early Macedonian emperors were veering towards this policy, but Romanus was the first Emperor to carry out an aggressive campaign. It might have been wiser to supply, by reforming or, better, abolishing the credit laws, some other safe investment of capital; but that was unthinkable in the tenth century. Romanus was more direct. In 922 he issued his first famous statute on pre-emption. By its terms magnates (οἱ δυνατοί) could only acquire estates, by purchase or by gifts, from the small proprietors, when they were their relatives; and in any case ten years had to elapse, during which the property could be redeemed, before the possession became permanent. In order of pre-emption, the first precedence was given to relatives, next to co-proprietors, then immediate neighbours and then to members of the same unit of taxation, and of the same community. It also attempted, by similar limitations, to stop and remedy soldiers' disposals of their land.[1]

Such a method was not likely to be successful, and nature conspired with the magnates. The winter of 928 was of the most remarkable severity—in Constantinople the ground was frozen

---

[1] *Leunclavius Novellae Constitutiones*, pp. 9–12; Zachariae, III, pp. 234 *et seq.*; Dölger, p. 72. Bury, appendix 12, in Gibbon, *Decline and Fall*, v, pp. 530 *et seq.*

for a hundred and twenty days. This brought about a terrible famine,[1] and, unluckily, was followed by a series of very poor harvests. In these circumstances all that the farmers could do to save themselves from ruin and starvation, was to pledge their lands to the magnates—the only pledge that the magnates would accept. And it soon became apparent that the necessary ten years would elapse before the farmers could possibly expect to be rich enough to redeem the land. Romanus again came to their rescue. In the autumn of 934 he issued another statute, cancelling all such transactions that had taken place since September 1st, 927; but he did not venture to be too severe, and made careful provisions about compensation for improvements, though these were arranged so as to make the magnates gain as little as possible. And severe penalties were laid on anyone who might attempt to break these laws in the future. A further clause ordained that owners who became monks might only bring the price of the land, not the land itself, with them to the cloister.[2]

These drastic laws were a brave attempt to check the evil, and at the time they may have had some success. Certainly they remained in force, and were copied in such distant provinces as Southern Italy. But, however well Romanus may have had them administered—and he seems to have been an excellent administrator—their effect was not lasting. Three years after his fall, Constantine Porphyrogennetus was obliged to issue a new statute on the same lines; and such statutes followed each other throughout the rest of the century. To the sad surprise of the Byzantines, this State intervention ended in failure, and things became worse than before. In the eleventh century the country-side was even more depopulated, and the magnates were even richer and more powerful. Local dynasties arose in Europe to combine with the families of Asia in dealing disastrous wounds to the authority of the crown.

The other statutes of Romanus's reign were only of minor importance. His predecessors had almost all been energetic law-givers, and recently Basil I and Leo VI had just finished the task of bringing Justinian's code, already revised by Leo III, fully

1 Theoph. Cont. p. 417.
2 *Leuncl. Nov. Const.* 37; Dölger, p. 77; Bury, *loc. cit.*

up to date. Romanus could rest on their laurels, and occupy himself merely with philanthropic schemes in the true tradition of Byzantine benevolent despotism. He added to the city recreation grounds, and he made the useful innovation of building hostels for litigants who had come up from the country. His charters, such as survived, nearly all are concerned with the endowment of churches and monasteries, work in which he took a much admired interest, though modern writers see in it rather a misguided piety that helped to undermine the Empire. He also would perform an occasional act of ephemeral indiscriminate charity as when he kindly, if foolishly, paid all his subject's debts and rents out of the Treasury—a proof that his reign must have been financially satisfactory. His laws, such as they were, seem to have been competently carried out, and his whole administration ran with a smooth efficiency.

Paternalism was the keynote of all Byzantine legislation. The Emperor treated his subjects like children, interfering in all their quarrels, controlling their careers and daily life, and doling out to them occasional arbitrary presents. The system was not wholly unsuccessful; and though in dealing with grave economic problems it pathetically broke down, we must remember the state of economic theory in those days and the position of the Empire islanded among barbarians, and be charitable to the zealous Emperors who acted according to their lights.

CHAPTER XII

The Fall of the Lecapeni

A STRONG usurper can rule till his death; a weak usurper is doomed. As old age came on, Romanus Lecapenus lost his health and his vigour, and acquired a conscience, and his hold over the government weakened. The young Lecapeni, who had long chafed under their father's control, saw him now publicly announce that he would give back the crown to the legal dynasty, that the forgotten Porphyrogennetus should follow him into the imperial supremacy,[1] and they realized that the future would pass them by, unless they struck first. But their sister, the wife of the Porphyrogennetus, herself well endowed with the ambition of the Lecapeni, was steadily watching them, jealous for her husband's interests. The air in the Palace was tense. Only the old Emperor, chatting piously for hours on end with his monks, or resting his weary body after the fatigue of government, seemed never to notice the storm that was driving up.

The populace of the city noticed it, for omens had directed their gaze. In December, 943, the Demi in the circus—the circus party-headquarters, that stood just opposite to the imperial throne—collapsed in a tempest.[2] A few months later there came to Constantinople from Armenia two 'Siamese twins', whose bodies were joined together facing each other. Romanus was disgusted, and firmly sent the evil portents away.[3] Then sinister tales began to be told about the reception of the Image of Edessa. Something was surely going to happen.

The reception of the Image of Edessa was the grand climax of Romanus's reign, but the hymns chanted in its honour were the swan-song of the Lecapeni. To the Greeks of his day the surrender of the image had been the most valuable result of all

---

1 Theoph. Cont. p. 435.   2 *Ibid.* p. 431.
3 *Ibid.* p. 433. They returned to Constantinople during the next reign, but soon one died, and the other could not be separated in time.

John Curcuas's victories; and indeed it might well be considered a symbol of the new spirit of conquest in the east. Its arrival therefore was accompanied with the most reverent ceremony. It arrived at the Bosphorus in August, 944; the Paracoemomene Theophanes had met it at the river Sagaris, and it crossed to Europe above the city. Romanus went to worship it privately at Blachernae; then, on August 15th it entered formally through the Golden Gate and was met by the three junior Emperors and the Patriarch—Romanus himself was too unwell to appear in public. A triumphal procession led by these anointed princes carried it through the city, and brought it to its resting-place in St Sophia. But strange miracles marred the proud pleasure of the Lecapeni; it was said that Romanus's sons could only see a blurred countenance on the picture, but the Porphyrogennetus clearly distinguished the features—a portent that the holy monk Sergius interpreted very unfavourably for the former. Moreover, as the image passed through the streets, a possessed man cried out suddenly: "Constantinople, take the glory and the blessing, and you, Constantine, your throne."[1]

The young Lecapeni did not improve their position by their conduct. Romanus, old and ill, made no attempt to control them but let them go unrestrained, like the sons of Eli to whom Sergius would frequently compare them.[2] Of their private excesses only vague hints have reached us; but of their political mischief we have one very definite example. In 943 Romanus wished to find a bride for his eldest surviving grandson, Romanus son of the Porphyrogennetus and Helena,[3] and thought of Euphrosyne the daughter of his faithful and distinguished friend John Curcuas.

---

1 Theoph. Cont. p. 432; *De Imagine Edessena*, p. 448; Symeon Magister, p. 470; Cedrenus, II, p. 321.

2 Theoph. Cont. p. 434. Liudprand on the other hand says that they revolted because they were tired of parental severity. That seems unlikely in view of the stories about their influence.

3 It must have been he and not Romanus son of Constantine Lecapenus, as Theoph. Cont. and the other chroniclers say. The Slavonic version of the Logothete (p. 41) alone calls it the Porphyrogennetus's son. The whole story becomes pointless if it was a Lecapenus involved, unless perhaps it was a son of Christopher's; but his son Romanus was dead. Besides we know that Romanus was looking for a bride for the Porphyrogennetus's son, whereas the other Romanus was, two years later, still of an age to be successfully castrated.

But this match, uniting the interests of the legitimate heir with those of the hero of the hour, did not at all suit the young Lecapeni; they insisted on the matter being dropped, and the young Romanus married shortly afterwards an illegitimate princess from Italy. But henceforward the Lecapeni looked on Curcuas with suspicion and jealousy—he was powerful and popular, and he must have hated the men that had stood between his daughter and the throne. Their first attempt to discredit him before Romanus failed, but in the end their persistency triumphed. Towards the end of 944 Curcuas was dismissed, and an imperial relative Pantherius became Domestic in his place.[1] At once Byzantine arms in the east met with disaster.[2]

As for Romanus himself, he was ruled by his conscience. Death seemed near to him, and he was frightened. He had stolen the throne, by intrigue and perjury, and the guilt weighed heavily on him. He was only an uneducated superstitious sailor with a strong leaning to religious practices. He began almost wildly to repent. He had always been attracted by the society of monks, now he had come hardly to see anyone else. Of these his most intimate friends were Photius's nephew, Sergius, a figure famed for uncompromising virtue, and Polyeuct, the future patriarch.[3] Under their influence he took to good works, to wholesale acts of indiscriminate charity or intolerant piety. The latter consisted in banishing from the Empire all Jews and all Armenians who would not convert to orthodox Christianity:[4] the former in extreme generosity with the public money; on one occasion he even remitted all the debts and rents in the city at a cost to the imperial purse of over nineteen centenaria.[5] But as he had originally no right to the imperial purse, Zonaras was justified in commenting that it was like cooking an ox and only giving the feet to the poor, and in adding that such repentance did not succeed in the eyes of the world, whatever it might do in the eyes of Heaven.[6] Romanus himself realized this, and

1 Theoph. Cont. pp. 426, 429.
2 Saïf-ad-Daula's victory in December 944 near Aleppo.
3 Theoph. Cont. pp. 433-4.
4 Maçoudi (Barbier de Meynard), II, pp. 8, 9; Chamich, II, p. 84.
5 Theoph. Cont. p. 429.
6 Zonaras, III, pp. 478-9.

his conscience still tormented him. In 943 when he made his will, he expressly gave his son-in-law the Porphyrogennetus precedence over his own sons; then assured that restitution would be made in the end, he returned to the company of his monks.[1]

But the end came sooner than he had expected. His sons realized quite well that on his death, if their brother-in-law came into power, they would be thrust into obscurity; monastic seclusion would probably be the best fate for which they could hope. Their only chance was a sudden *coup*. Their action may have been unfilial, but it was not unnatural; fear alone might have dictated it, and in addition they were ridden with ambition. Accounts differ as to how the intrigue started. Later chroniclers, who for some reason disliked the Porphyrogennetus, accuse him of having incited the sons against their father; but, whatever Helena may have done, such subtle villainy was very alien to his amiable mildness. It seems that Stephen Lecapenus was the ringleader, and that his brother Constantine, a finer character, was rather unwillingly dragged into it—Stephen as the elder had more at stake. Working with them was Marianus Argyrus, an ex-monk, the Protospatharius Basil Petinus (who, in Cedrenus's account, was the diabolic agent of the Porphyrogennetus), and Manuel Curtices, together with a few less prominent conspirators, a Stratege Diogenes, a certain Clado and a Philip.[2]

It was the custom of everyone to leave the Palace for the six midday hours, during which time there was no admission to the precincts. On December 20th, 944—he had ruled now for two days over a quarter of a century—Romanus lay ill in his chamber. Stephen and Constantine Lecapenus managed secretly to smuggle in their supporters, and during these uninterrupted hours seized hold of the ill old man, and put him into a boat waiting at the private Palace harbour. Before anyone in the city was aware of the least disturbance, Romanus had already been carried over the sea to the little island of Prote—nearest of the Princes' Islands—and was being transformed, probably not unwillingly, into a monk. Thus, quietly and smoothly, his reign

1 Theoph. Cont. p. 435.
2 *Ibid.* pp. 435, 438; Cedrenus, II, pp. 32 *et seq.*; Logothete (Slav), p. 42.

was brought to an end. His sons had now to consider how to deal with their brother-in-law.

But soon rumours began to rush through the city, that Romanus was deposed and that Constantine Porphyrogennetus's life was being threatened. The citizens heard of the old man's fate with equanimity—they had liked him, but after all he was only an elderly usurper—but the danger to the legitimate Emperor roused them to fury. Mindful for the first time for years of the son of Leo, the grandson of Basil, the purple-born child over whom so many storms had raged, crowds gathered at the Palace gates demanding vociferously their Emperor; and they would not disperse until Constantine Porphyrogennetus showed himself bareheaded before them all. The Lecapeni brothers were aghast; they had not rid themselves of their father in order to be ruled by their brother-in-law. But they dared not go against public opinion so uncompromisingly expressed. The Porphyrogennetus had been intended to follow his father-in-law; but, defended by the inexplicable love of his people, and further supported by the Roman and Provençal ambassadors and the envoys from Gaeta and Amalfi, he had instead to be admitted as Senior Emperor.[1]

The state of affairs was too uncomfortable to last for more than forty days; but meanwhile the three Emperors kept an outward appearance of amity and divided the spoils. To the Porphyrogennetus as senior fell the appointment of the most important posts; the Lecapene Pantherius was removed and Bardas Phocas, hereditary foe to the Lecapeni,[2] became Domestic of the Schools, while the navy went to Constantine Gongylius, one of the family so devoted to the Empress Zoe, perhaps even one of the brothers that had been her prominent supporters twenty-five years before. But the Lecapene conspirators were also rewarded. Basil Petinus became patrician and chief hetaeri-arch, Marianus Count of the Stables, and Curtices patrician and Drungarius of the Watch.[3] Between the two factions the whole personnel was changed.

1 Liudprand, *Antapodosis*, v, pp. 142 *et seq.*—a first-hand account given him by the Provençal Ambassador, Bishop Siegfried.

2 He was a brother of Romanus's old rival, Leo, but had served under Romanus—e.g. against the Russians in 941.

3 Theoph. Cont. p. 436.

The arrangement was clearly ephemeral, and in view of the popular intervention there could only be one end to it—an end which the Augusta Helena continually urged her husband to hasten.[1] Eventually, after the Lecapeni had in vain tried to lure Constantine to a fatal breakfast party, Constantine, in his turn, suddenly arrested them at dinner on January 27th, 945, and sent them as prisoners after their father.[2] And thus, ignominiously, the whole Lecapene episode was closed.

Stephen and Constantine Lecapenus were first taken to the Princes' Islands, and there on the shore of Prote their father was waiting to greet them. According to the Greek chroniclers, who were fond of apt biblical quotations, he merely murmured the words of Isaiah (i. 2); but Liudprand puts a different and more credible speech in his mouth—a speech of bitter sarcasm, in which he thanked his sons for not neglecting him and regretted the monks' ignorance of the correct etiquette for receiving Emperors. The miserable young men had not to endure their father's taunts for long; Stephen was sent on to a prison at Proeconnese and later was moved to Rhodes, then Mitylene; Constantine was taken to Tenedos and then to Samothrace.[3]

Meanwhile, the Palace was cleared of the remaining Lecapeni. As a wise precaution, Romanus's grandsons were gently put out of the running for the throne. Christopher's son Michael was degraded and made a cleric, becoming later Magister and Rector.[4] Constantine Lecapenus's son Romanus was castrated, and later rose to the rank of Patrician and Prefect.[5] The wives of the fallen emperors fade from history, no doubt into monastic seclusion; Romanus's daughters had been by their marriages reduced to the safety of private stations: all except Helena, now triumphant sole Empress. The other members of the family were inviolable, Theophylact on his patriarchal throne and Maria in Bulgaria. There was, however, one more survivor from the ship-

---

1 Logothete (Slav), p. 42; Cedrenus, II, pp. 323-4.
2 Liudprand, *ibid.* pp. 43-44. He says that Constantine hastily called in the help of loyal Macedonian troops, on the advice of one Diavolinus, who betrayed the breakfast plot. He has clearly muddled this *coup* with Stephen's plot in 947.
3 Liudprand, *loc. cit.*; Theoph. Cont. p. 437.
4 Theoph. Cont. p. 438.   5 *Ibid.* p. 426.

wreck, Romanus's only bastard, Basil, the son of a Bulgarian woman, still little more than a boy, the protégé of his half-sister Helena, who destined a great part for him in the future. Stephen's allies deserted him in time and outlasted his fall; but all, to the delight of the pious chroniclers, met with highly unpleasant ends. Basil Petinus, after a long and discreditable career, was sent under Romanus II, trembling for his life, to die in a dreary exile. Marianus Argyrus, who was soon to conduct a large expedition to Italy, eventually was killed by a tablet thrown by a woman. Curtices lost his life on the Cretan expedition of 949. Diogenes the strategos died of terrible lance wounds; Clado and Philip and others lost their noses and ears after a conspiracy.[1] Of Romanus's former servants, the excellent Theophanes alone kept his post a little longer: while as though to mark the passing of an epoch, an earthquake opened a chasm right through the houses of Romanus Saronites, Romanus's son-in-law, and John Curcuas.[2]

In the island of Prote, Romanus, uncomplaining, passed his days in earnest repentance. His conscience hurt him still; and at last one night he dreamed a terrible dream. He saw a vision of Hell whither were being goaded his own son Constantine, and Anastasius, Bishop of Heraclea. He himself was to have followed, but the Virgin Mary stretched out her hand and saved him. Soon afterwards he learnt that not only had the bishop died that very night, but also Constantine, in an attempt to escape from prison, had killed his chief gaoler, and had himself been killed by the rest of the prison staff. This sinister vision, so accurately fulfilled, braced Romanus up to a still greater act of repentance; he would seek salvation by acknowledging his sins in public and publicly suffering humiliation. On Holy Thursday (946?[3]) before three hundred monks, chosen for their holiness from as far off as Rome itself, Romanus read out from a book all his sins one by one and asked forgiveness for each, while the monks chanted "Kyrie Eleison". Then, before the Communion table, he was whipped and insulted by a little neophyte, amid the tears of all

1 Theoph. Cont. pp. 438, 479.
2 *Ibid.* p. 441.
3 The year is never given, but 946 seems the best date—945 would be too early, but it was apparently some time before Stephen's conspiracy in 947.

the witnesses. The book of his sins was carefully sent to Mount Olympus, to the holy monk Dermocaetes, with some money and a request that his fellow-monks should fast for a fortnight praying for the ex-Emperor's soul. The request was granted; and one night, as Dermocaetes was praying, a voice cried out thrice, "God's mercy has conquered". Dermocaetes looked at the book and found it empty of writing. The monks, praising God for the miracle, sent it back to Romanus, in whose tomb it was buried.[1]

God had accepted this last atonement and Romanus could rest in peace. But even now the call of the world was too much for him. His faithful friend Theophanes and the Patriarch Theophylact entered into one more conspiracy on his behalf, and after some persuasion, he agreed to their plans. The attempt was never made, the government discovered the plot too soon. Theophylact from his position was sacrosanct, and could return to his horses unscathed; but Theophanes was deposed and driven into exile, and with him his accomplices, George the Protospatharius and Thomas the Primicerius. Romanus remained on a pious monk in Prote. In December, 947, another plot was discovered. Michael Diabolinus betrayed a number of officials working in favour of Stephen Lecapenus. They all lost their positions and their noses and ears, or suffered scourging and public humiliation.[2]

Neither Stephen nor Romanus was to return to the city, save as a corpse. For that return Romanus had not long to wait. On June 15th, 948, death came to him. His body was carried back to Constantinople, to lie at his wife's side in the monastery of the Myrelaeum.[3]

Of the rest of the family there is little more to be said. The ex-Emperor Constantine was dead. The ex-Emperor Stephen lived on, respected by all who saw him, in exile for nineteen years; his sudden death, like all sudden deaths of that period, was attributed to the hand of the Empress Theophano. Theophylact the Patriarch enjoyed his sporting if scarcely clerical life

1 Theoph. Cont. pp. 439–40. Romanus must still have been treated as a figure of great dignity if so widely sought a collection of monks would be made for him.

2 *Ibid.* pp. 400–1.

3 *Ibid. loc. cit.*

for several years more, but his horses in the end proved his ruin; in 954 a severe riding accident turned him into a complete invalid, and two years later he died.[1] Of the next generation, Maria lived on nearly twenty years longer on the Bulgar throne, dying about 965.[2] Michael and Romanus Lecapenus led apparently not undistinguished lives, but avoided the limelight sufficiently for their ultimate fate to be unknown. Only the Empress Helena and the bastard Basil triumphed fully. Basil succeeded, on Theophanes's exile, to the post of Paracoemomene. From that eminence he aided his half-sister, so it was said, in gaily selling justice while her imperial husband wrote books, painted pictures and drank.[3] Basil had a long, prominent and for the most part prosperous career before him, only to pass from history some forty years later, under Helena's grandsons. Helena herself met the fate of her father, being thrust into a monastery by an unfilial son. With the death of all these the Lecapene name died too.

So fell the Lecapeni who made the strongest challenge to legitimacy that the Macedonian house had to face. But for his sons Romanus might have died on the throne; but the ultimate conclusion was inevitable. The Macedonian house was built on too steadfast a foundation, by Basil its founder and by Leo the Wise. The reign of the Lecapeni had lasted a quarter of a century, little enough time compared to the two centuries of the Macedonians, and, compared to the thousand years of Byzantium, the tiniest episode. Nevertheless, the episode was not entirely shameful, and it has its proper mansion in history.

1 Theoph. Cont. p. 444; Cedrenus, II, p. 324.
2 Cedrenus, II, p. 346.   3 *Ibid.* pp. 325–6.

CHAPTER XIII

Romanus and his Reign's place in History

IT remains now to put the episode into its proper perspective. During the seventh and eighth centuries the Empire had been in a long eclipse. The shock of the Saracen onrush, the climax of so many barbarian invasions, had fallen too heavily on it; its energies were spent in preserving Asia Minor and even the capital itself. The provinces to the east and south had all been lopped off, and gradually the west had slipped from the imperial grasp, till only Sicily remained. The Isaurian emperors were great reformers and did much to reorganize the internal machinery; but they cut the ground away from beneath their feet by the folly of iconoclasm. It was not until the middle of the ninth century that the Empire retrieved religious union, and, with its old Roman organization gone and in its place the new strong centralized administration that we must call Byzantine, it could pause to survey the world around. At this moment Basil the Macedonian burst upon the scene.

Basil was fortunate in his time. Under Theophilus and Saint Theodora, peacemaker to the Church, the Empire had flourished; and the drunken Michael's orgies had been bad enough to make people welcome a usurper, but not bad enough, under Bardas's care, materially to damage this prosperity. Moreover, though in the west the Saracens were stealing Sicily, in the east the Califate was sinking and, see-saw-wise, the glory of the Empire re-arose, while the great Slav block to the north was being civilized and stabilized by a series of brilliant Christian missions. Basil took advantage of it all. In the east by the destruction of the Paulicians he showed that the Empire would stand no nonsense from rebel heretics; in the west his generals reconquered Southern Italy. At home he kept a firm control and set about bringing the administration and the laws fully up to date. But he left two great problems unsettled. The first was the problem of Bulgaria; during the dark centuries a huge

Bulgarian Empire had arisen in the Balkans, and its Christianizing had not had the effect that Byzantine statesmen had hoped. Its monarchs were too clever to become the humble vassals of the Basileus; they began to think themselves as good as him. The second problem was the relations between Church and State, a problem brought into prominence by the Patriarch Photius. Under Basil's successor Leo the problems grew more tense. Boris of Bulgaria was followed by Symeon, more ambitious than his father and a better general; and a sequence of misadventures brought the Church government question to a crisis. Leo's unfortunate marital tragedies rent the whole Empire, and threatened the existence of his dynasty. Leo himself won his way, but only for his lifetime; trouble would certainly follow his death. At the same time there was a slight renascence among the Califs at Bagdad.

When Leo died the better days seemed drawing to a close. The pleasure-loving Alexander would not trouble himself with the government, content to allow the ecclesiastical enemies of his brother to have their vengeance. Party warfare flared through the State. And Bulgaria declared war; Symeon was thinking of himself attaining to the throne of the Caesars. The regency council was no better than Alexander, and fell in confusion. Under the Empress Zoe there was a revival. In Armenia and in Italy her troops showed that the Empire was still the greatest power. But Zoe was only a party leader, and she made an unlucky mistake. She staked everything on a direct defeat of the Bulgars, but her servants failed or betrayed her and she lost. The wash that followed in the disaster's wake sank her; but out of the waters there emerged in triumph a figure, unknown to most of the onlookers, the admiral Romanus Lecapenus.

Romanus had won and kept his power only by the most meticulous care. His one asset was his fleet, large and unscathed and apparently devoted to him. On the other hand, he had been a traitor to his country; he came into prominence only as a party leader, a rival to the Empress and the aristocracy that she supported; he was himself of very humble origin—so that every ambitious man in all the Empire might feel himself as good as his new lord and wish to emulate him—and all the more reput-

able older statesmen (such as the Magister Stephen) declined
to have anything to do with him; the perjury that he had employed had been too crude and shameless. Yet Romanus succeeded. Tact enabled him to use and yet to control the Patriarch
Nicholas; forbearance and mildness gradually overcame the
hostility of most of his opponents. He never made the slightest
threat against the life of the Porphyrogennetus, however much
he may have hoped for his death, treating him on the contrary
as one of his own family; and he always officially dissociated
himself from any severe punishment undergone by fallen enemies.[1] But all the time he was watching with unremittent
closeness to nip any conspiracy in time. His remarkably sure
judgment in the choice of servants helped him further, and so,
in time, he had a complete and firmly established hold over the
whole organization of government.

Once firmly established he was able to face Leo's problems,
the Church and Bulgaria. For both he employed a simple
remedy, patience. With the Church he flattered and cajoled
Nicholas till the fierce old man died; then, with a cynicism in
strange contrast to his usual piety, he appointed two nonentities
and his amiable son in his place, and had no more trouble from
patriarchal insubordination. With Bulgaria, he made no attempt
to send out expeditions to ravage and destroy Symeon's Empire.
Such a method had failed; he was content to wait in Constantinople, adequately guarding the city and occasionally sending out
troops to protect the suburbs. He peacefully waited while
Symeon battered himself again and again against the inviolable
walls, and further embarrassed him by rousing Serbs every few
years to attack him in his rear. Such a method meant the temporary sacrifice of Thrace, but it was worth while. Symeon
would march up to the city unopposed; he could always in the
end beat the Serbs; but the long process utterly exhausted
Bulgaria. As soon as Symeon died and his iron grip relaxed,
his Empire fell to the ground, and the Bulgars asked humbly for
peace. Here again Romanus showed a fresh wisdom. Titular
concessions meant nothing to him; he gave them freely, and in
return won real advantages, peace in the first place, then land

1 E.g. the blinding of Leo Phocas.

and influence. The Bulgars, the menace of the Empire for over a hundred years, suddenly ceased to count.

Thus, before he had been eight years on the throne, Romanus could present the Empire with the solution of its two greatest problems. He now turned to the East. Hitherto, for centuries, imperial arms had been here on the defensive. Occasional emperors, such as Theophilus and Basil, had invaded Saracen land, but their expeditions were primarily grand counter-raids. Basil had taken a new step by annexing territory over the frontier; but he only took the land that had been occupied by the heretic Paulicians.[1] Leo followed his father's example and also annexed some Armenian land, the principality of Teces beyond the upper Euphrates—a step of considerable importance in the historical geography of the frontier. Zoe advanced even further; at the time of the truce of 917 she seems to have taken possession of enough Saracen or debatable territory to turn the Lycandian clisura into a theme; and that same truce had kept off the Saracens while the Empire suffered the worst blows of the Bulgar war. But it was left to Romanus to change the whole state of affairs. From already a year before the Bulgar peace and onward till the close of the reign, John Curcuas, the general that Romanus had appointed, conducted a consecutive series of aggressive campaigns far into Armenian and Saracen country; and these were not mere raids and forays but definitely had conquest in view. The capture and annexation of Melitene and all its territory in 934 suddenly opened the eyes of the world to what was happening. The Califate's brief revival was over, and the Moslem Empire was in disruption; even the prowess and power of Saïf-ad-Daula was useless to check the Christian advance. By the time of Romanus's fall the imperial frontier ran beyond the upper waters of the Tigris, and many Moslem cities, Samosata, the cities of Lake Van, and Erzerum, all acknowledged the supremacy of the Basileus. They were not vast conquests, it is true, but they were the first; they marked the turning-point. Henceforward the old order was changed; now it was the Christians that attacked and the Moslems that struggled in vain to

---

[1] I exclude the passage to and fro between Greek and Saracen of frontier fortresses such as Lulum, finally won for the Greeks by Basil.

keep them off. John Curcuas had brought a new spirit to the
soldiers of the eastern front; he had paved the road over which
the imperial armies would march, to Lebanon and to the mountains of Persia, once more.

In Italy the reign had no such significance. The Byzantine
apogee was reached when Zoe's troops won the battle of the
Garigliano; Romanus was merely staving off an inevitable
decline. In Illyricum, over which Romanus never troubled
himself, ground was, if anything, lost. But with regard to the
nations of the north, his government was of the highest importance. The collapse of Bulgaria suddenly brought Byzantium
after a very long break into full relations with the huge nomad
tribes. Romanus and his ministers had therefore to work out
the policies that should be pursued with regard to them, the
wise, delicate policies that the Porphyrogennetus has recorded
for posterity. The rules devised were all in the proper Byzantine
tradition; nevertheless, they were clearly the work of a fine
intelligence, and were followed successfully for many years to
come.

Internally, apart from his ecclesiastical settlement, Romanus's
reign needs no comment. He was the first Emperor to introduce
land legislation against magnates; but in that, as in all his internal
administration, he was merely following the orthodox Macedonian tradition. And even when he brought the Church under
his control by appointing a prince as Patriarch, he was merely
copying an idea evolved by Basil and by Leo.

It is in its foreign aspect that Romanus's reign finds its high
place; and there it little deserves the oblivion into which it has
fallen. It was the time when the Empire cast off her troubles
from her and rose up towards her greatest splendour, when she
turned the last corner before her golden path under the great
warrior-Emperors, Nicephorus, John and Basil. As such, it was
a memorable reign.

How much this was due to Romanus himself is less easy to
say. Would another man on the imperial throne have achieved
the same success? To some extent Romanus met with great good
luck. The decline of the Califate gave an opportunity on the
eastern front; the feebleness of Symeon's successor inevitably

weakened Bulgaria. Except for the religious schism the Empire
was well organized at home. The military victories were almost
all entirely due to John Curcuas; the diplomatic victories were
probably won by Theophanes.

Nevertheless, however much the weakness of Bulgaria and the
Califate may have helped, another man would have found it
hard to be in a position to use them. Had Romanus not risen
to the throne the government would almost certainly have fallen
to a coalition, cemented by marriage, between Zoe and Leo
Phocas; and Zoe, though clever, was injudicious and rash, and
Leo was not even clever. It is difficult to believe that they would
have been able to use the advantages—that they would have
been able to wait in patience till Symeon died exhausted.
Romanus, emerging at a moment of disaster for Byzantium,
succeeded, despite the humility of his origin and the difficulties
of his position, not only in establishing himself firmly enough
to consider foreign wars but also in building around him sufficient
peace and stability to make foreign action effective. All the fine
organization of Byzantium would have been valueless without
concord in the highest departments of the State. Also, though
John Curcuas and Theophanes were the actual agents of most
of the reign's triumphs, in the end everything depended on the
Emperor. It was he that discovered and appointed them; it was
he that gave them the support without which they could do
nothing. All the accounts of his rule picture it as a very personal
affair; it was he that devised the poor-relief in the winter of 928;
it was he that passed sleepless nights in 941 thinking out how
to meet the Russian pirates. He was the Emperor; the glory of
the reign should be his.

Yet for all his splendid statecraft, as a man he remains faintly
drawn, a dim and homely figure in the terrific picture gallery of
the Emperors of the East. The only portraits of him that still
exist, rough portraits on his coins, show merely an amiable old
man with a very long beard. He had singularly few vices—
except for the wholesale perjury that lifted him to the throne,
and a worldly cynicism in his appointments to the Patriarchate,
justified probably by his genuine faith in Caesaropapism—and
he repented very sincerely of his usurpation: though he never

offered to return the crown during his own lifetime to its proper
owner. He was moral as mediaeval monarchs went, leaving only
one bastard behind him, born long after his wife's death. He
was pious, with a crude piety that befitted an old sailor, and
humble in his dealings with the holy. He was generous, particularly with the public purse. He was clement, disliking and
almost always avoiding bloodshed, except with barbarian pirates
who did not count. He was a deeply affectionate husband and
father, all too forbearing in his treatment of his sons.

Yet all these excellent virtues and all the good qualities of his
statesmanship leave him an unromantic figure, a figure without
charm. His servants were apparently fond of him and worked
for him loyally; the fleet when he commanded it was apparently
devoted to him, and the general crowds liked him for his generosity
and kindness and his admirable piety. Yet when he fell, none
lifted a finger to save him, except Theophanes and the worthless
Theophylact. The populace to whom he had given so much
barely noticed his fall, reserving all their enthusiastic attention
to the Porphyrogennetus, who had never done anything for
them. Partly this must have been due to his lack of education;
for the Byzantines were all great intellectual snobs, and such
a lapse in the line of cultured Emperors must have been dis-
tressing to the national pride. Yet somehow Romanus inspired
one very remarkable and quite inexplicable friendship; the
mysterious Logothete, whose chronicle formed the basis of all
the history of the years, writing at a time when Lecapene sentiments cannot have been commended, treats of him with an
obvious affection and admiration that nothing in the text fully
justifies; and he even, many years later, showed his fondness for
the family, when Stephen Lecapenus died in exile, by writing
him a little elegy. Perhaps the gentle, bearded face hid an attrac-
tion that just a chosen few, like Theophanes and the Logothete,
fully realized and never forgot. His reign was a great reign; and
so he too must have had something of greatness in him.

And, for all his homeliness, he too can give us ground to
moralize. His story is a fable, told on a grand scale, of the
thanklessness of ambition. Step by step, dishonest and for-
sworn, he had mounted to the throne; and there he had reigned

in splendour, bringing glory to the Empire. But retribution reached him in the end, and his days and nights were filled with the aching wounds of conscience. All the pious charity that an Emperor could perform he performed; he carefully planned that his victim should recover all his rights. But God was inexorable and sent him tribulation. He fell; and shorn as a monk he wondered wearily: had it been worth while? And at last he knew and made answer: "He reigns more gloriously who serves the humilities of the servants of God, than he who orders the mighty sinners of the world".[1]

Romanus was punished very hardly; but such are the wages of ambition. Only when the holiest monks in Christendom had heard the full tale of his sins and had chanted the Kyrie Eleison over his humbled form—only when God in a miracle had wiped his sins away—only then could he await in calmness the dread summons of Death, turning from the domes and towers of the city shimmering across the dark sea, and gazing steadfastly at the peaks of holy Olympus, where the snow lies late into the summer....

Ἔξελθε, Βασιλεῦ, καλεῖ σε ὁ Βασιλεὺς τῶν βασιλευόντων καὶ Κύριος τῶν κυριευόντων.

1 Liudprand, *Antapodosis*, p. 145.

APPENDIX I

The Date of the Interview between Romanus and Symeon (Chapter v, p. 90)

IN attempting any chronology of the Bulgarian war, the first necessity is to fix the date of the interview between Romanus and Symeon. The Greek chroniclers who are our sources for this important climax, one and all give it impossible dates. From the fact that Nicholas the Patriarch was one of the actors, we know that the interview took place before May, 925, the year of his death. The last date before the interview given in the chronicles is February, 922, the date of the Empress Theodora's death; but from the intervening events chronicled it is reasonable to regard 923 as the earliest possible year.

The Greek chroniclers are unanimous in saying that Symeon invaded Thrace (in the campaign that ended in the interview) in September in the second indiction, that is to say, either 913 or 928. Both dates are obviously impossible. About the date of the interview itself they are less unanimous. All the earliest chroniclers agree that it took place on the πέμπτη ἡμέρα (Symeon Magister adds τῆς ἑβδομάδος); Georgius Monachus Continuatus then says that the day was November 19th; Leo Grammaticus, Theodosius of Melitene, Theophanes Continuatus, and the later chroniclers, Cedrenus and Zonaras, call it November 9th; Georgius Hamartolus (Muralt's edition) and Symeon Magister call it September 9th. The Slavonic version of the Logothete translates πέμπτη ἡμέρα as *tchetvrtok*, Thursday, and gives the date November 9th. Nestor, who drew on Greek sources, solves the problem to his own satisfaction by altering the indiction and giving the date Thursday, November 19th, 929, an actual day; but he can be ignored.

Professor Zlatarsky, in his endeavour to place the interview in 923, takes the words πέμπτη ἡμέρα to mean the fifth day after Symeon's arrival at the city. Symeon Magister is the only authority to add the words τῆς ἑβδομάδος, and he is notoriously the latest and least important of the synoptic chroniclers. The day of the week therefore becomes immaterial. The theory is ingenious, but, I think, untenable. In the Greek of the period πέμπτη ἡμέρα ordinarily means Thursday, and it seems too highly improbable that it should mean anything else here. Professor Zlatarsky ignores the *tchetvrtok* of the Slavonic version of the Logothete (in 1896, when he first advanced his theory, it had not been published; but he has not altered it since) which shows that the Slavonic translators, like the redactor of 'Symeon Magister', naturally understood Thursday to be meant; and we have no reason to translate differently to them.

Accepting, as we must, that the day was Thursday, the problem narrows down. In this decade November 19th fell on a Thursday only in 929, November 9th in 920 and 926, and September 9th in 924. Krug accepts this last date, pointing out how easily a careless scribe of the basic chronicle might have become muddled between month and day and make both the ninth; the redactor of 'Symeon Magister' noticed the discrepancy, and corrected it, though he was not thorough enough to correct the indiction. The idea is permissible, and Muralt accepted it. On the other hand, it may well be argued that the indiction rather points to the year 923; a scribe might easily confuse the 2nd and 12th indictions, but scarcely the 2nd and 13th. But then we cannot find a suitable Thursday in 923.

So much for the internal evidence. When we come to consider the date in the light of other affairs, the first thing to remark is that November is an extraordinarily late season in the year for Symeon to have brought his army to Constantinople. Not only would no sensible commander of that date have thought of conducting a campaign so late into the Balkan winter; but also, if, as we are told, he invaded Thrace in September, and apparently met no opposition and indulged in no sieges or divagations, one cannot imagine how he managed to take so long coming through Thrace, a journey at the most of about a hundred miles. September is a far likelier month as regards both the season for campaigning and the length of time spent in the journey —we may legitimately assume that perhaps he crossed the actual frontier during the last week of August: though if he made forced marches, intending a sudden attack, there is no need to make even that emendation.

If we accept September instead of November, it then is obviously wisest to accept the whole Thursday, September 9th, 924, and to give up any attempt to explain the wrong indiction number. And if we look at the general history of the Empire we find additional and, I think, conclusive reasons for following that course. Bulgarian history is not very helpful; we know that either in 923 or 924, presumably in whichever year they did not come to Constantinople, the Bulgars conducted a Serbian campaign; but the dates are interchangeable. The history of the Empire is more decisive. First, in passing, we should remember that the Patriarch Nicholas wrote only two letters to Symeon between the interview and his own death. Both letters from their tone seem to have been written soon after the interview, and the second was written when Nicholas's health was breaking up, presumably soon before his death. But what is most indicative is Romanus's foreign policy with regard to the Moslems during 923 and 924. In 924 Romanus suddenly approached the Calif's Court with suggestions for a truce. The situation on the eastern front provided no reason for such a move; but Romanus desired peace eagerly enough to accept the humiliating clause of the Moslems that the truce should not take place till after their summer raids. Clearly Romanus was alarmed by some danger from another part of the Empire. In 923 he showed no such alarm; it is therefore only reasonable to assume that the alarm in 924 was due to news of Symeon's projected grand attack on the capital.[1]

The date of this transaction, which is known, seems to be the final proof. I therefore have no hesitation in placing the interview between Symeon and Romanus on Thursday, September 9th, 924.[2]

1 The transactions with the African Moslems are equivocal. Symeon's abortive alliance with them probably took place in 923, but as there are no means of assigning accurately the season of the year nor of telling how long elapsed between the negotiations and Symeon's invasion, we must fall back on the other evidence.

2 Theoph. Cont. pp. 405, 407; Symeon Magister, pp. 735, 736; Georgius Monachus, pp. 898, 899; Leo Grammaticus, pp. 310, 311; Theodosius Melitenus, pp. 219 *et seq.*; Georgius Hamartolus, pp. 824 *et seq.*; Logothete (Slav), p. 134; Nestor, p. 26; Nich. Myst. Ep. xxx, xxxi, pp. 185 *et seq.*; Krug, *Kritischer Versuch*, pp. 155–160; Muralt, *Essais de Chronographie Byzantine*, p. 502; Zlatarsky, *Zbornik*, xiii, pp. 200 *et seq.* n. 11; Dölger, p. 74.

APPENDIX II

The Date of the Visit of King Ashot to Constantinople
(Chapter vii, p. 131)

THE date of King Ashot's visit to Constantinople has been a stumbling-block to most historians of Armenia. We know that after the collapse of Armenia under Sembat and its devastation by the Moslems, Ashot, Sembat's heir, journeyed to Constantinople, and was replaced by Greek help. The date is naturally of considerable importance for the history of the Greco-Arab wars. Saint-Martin, the first eminent occidental historian of Armenia, dated it in 921, and every subsequent historian, with the exception of Dölger, has followed his lead.

The evidence falls under three headings, Greek, Arab and Armenian. The Greek chroniclers in unison place Ashot's visit to Constantinople during the regency of the Empress Zoe, who received him with honour. From the context the visit took place just before the fall of Adrianople in September, 914. The Arab chroniclers naturally do not concern themselves with the visits of Armenian princes to Constantinople; they do, however, deal with Greco-Armenian campaigns. In 915 the Greeks conducted a large and on the whole successful offensive on the Euphrates frontier and against Tarsus; whereas in 921 no campaign is recorded and in 922 their slight aggressive movement against Melitene (their only offensive action that year) was a failure. The Armenian historians tell many varied stories. John Catholicus, the only contemporary writer, unfortunately gives only two dates in all his works and one is forty years out; during these years he gives none. On the other hand, when telling of the letter that he wrote to the imperial court in reply to the invitation to Ashot, he gives the address as being to the Emperor Kosdantianós (Constantine), not Romanus. Also, considering that John died in 925 and apparently stopped writing in 924, it seems unlikely that he would have dealt so scantily with the years 913 to 921 and so fully of the last three.[1] Of the other Armenian historians, Samuel of Ani kills Sembat in 915 and says that Armenia was without a master for seven years; Asoghic says that after Sembat's death (undated) his son Ashot fled to Constantinople to the Emperor Leo, and that Romanus in the second year of his reign sent 'Demestikos'—the

---

[1] He kills Sembat on p. 233: sends Ashot to Constantinople, p. 283; Ashot returns from Constantinople, p. 292; and the history closes, p. 369.

Domestic—to Dovin; Vardan the Great makes Ashot be crowned by
the Emperor Leo in 921 and then tells of his wars with Gagic and
Sbarabied; the Siounian history dates Sembat's fall in 913 and on the
next page, as though telling of an immediately subsequent event, says
that Ashot was sent back by the Emperor Romanus; Thomas
Ardzrouni has no relevant information to give. In more modern
times Chamich dated Ashot's return in 921, but he gives no
references.

Here the consensus of opinion seems to be in favour of 921–2:
though John Catholicus, whose evidence, being contemporary, is
much the most valuable, is equivocal, leaning if anything towards an
earlier date. The others' dates can to a certain extent be explained
by the fact that the Armenians (like the Italian Liudprand) imagined
that Romanus Lecapenus followed immediately after Alexander on
the imperial throne. This would make Asoghic's and the Siounian
versions harmonize with the earlier date—and with regard to the
former we may notice that in 922 the Domestic cannot have been to
Dovin as he was fully occupied in Thrace. Samuel of Ani starts with
an error; Sembat certainly died in 913; but Armenia may well be
considered to have been without a master for seven years, as civil war
and chaos were rife before Sembat's death and were not ended till
some years after Ashot's return. Vardan alone gives the date quite
clearly as 921, and so can probably be ignored; an error is easily
intelligible.

Certainly where the Armenians give undated or inherently con-
flicting accounts, it is ridiculous not to accept the definite dating of
the Greek chroniclers, who are positive that Ashot was received by
Zoe; except for this suspect Armenian evidence there is no reason to
doubt their statement, particularly when the Arab chroniclers' evidence is in harmony with it. Saint-Martin in choosing the later date
either must have attempted to write Armenian history without
reading the pertinent Greek records or must have considered later
Armenian authorities preferable to almost contemporary Greek;
either alternative presents a most discreditable lack of historical
sense. It is incredible that so many historians should have followed
his lead; Rambaud, who knew and valued the Greek sources, is reduced to saying on one page that in 920 Nicholas wrote inviting
Ashot to Constantinople, and on the next that Ashot came in answer
to the invitation to find Nicholas fallen from power and Zoe ruling
instead. Rambaud was well aware that in 920 Zoe had been already
for a year immured in the final seclusion of a monastery. Dölger is the
first historian to point out Saint-Martin's flouting of the Greek
evidence; but his work, dealing as it does with Greek documents and
authorities, has not been noticed by writers on Armenian history.
It is to be hoped however that they will realize the folly of ignoring the

Greek authorities and will place Ashot's visit to Constantinople in the year 914.[1]

1 Theoph. Cont. p. 387; Georgius Monachus, p. 879; Logothete (Slav), p. 127, etc.; Tabari, *V.P.* p. 19; Arib, *V.P.* p. 56; Ibn-al-Asir, *V.P.* pp. 104, 105, 106; John Catholicus, pp. 283, 292 *et passim*; Samuel of Ani, p. 435; Asoghic, pp. 23–25; Vardan, p. 111; *Histoire de la Siounie*, pp. 116, 117; Chamich, II, pp. 49 *et seq.*; *Saint-Martin*, notes to John Catholicus, p. 420: *Mémoires*, pp. 361–2; Rambaud, pp. 503, 504; Vasiliev, II, pp. 216, 217; Dölger, I, I, p. 69.

APPENDIX III

The Fixed Rate of Interest and of Retail Profits
(Chapter i, p. 23 and xi, p. 225)

IN view of Romanus's land legislation and indeed the whole circumstances of Byzantine financial life, it is perhaps best to give the provisions of the 'Rhodian Code', the laws which, by fixing firmly the rates of interest that could be derived from invested capital, drove the rich into seeking investments in real property and land. In the early years of the Empire the rate of interest of an ordinary transaction had been fixed at 6 per cent.; if the lender was a magnate it was 4 per cent.; if a professional usurer, 8 per cent.; and for transmarine speculation it was 72 per cent.—a proof not only of the risks that merchant ships ran in the uncharted unlit seas, but also of the profits that a successful transmarine speculation would make. By the tenth century the position had slightly changed, to the advantage of the lender. The unit became 72, the number of nomismata in a pound of gold, and interest was reckoned as 6 per cent. of 72 and so on: so that the ordinary interest became 8·33 per cent., magnates' 5·55 per cent., and professional usurers' 11·11 per cent. It was thus possible to draw quite a good income through advancing capital, even for the magnates; but they naturally chafed under restrictions that made their investments less profitable than those of other classes. Land could, however, usually be made to produce a better profit besides giving the possessor a certain amount of political power. It was therefore hardly surprising that the magnates devoted their wealth to the building up of huge estates, to the alarm of the imperial government.

It was, however, also possible to secure a good gilt-edged investment by buying a life annuity or a title, such as that of protospatharius, which brought in 10 per cent. of one's outlay for life; or the less greedy but more provident could secure an income of about 2½ per cent. by purchasing outright a minor post at Court which they could either resell or leave to their heirs.

Similar restrictions hedged round the retail trade. Merchants retailed their goods at a fixed profit of 16¾ per cent. Middlemen were dispensed with; the retailers were all banded together according to their trades into corporations which bought the raw material or the wholesale goods and divided them up among the members. The shopkeepers had many other rules to keep, under a penalty of large fines to the State; the government, acting through the Prefect of the City, fixed wages and hours, superintended the quality, and forbade goods to be kept speculatively in reserve and forced down prices during a scarcity. There were even religious restrictions—soap-makers, for example, were not allowed to manufacture out of animal fats during Lent. The great concern of the government was to supply Constantinople with every necessity. Consequently the export trade (except of luxuries) was neglected or actively discouraged; salt fish might not be exported at all. The corporations, so restricted, never rose to political power. Moreover, the government could call on them to undertake certain civic duties, both to act as expert valuers and to do police-work; and if required they had to work for the State without a contract.

In conclusion it must be remembered that a vast amount of capital was still invested in slaves—acquired either from the Russian merchants or as prisoners of war. In domestic service they were now rare; but on the land and still more in the mines and the factories they provided the bulk of the unskilled labour. The State was by far the greatest slave-owner, but rich individuals owned enormous numbers; the widow Danielis bequeathed thousands to the Basileus at her death. Those in private hands were on the whole better treated than those owned by the State, who used them with considerable rigour.[1]

1 For this appendix see *Le Livre du Préfet, passim*; Bury, Appendix XIII in Gibbon's *Decline and Fall*, v, pp. 533–4, and Macri, *L'Économie Urbaine*, pp. 35 *et seq. passim*.

BIBLIOGRAPHY

NOTE. The following abbreviations are used in the
bibliography and in the footnotes to the text:

B.Z. Die Byzantinische Zeitschrift. Leipzig, 1892– .
Camb. Med. Hist. The Cambridge Medieval History. Cambridge,
1911– .
C.S.H.B. Corpus Scriptorum Historiae Byzantinorum. Bonn, 1828–
97.
D.A.I. Constantine Porphyrogenitus, *De Administrando Imperio*—
see below.
D.C. Idem, De Ceremoniis Aulae Byzantinae—see below.
D.T. Idem, De Thematibus—see below.
E.H.R. The English Historical Review. London, 1886– .
H.Z. Die Historische Zeitschrift. Munich, 1860– .
I.R.A.O. Imperatorskoe Russkoe Archaeologicheskoe Obschestvo, trudi.
St Petersburg, 1861–98.
J.H.S. The Journal of Hellenic Studies. London, 1881– .
M.A.I. L. A. Muratori, *Antiquitates Italicae Medii Aevi.* Milan,
1738–42.
M.G.H. Monumenta Germaniae Historiae, scriptores, ed. G. H.
Pertz, etc. Hanover, 1826–96.
M.P.G. J. P. Migne, *Patrologia Cursus Completus, series Graeca.*
Paris, 1857–66.
M.P.L. Idem, Patrologia Cursus Completus, series Latina. Paris,
1844–55.
M.R.I.S. L. A. Muratori, *Rerum Italicarum Scriptores.* Milan,
1723–51.
R.E.A. La Revue des Etudes Arméniennes. Paris, 1921–
R.E.G. La Revue des Etudes Grecques. Paris, 1887– .
S.N.U. Sbornik za Narodni Umotvorenia. Sofia, 1889– .
S.R.H. Scriptores Rerum Hungaricarum, veteres ac genuini. Vienna,
1746.
Theoph. Cont. Theophanes Continuatus—see below.
Viz. Vrem. Vizantyiski Vremennik, *Byzantina Chronica.* St Peters-
burg, 1894–1916.
V.P. A. A. Vasiliev, *Vizantia i Arabyi,* vol. II, *Prilozhenia*—see
below.
*Z.K.T. Zbornik Kralja Tomislava u spomen Tišučugod isnjiče Hrvats-
koga Kraljevtsva.* Pošebna djela Jugoslavenske Academije
Znanosti i Umjetnosti, Knjiga XVII. Zagreb, 1925.

I

ORIGINAL SOURCES

A. GREEK AND·SLAVONIC

Cameniata, Joannes. *De Excidio Thessalonicae. C.S.H.B.* 1838.

Cedrenus, Georgius. *Synopsis Historiae. C.S.H.B.* 1838–9.

Codinus, Georgius, Curopalata. *De Officialibus Palatii Constantinopolitani et de Officiis Magnae Ecclesiae. C.S.H.B.* 1839.

Constantine of Rhodes. *Works.* Ed. E. Le Grand. *R.E.G.* vol. ix.

Constantine Porphyrogenitus. *De Ceremoniis Aulae Byzantinae; De Thematibus; De Administrando Imperio.* 3 vols. *C.S.H.B.* 1829–40.

—— *Narratio de Imagine Edessena. M.P.G.* vol. cxiii.

Digénis Akritas. Publ. E. Le Grand. (Bibliothèque Grecque Vulgaire.) Paris, 1902.

Georgius Hamartolus. Ed. Muralt. St Petersburg, 1859.

Georgius Monachus Continuatus. *Chronicon. C.S.H.B.* 1838.

Glycas, Michael. *Annales. C.S.H.B.* 1836.

Joel. *Chronographia. C.S.H.B.* 1837.

Leo Diaconus. *Historia. C.S.H.B.* 1828.

Leo Grammaticus. *Chronographia. C.S.H.B.* 1842.

Leo Sapiens, Imperator. *Opera. M.P.G.* vol. cvii.

Liber de Re Militari, Incerti Scriptoris Byzantini Saeculi X. Ed. Vari. Leipzig, 1901.

Livre du Préfet, Le. Ed. J. Nicole. Geneva, 1893.

Manasses, Constantinus. *Synopsis Historica. C.S.H.B.* 1837.

Nicephorus Phocas, Imperator. *Velitatio Bellica. C.S.H.B.* 1828.

Nicholaus Mysticus, Patriarcha. *Epistolae. M.P.G.* vol. cxi.

Philotheus. *Cleterologium.* In Bury, *Administrative System*—see below.

Romanus Lecapenus, Imperator. *Epistolae.* Ed. Sakkelion, Deltion, vol. ii. Athens, 1883.

Symeon, Logothete. *Epitaph on Stephen Lecapenus.* Ed. Vasilievsky. *Viz. Vrem.* vol. iii.

Symeon, Magister. *Chronicon. C.S.H.B.* 1838.

Theodosius Melitenus. *Chronographia.* Ed. Tafel. Munich, 1859.

Theophanes Continuatus. *Chronographia. C.S.H.B.* 1838.

Vita Sancti Euthymii. Ed. C. de Boor. Berlin, 1888.

Vita Sancti Lucae Minoris. M.P.G. vol. cxi.

Zonaras. *Epitome Historiarum. C.S.H.B.* 1841–97.

Chrabr, Monach. On the Alphabet. In Kalaidovitch, *op. cit.* below.

John, Exarch. *Shestodnnie.* In Miklosich, *Chrestomathia Palaeo-Slovenica.* Vienna, 1861.

Nestor, Chronique dite de. Ed. and trans. L. Leger. Paris, 1884.

Simeon, Logothete. *Lietovnik.* Ed. Sreznevsky. St Petersburg, 1905.

B. LATIN

Annales Barenses. *M.P.L.* vol. CLV.
Annales Beneventani. *M.G.H.* vol. III.
Annales Casinates. *M.G.H.* vol. III.
Annales Cavenses. *M.G.H.* vol. III.
Annales Fuldenses. *M.G.H.* vol. I.
Annales Quedlinburgenses. *M.G.H.* vol. III.
Anonymi Historia Ducum Hungariae. In *S.R.H.*
Chronicum Amalphitanum. *M.A.I.* vol. I.
Chronicum Salernitanum. *M.G.H.* vol. III.
Chronicum Sancti Monasterii Casinensis. *M.R.I.S.* vol. IV.
Chronicum Vulturnense. *M.R.I.S.* vol. I, pt. II.
Dandolo, Andrea. *Chronicum Venetum*. *M.R.I.S.* vol. XII.
Flodoardus. *Annales*. *M.P.L.* vol. CXXXV.
Joannes Diaconus. *Chronicum Venetum*. *M.G.H.* vol. VII.
Leo Ostiensis. *Chronicon Monasterii Casinensis*. *M.G.S.* vol. VII.
Liudprand. *Opera*. Ed. Bekker (*Scriptores Rerum Germanicarum*). Hanover, 1915.
Lupus Protospatharius. *Annales*. *M.P.L.* vol. CLV.
Presbyter Diocleaè. *De Regno Slavorum*. In Lucius, *op. cit.* below.
Ranzanus, Petrus. Indices. In *S.R.H.*
Restius, Junius. *Chronica Ragusina*. *Monumenta Spectantia Historiam Slavorum Meridionalium, scriptores*, vol. II. Zagreb, 1893.
Thomas Archidiaconus. *Historia Salonita*. In Lucius, *op. cit.* below.
Thwrocz, Joannes de. *Historia*. In *S.R.H.*

C. ARABIC

Cronaca Siculo-Saracena di Cambridge. (With parallel Greek text.) Ed. Costa Luzzi. In *Documenti per Servire alla Storia di Sicilia*. Palermo, 1890.
Eutychius of Alexandria. Trans. in *M.P.G.* vol. CXI.
Ibn Foszlan. *De Chazaris*. Trans. Fraehn. St Petersburg, 1822.
Ibn Shaprut, Hasdai. *Letter to Chazar King*. Trans. in Harkavy, *op. cit.* below.
Maçoudi. *Les Prairies d'Or*. Trans. Barbier de Meynard. Paris, 1861.
Yachya of Antioch. Trans. Kratchovsky and Vasiliev, in *Patrologia Orientalis*, vol. XVIII. Paris, 1924.

Selections in the Prilozhenia to Vasiliev, *Vizantia i Arabyi*, vol. II —see below—of the following: Al-Birzali, Al-Hamdan, Al-Makin, Arib, Eutychius of Alexandria, Ibn Adari, Ibn-al-Asir, Ibn Haldin, Ibn Kesir, Ibn Zafir, Kemaleddin, Kitabu'l-Uyun-wal-Hadarik, Maçoudi, Nuweiri, Sibt-ibn-al-Djauzi, Tabari, Yachya of Antioch and Zahabi.

D. ARMENIAN AND CAUCASIAN

Ardzrouni, Thomas. *Histoire des Ardzrouni.* Trans. Brosset, in *Collection d'Historiens arméniens.* St Petersburg, 1874.
Asoghic, Stephen. *Histoire Universelle.* Trans. Dulaurier et Macler. Paris, 1883.
John VI, Catholicus. *Histoire d'Arménie.* Trans. Saint-Martin; ed. Lajard. Paris, 1841.
Orbelian, Stephen. *Histoire de la Siounie.* Trans. Brosset. St Petersburg, 1864.
Samuel of Ani. *Table Chronologique.* Trans. Brosset, in *Collection d'Historiens arméniens.*
The Georgian Chronicle. Trans. in Brosset, *Histoire de la Géorgie—* see below.
Vartan, called the Great. *Vseobschaya Historia.* Trans. Emin. Moscow, 1861.

II

MODERN WORKS

The works marked with an asterisk (*) are those of greatest importance, either as valuable general histories or because they deal competently with important particular points.

Adonts, N. G. *Armeniya.* St Petersburg, 1908.
*Amari, M. *Storia dei Musulmani in Sicilia.* Florence, 1854.
Anderson, J. G. C. The Road-System of Eastern Asia Minor. *J.H.S.* vol. VII.
Andreades, A. *Le Montant du Budget de l'Empire Byzantin.* Paris, 1922.
—— La Population de Constantinople. In *Metron.* Rovigo, 1920.
—— La Vénalité des Offices en Byzance. *Nationale Revue Historique de Droit Français,* vol. IV, 1921.
Armingaud, J. *Venise et le Bas-Empire.* Paris, 1867.
*Baynes, N. H. *The Byzantine Empire.* London, 1926.
Besta, E. *La Sardegna Medioevale.* Palermo, 1908.
Boak, A. E. R. and Dunlap, J. E. *Two Studies in Later Roman and Byzantine Administration.* New York, 1924.
Brooke, E. W. Arabic Lists of the Byzantine Themes. *J.H.S.* vol. XI.
*Brosset, M. F. *Histoire de la Géorgie.* St Petersburg, 1849.
—— *Les Ruines d'Ani.* St Petersburg, 1860–1.
*Bury, J. B. Appendices to Gibbon—see below—vols. V and VI.
* —— *History of the Eastern Roman Empire* (802–67). London, 1912.

*Bury, J. B. The Ceremonial Book of Constantine Porphyrogennetos. *E.H.R.* vol. XXII.

* —— *The Constitution of the Later Roman Empire.* Cambridge,1910.

—— The Great Palace. *B.Z.* vol. xx.

* —— *The Imperial Administrative System in the IX Century.* British Academy, Supplementary Papers, I. London, 1911.

* —— The Naval Policy of the Roman Empire. *Centenario della Nascita di M. Amari.* Vol. II. Palermo, 1900.

* —— The Treatise De Administrando Imperio. *B.Z.* vol. xv.

*Bussell, F. W. *The Roman Empire.* London, 1910.

*Cambridge Medieval History, The. Vols. III and IV. Cambridge, 1922–3.

*Chamich, M. *History of Armenia.* Trans. Avdall. Calcutta, 1827.

*Dalton, O. M. *Byzantine Art and Archaeology.* Oxford, 1911.

Diehl, C. *Byzance, Grandeur et Décadence.* Paris, 1919.

—— *Choses et Gens de Byzance.* Paris, 1926.

—— *Etudes Byzantines.* Paris, 1905.

—— *Figures Byzantines.* Paris, 1906–8.

—— *Histoire de l'Empire Byzantin.* Paris, 1919.

* —— *Manuel de l'Art Byzantin.* Paris, 1910.

*D'Ohsson, C. *Les Peuples du Caucase.* Paris, 1828.

*Dölger, F. *Corpus der Griechischen Urkunden des Mittelalters und der Neueren Zeit.* Reihe A, Abteilung I. Munich, 1924.

*Drinov, M. S. *Yuzhnie Slavyane i Vizantiya v X Vieke.* Moscow, 1875.

*Du Cange, C. du F. *Familiae Augustae Byzantinae.* Paris, 1680.

Duchesne, L. *Les Premiers Temps de l'Etat Pontifical.* Paris, 1911.

Dvornik, F. *Les Slaves, Byzance et Rome.* Paris, 1926.

Ebersolt, J. *Le Grand Palais et le Livre des Cérémonies.* Paris, 1913.

—— *Les Sanctuaires de Constantinople.* Paris, 1921.

Ebersolt, J. and Thiers, A. *Les Eglises de Constantinople.* Paris, 1913.

*Farlati, D. *Illyricum Sacrum.* Venice, 1751.

Ferradou, A. *Des Biens des Monastères à Byzance.* Bordeaux, 1896.

Finlay, G. *History of Greece.* Oxford, 1877.

*Fraehn, C. M. *De Chazaris Excerpta ex Scriptoribus Arabis.* St Petersburg, 1822.

*Gay, J. *L'Italie Méridionale et l'Empire Byzantin.* Paris, 1904.

*Gfrörer, A. F. *Byzantinische Geschichten.* Graz, 1872–7.

*Gibbon, E. *The Decline and Fall of the Roman Empire.* Ed. J. B. Bury. London, 1909–14.

*Golubinski, E. E. *Kratkyi Ocherk Pravoslavnyikh Tserkvei.* Moscow, 1870.

*Gregorovius, F. *History of Rome in the Middle Ages.* Trans. Hamilton. London, 1894–1902.

Gruber, D. Iz Vremena Kralja Tomislava. In Z.K.T.

Harkavy, A. Y. O Khazarakh i Khazarskom Tsarstvie. I.R.A.O. vol. XVII.

Hergenröther, J. A. S. *Photius, Patriarch von Konstantinopel.* Ratisbon, 1867–9.

Heyd, W. *Histoire du Commerce du Levant au Moyen Age.* Leipzig, 1885.

*Hirsch, F. *Byzantinische Studien.* Leipzig, 1876.

* —— *Kaiser Konstantin VII Porphyrogennetos.* Berlin, 1873.

Hodgson, F. C. *The Early History of Venice.* London, 1901.

Huart, C. *Histoire des Arabes.* Paris, 1912.

—— Une Razzia en Arménie au Xme Siècle. R.E.A. vol. I, pt. I.

Hubschmann, H. Die Altarmenische Ortsnamen. *Indogermanische Forschungen.* Vol. XVII, Strassburg, 1904.

Iorga, N. *Formes Byzantines et Réalités Balkaniques.* Paris, 1922.

Jewish Encyclopaedia, The. Article on Chazars. New York, 1907.

Jireček, C. G. *Geschichte der Bulgaren.* Prague, 1876.

—— *Geschichte der Serben.* Gotha, 1911.

Kalaidovitch, K. F. *Ioann Eksarkh.* Moscow, 1824.

Klaic, V. Prilozi Hrvatskoj Historiji za Narodnik Vladara. In Z.K.T.

*Kluchevsky, V. O. *History of Russia.* Trans. Hogarth. London, 1911.

*Krumbacher, K. *Geschichte der Byzantinische Litteratur.* Munich, 1897.

Kukuljević, J. Tomislav, prvi Kralj Hravtski-Sakcinski. In Z.K.T.

Kulakovski, Y. A. *Alanyi po Sviedienam Klassicheskikh i Vizant-yiskikh Pisatelei.* Kiev, 1899.

—— *Proshloe Tavridyi.* Kiev, 1914.

Laurent, J. *L'Arménie entre Byzance et l'Islam.* Paris, 1919.

—— *Les Origines Mediévales de la Question Arménienne.* Paris, 1920.

Lebeau, C. *Histoire du Bas-Empire.* Ed. Saint-Martin and Brosset. Paris, 1824–36.

Le Quien, M. *Oriens Christianus.* Paris, 1740.

*Lucius, J. *De Regno Dalmatiae et Croatiae.* Amsterdam, 1666.

Luzzatto, P. *Notice sur Abou-Iousouf Hasdaï Ibn-Schaprout.* Paris, 1852.

*Macri, C. M. *L'Economie Urbaine dans Byzance.* Paris, 1925.

Mamboury, E. *Constantinople.* Constantinople, 1925.

Manoilovitch, G. Introduction to Z.K.T.

*Marquart, J. *Osteuropäische und Ostasiatische Streifzuge.* Leipzig, 1903.

Mishev, D. *The Bulgarians in the Past.* Lausanne, 1919.

Muir, Sir W. *The Caliphate.* London, 1891.

*Muralt, E. de. *Essai de Chronographie Byzantine.* St Petersburg, 1855.

*Muratori, L. A. *Annali d'Italia.* Milan, 1744.

Neumann, C. Die Byzantinische Marine. *H.Z.* vol. xxxvii.

Oman, C. W. C. *History of the Art of War.* The Middle Ages. London, 1898.

—— *The Byzantine Empire.* London, 1892.

Palauzov, S. N. *Viek Bolgarskavo Tsarya Simeona.* St Petersburg, 1852.

Pierce, H. and Tyler, R. *Byzantine Art.* London, 1926.

Platon, G. Observations sur le Droit de προτίμησις. *Revue Générale du Droit,* vols. xxvii–xxix. Paris, 1903.

*Popov, N. A. *Imperator Liev VI Mudryi.* Moscow, 1892.

Rački, F. *Ocjena Starijih Izvora za Hrvatsku i Srbsku Povjest Sredjega Vieka Književnik.* Zagreb, 1864.

*Rambaud, A. *L'Empire Grec au Xme Siècle: Constantin Porphyrogénète.* Paris, 1870.

—— *Etudes sur l'Histoire Byzantine.* Paris, 1912.

Ramsay, Sir W. M. *The Historical Geography of Asia Minor.* Royal Geographical Society, Supplementary Papers iv. London, 1890.

Regling, K. Ein Goldsolidus des Romanus I. *Zeitschrift für Numismatik,* vol. xxxiii. Berlin, 1922.

Rostovtsev, M. I. *Iranians and Greeks in South Russia.* Oxford, 1922.

Šafařík, P. J. *Slavische Alterthümer.* Leipzig, 1843.

*Saint-Martin, J. *Mémoires Historiques et Géographiques sur l'Arménie.* Paris, 1818.

Schlumberger, G. L. *Mélanges d'Archéologie Byzantine.* Paris, 1895.

—— *Sigillographie de l'Empire Byzantin.* Paris, 1894.

*Šišić, F. von. *Geschichte der Kroaten.* Zagreb, 1917.

—— *Priručnik Izvora Hrvatskoj Historije.* Zagreb, 1914.

*Soloviev, S. M. *Istoriya Rossyi.* Moscow, 1851.

Srebnic, J. Odnosaji Pape Ivana X prema Bizantu i Slavenima na Balkanu. In *Z.K.T.*

Strzygowski, J. *Die Baukunst der Armenier und Europa.* Vienna, 1919.

Testaud, G. *Des Rapports des Puissants et des Petits Propriétaires Ruraux.* Bordeaux, 1898.

Tournebize, F. *Histoire Politique et Religieuse de l'Arménie.* Paris, 1910.

Uspenski, F. G. *Rus i Vizantiya v X Vieke.* Odessa, 1888.

*Vambéry, A. *Die Ursprung der Magyaren.* Leipzig, 1882.

*Vasiliev, A. A. *Vizantiya i Arabyi.* St Petersburg, 1900–2.

Vasilievsky, V. G. *Russko-Vizantyiskiya Izsliedovaniya.* St Petersburg, 1893.

Vivien de Saint-Martin, L. *Etudes de Géographie Ancienne et d'Ethnographie Asiatique.* Paris, 1850.

Wroth, W. W. *Imperial Byzantine Coins in the British Museum.* London, 1908.

*Zachariae von Lingenthal, K. E. *Geschichte des Griechisch-römischen Rechtes.* Berlin, 1892.

* —— *Jus Graeco-Romanum.* Leipzig, 1856–84.

*Zlatarsky, V. N. *Istoria na Blgarskara Drjava.* Sofia, 1918–27.

—— Izvestiata za Blgaritie v Khronikata. *S.N.U.* vol. xxiv.

* —— Pismata na Imperatora Romana Lakapena. *S.N.U.* vol. xiii.

* —— Pismata na Patriarkha Nikolaya Mistika. *S.N.U.* vols. x–xiii.

APPENDIX IV

Genealogical Trees

I. The Lecapeni.[1]

II. Balkan Royal and Princely Houses.[2]
1. The Bulgarian Tsars.
2. The Serbian Princes.

III. Armenian Royal and Princely Houses.
1. The Royal Bagratids of Armenia.
2. The Bagratids of Taron.
3. The Ardzrouni of Vaspourakan.
4. The Orbelians of Siounia.

IV. Iberian Princely Houses.
1. The Bagratids of Karthli (The Curopalates).
2. The Bagratids of Tao and Ardanoudj.

V. The Royal House of Abasgia.

[1] The genealogy of the chief Byzantine families, such as the Macedonian dynasty itself or the Phocae, is given fully in Du Cange, *Familiae Augustae Byzantinae* (though he makes a curious and obviously impossible abridgement in the generations of the Argyri). I therefore only give the tree of the Lecapeni.

[2] I have not attempted a genealogy of the Croatian monarchs, as I consider their relationships and even their sequence too obscure for such treatment.

INDEX

N.B. Except in the case of monarchs, persons with two known names are to be found under their surnames—e.g. for John Curcuas, see Curcuas not John. Where the second name is merely a title—e.g. John Mysticus —see the first name.

DATE DUE

1/13			
OCT 3 1974			
OC 8 '76			
GAYLORD			PRINTED IN U.S.A.